STEVE AND THE TIGER

Riding the Americas

Enjoy the ride!

Steve Stewart

STEVE AND THE TIGER
Riding the Americas

STEVE STEWART

BROWN
DOG
BOOKS

Published under licence by Brown Dog Books and The Self-Publishing Partnership, 7 Green Park Station, Bath BA1 1JB

www.selfpublishingpartnership.co.uk

ISBN printed book: 978-1-78545-076-1
ISBN e-book: 978-1-78545-077-8

Cover design by Kevin Rylands
Internal design by Tim Jollands

Printed and bound by CPI Group (UK) Ltd, Croydon CR0 4YY

FRONT COVER PHOTO
Riding away from the Brooks Mountains towards Prudhoe Bay.

Contents

Introduction

Growing up in Scotland in the 60s and 70s I only knew one person with a motorcycle and he only ever rode around the streets and back roads of my local town. It was during a school trip to Urquhart Castle on the shores of Loch Ness as a teenager that I became aware that you could go touring and on holiday on a motorcycle. I met a couple of Germans who were riding around Scotland on motorbikes. They looked; cool, interesting, different, and adventurous and I thought to myself, someday I'm going to do that.

A few years later I got my first bike and short trips around my local area and Scotland followed. I then planned a bigger trip with my girlfriend Margaret (Mags) (who would later become my wife) to go on a touring holiday to Torquay in Devon, England. So at 18 years old I set off on my first tour, two up on a little Kawasaki Z250 four-stroke. We were fully loaded, complete with camping gear and panniers, and rode all the way from Airdrie to Torquay – a distance of over 500 miles (seemed a lot at the time). That was in 1980, when the M74 didn't exist as it was still the A74. It was a long trip south and an even longer trip back north. It rained continuously and the little Kawasaki struggled with the added burden of three gallons of scrumpy cider, two of which were tied on the panniers and the other was on the seat between Mag's legs. But I loved it and it gave me a taste for touring that would inspire me to go further afield.

However, my motorcycle touring was going to have to wait, because I decided a career in the Army as a paratrooper would be a great way of seeing the world. But motorcycling was to play a key part in my first few years, as injuries from a crash resulted in a medical board, where I was declared no longer fit for parachuting. This left me with two choices; leave or transfer to another unit. I chose the latter. As I was only barred from parachuting, I chose to transfer to the British Army's only complete commando regiment, 29 Commando Regiment RA. After successfully completing the All Arms Commando Course, I moved to Plymouth, where I would spend all but two of the next 26 years with the regiment.

And I did indeed travel the world, both on training exercises and multiple Operational Deployments. I even had the privilege of riding a motorcycle as part of my job and deployed to Kuwait on Operation Telic (Iraq War 2003) on a Harley Davidson MT350. For those unfamiliar with this bike, it is an off-road motorcycle of sorts, as in it has knobbly tyres and is rugged. But like its road-going cousins it was very heavy and cumbersome! Alas, it was to end in tears and a trip back through the casualty evacuation chain to Selly Oak Hospital in Birmingham, but that's another story.

My years in the Army meant that my touring was limited to short trips during leave periods. Over the years I have toured all over Europe, mainly going to see Moto GPs and World Superbike races. I have been to almost every circuit; some more than once, some more than twice and my particular favourite, Valencia, six times. On other occasions I would ride through Europe to join my family, who had flown out to a holiday destination, before riding back at the end. I'd even managed to ride a Harley Davidson through the Blue Ridge Mountains of Virginia for a week during an exercise in the USA. Some trips were just long weekends, whilst others were for two or three weeks. Sometimes I went with my wife riding pillion and sometimes with friends and colleagues, but the majority were solo. I always preferred riding alone as it meant more freedom; to do what

I wanted, ride where and when I wanted, for as long as I wanted and as fast as I wanted.

All of these trips were done on sports bikes (except for my short Harley trip), sometimes with minimal kit (a small backpack) and other times with a full range of camping equipment and panniers.

Over the years I have also raced enduro and motocross and suffered a fair amount of injuries and broken bones, some due to work but most due to motocross accidents. Yet nothing has ever dampened my enthusiasm for riding and travelling and my aim to do a once-in-a-lifetime big dream trip someday.

The big trip was never far from my mind and was always being fuelled by reading books and magazine articles about motorcycle touring. One in particular stuck in my mind; *Bike* magazine ran an article about packing in your job, riding off on your motorcycle to exotic countries and seeking adventure. It reaffirmed my aim to do likewise someday. They then serialised Dan Walsh's travels in South America and this inspired me even more. But I was still in the Army, enjoying my life and my career, and promotion prospects were good, so the dream trip would have to wait.

Fast forward to 2013 and the government were rolling out a programme of redundancy as part of the defence cuts in an effort to reduce numbers in the Armed forces. It ran in three tranches and when tranche three of the programme was announced, I was pleased to see that my rank (Captain) and job spec made me eligible to apply for redundancy and early retirement. I still had a few years left but I wasn't getting any younger, so I carefully weighed up all the pros and cons of either staying in, or retiring with the redundancy package. After a lot of thought, and discussions with my wife, we decided the package was too good an opportunity to miss, so I applied. Six months later I received a letter informing me that I had been successful in my application for redundancy.

I retired aged 51 and set about fulfilling my dream of riding a motorcycle somewhere exotic, adventurous and further afield. And it would all be funded by my redundancy payment. My wife had agreed to let me go travelling for six or seven months before getting a job, so then I had to decide where I was going, and when. As I said, I have travelled around most of the world with the Army, but had never been to South America. The two books that inspired me most were; Dan Walsh's *These Are the Days that Must Happen to You* and Lois Pryce's *Lois on the Loose,* both of whom rode through the Americas, so it was an easy choice; that was where I was going. It is also easy administratively as there is no requirement for carnets or visas anywhere in the Americas for British citizens; all you have to do is get there.

Now, when I told my family and friends about my plans to ride through the Americas they all asked the same question: isn't that dangerous? Which made me laugh, because during my service in the Army, I deployed on numerous operational tours (including four to Afghanistan) and none of them ever showed any concern, or asked if it was dangerous. My wife and family just thought that was normal because it was my job. Now I was about to embark on a motorcycle trip to South America, they all thought it was dangerous and were concerned for me.

I had a loose plan of riding from the bottom of South America (Ushuaia) to the top of Alaska (Prudhoe Bay). Most Adv (adventure) riders do this route north to south, but I wanted to get away as soon as possible so planned to leave at the end of February. This would allow me to get to Ushuaia before the onset of the southern hemisphere's winter and then over the next six months ride to Alaska before the first snows arrived in the north. So time was my constraining factor; I needed to get to Alaska before September. Six months, more than enough time to ride the Americas. I am not a professional writer or journalist and this book is about my trip written in my own words. I've tried to cover everything from preparing to go, documentation and bike selection to the equipment and the gear I took with me. And the trip is as it happened on a day-to-day basis; where I rode, what I did, crashes, injuries, police corruption, attempted robbery, personal bereavement, and some of the interesting characters I met on the way. I hope you enjoy reading it and hopefully I can inspire you to get out there and ride your bike on your own dream trip someday.

1.
Planning and Preparation

Bike selection

I had originally intended on buying a KTM 690 as I've been racing the SXF250 for the past few years, so I figured it would be familiar and I wanted to venture further off the beaten track. However, a crash at the beginning of last season (22 March to be precise) resulting in a dislocated and broken glenoid socket (shoulder) followed by a bone graft and shoulder reconstruction, forced a change of plan. I would need something a bit more comfy and road-orientated but with a bit of off-road capability.

I looked at the BMWs but found them too big for me even though I'm 5ft 9in'? Also (BMW riders don't take offence) I was the only one in the shop without grey hair! I checked out the Yamaha Ténéré as well, but didn't like the look of it, simple as that; it's all about the look. Having owned a few Triumphs over the years I decided to fly the flag for British industry and chose the Triumph Tiger 800XC as the reviews were good, it looks good and it's BRITISH!

The next decision was whether to buy new or second-hand. I went for a second-hand 2012 Tiger with 1,900 miles on it that had just had its second service. I bought it from a nice bloke in Devizes for

£6,500 (saving over two grand) and rode it back to Plymouth. It was fitted with; centre stand, heated grips, sump guard, aftermarket screen and engine crash bars, so was a real bargain. I have since made more modifications and added more extras, which I'll cover later. The ride back was great; 160 miles in driving rain and a strong side wind (nothing like I was to experience later in Patagonia), but the bike coped very well and my first experience of heated grips was great. So far so good and I was happy with my choice. With the saving I made on the bike I bought a set of Metal Mule 38-litre panniers (hand made in Sussex), which came complete with mounting frames, and a smaller narrower exhaust. This meant both panniers were the same size and width when fitted so they looked better, and the Tiger sounded better with the new sportier exhaust.

Personal administration, medical and insurance

Documentation was fairly straightforward as no visas are required for the Americas. I had several copies of all my documents made; passport, V5 vehicle registration, Driver's Licence (both parts), International Driving Permit and Yellow Fever certificate (needed for most countries), and also scanned and saved them to a USB memory stick. One set of copied documents I hid on the bike and the other I left at home, so in the event of losing anything I would have plenty of backup, just in case. Money-wise, I purchased two pre-paid travel cards; My Travel Cash and Kalixa, similar to credit cards and accepted in most places, only it's your money so no bills or interest to pay. I would load them via bank transfer from my current account as and when required.

For the motorcycle, third-party insurance is required in most countries and can usually be bought at the border crossing points. Dakar Motos (Buenos Aires) sorted out my third-party insurance for

Argentina, which I would need in order to clear the bike through customs when it arrived. It would also cover surrounding countries; Peru, Chile and Bolivia, and was cheap at around £10 a month.

Health-wise before leaving the Army I made sure all my vaccinations were up to date and any I didn't have I arranged to have done. I only required one and that was a series of rabies jabs, not mandatory for the Americas but they were free, so I got them anyway. I also got antimalarial tablets for when I reached the tropics. I had seen the orthopaedic consultant regarding my reconstructed shoulder back in November and it had healed very well so I was given the all-clear. Other than that, I had been gradually building up the strength and was about 80/90per cent back to normal.

However, this still caused some problems getting motorcycle travel/medical insurance as the start date for my trip was less than a year since the injury. That, along with all my other ailments (too many to mention), meant insurance was difficult to get – apparently I'm a risk! At one point I didn't think I was going to get cover as I had been turned down by several companies. I seriously considered going without cover or delaying the trip until a later date. Thankfully, I had to do neither as I eventually got full motorcycle travel/medical cover from a company called Holiday Safe. There was an excess of £150 added on top of the standard cover, which I thought was reasonable.

In preparation for the South and Central American part of my trip, where they all speak Spanish, I did a 10-week (one evening a week) beginners' Spanish course with Atlantic Languages in Plymouth. This was paid for by the Army as part of my pre-release. One night just before Christmas as I was riding into town for my Spanish class, down a 40mph dual carriageway with a bus lane and a slip road that all converge, I was sideswiped by a large white van that cut across the bus lane towards the exit slip road. The loud bang as he hit me was horrendous and I was sent careering across the road towards the underpass wall. I thought I was off for sure.

I took the full impact on my right elbow and I thought my trip was over before it had begun; I also thought I was taking another visit to the hospital. But somehow I managed to stay upright, more by luck than skill, and the fact that the Tiger is a big old beast helped. My elbow was a bit sore but my shoulder seemed to take it well, so other than a racing heart and slightly soiled underwear, both the Tiger and I escaped undamaged. My Spanish was still poor but I was hoping it would improve when I got there.

Planning

I used the military acronym of KISS (Keep It Simple Stupid) for this trip so all I had planned was a start point, date and a rough timescale of six or seven months; any longer and I might not have a wife to return to! I would be starting in Buenos Aires at the beginning of March and riding approximately 2,000 miles south to Ushuaia. Then I'd simply turn around and head north to Alaska, about 16,000 miles as the crow flies, visiting as many countries as possible on the way up. Once in Prudhoe Bay it would then be another turn around and head south to somewhere (?) in the USA to arrange my return. I had a lot of places and things in my mind that I wanted to see and visit along the way, so the route would not be direct. That's it: really simple, no time schedule (apart from reaching Alaska before winter), no accommodation booked, just taking each day as it came and riding where the road or track took me.

The bike was flown out by James Cargo and it was all very straightforward. I dropped it off at their depot near Heathrow with a quarter-tank of fuel; it was then packed into a crate and shipped by air freight to Buenos Aires, where I would collect it from customs at the airport. I flew out the day after my bike on an Alitalia jet from Heathrow via Rome to Buenos Aires. I had pre-booked a hotel for the first five days while I waited on the bike; this allowed me to get over the jet-lag and sort out all the customs stuff, but that was it as far as the planning went.

Bike gear

Givi HPS X 01 helmet. RST Pro Series adventure suit. Halvarrsons summer gloves. Alpine Star winter gloves. Falco adventure boots. Neck warmer. Ski mask.

Tools

I wanted to be as self-sufficient as possible and took a comprehensive tool kit and spares pack, which are listed below:

Chain breaker. Socket (front sprocket). Front and rear spindle sockets. Junior hacksaw. Spanners: 6–17mm and adjustable. Tyre levers: 2x13in, 1x10in. Socket set: 5–19mm. Mole grips. Stubby hammer. Screwdriver multi bits. Allen and Torque keys. Pliers/wire snips. Multi meter. Jump leads. Mini 12v air compressor. Tyre pressure gauge. Bicycle hand pump.

Spares

Spares for the trip were mostly consumables so I could service and carry out minor repairs on the road:

Chain. Chain links. Rear sprocket. Front sprocket. Brake and clutch levers. Fork seals. Wheel bearings. Throttle and clutch cable. Gear lever. Assorted glues, sealants and steel epoxy. Hose clamps. Cable ties. Tapes: gaffer, hose, electric. Tent/roll-mat repair kit. Assorted nuts/bolts. Clear plastic tubing. Inner tubes (front and rear). Puncture kit. Sump plug and washer. Fuses. Spare bulbs. Brake pads. Spark plugs x 3. Oil filter. Air filter x 2.

Extras and modifications fitted

Fog lamps. Front mudguard risers and extension. Rear shock mud guard (modified KTM off-road) fixed just under the battery box. Span adjustable brake and clutch levers. Folding gear shifter. Scottoiler. Plastic tool tube (fitted on opposite side to exhaust). Side stand cut-out switch protector and base plate. Top box (made from old aluminium camera case). Oxford bar-mounted clock (because I can't read the one in the display). 12v charging socket.

Navigation

Daily route planning would be done with maps for route planning/navigation and I'd taken the Garmin Nuvo 250 satnav from my car. I had South American and North American maps on a micro sim-card purchased from Garmin. As it was from my car, I had Velcro-d it on to a bracket on my windshield frame so it could be easily removed. Power would be provided from a 12v socket attached to my handlebars. I also had all the waterproof paper maps that I required for South America, Central America and Mexico and would get North America in country.

Communications and electrical equipment

For communication back home I would be using Wi-Fi and internet when available in towns, hotels, hostels etc. After some research, I had chosen to use Google hangouts for this and have bought a Samsung Chromebook especially for this purpose. I had been testing it out and was more than happy with it; very fast and it met my limited IT needs. I would also be carrying my mobile phone but only for the odd call home and for emergency use. The only other electrical equipment was my trusty old mp3 player loaded with plenty of Johnny Cash and country music, and not forgetting a digital camera. All of my electrical kit could be charged and run from my bike, which has two 12v dc sockets and has a power output of 645 watts.

Camping equipment

I was hoping to camp as much as possible, one because I enjoy it and two because it's cheaper. However, I would use hotels, motels or hostels every week or two, either to rest or carry out some administration. All of the camping gear, except for the tent, roll mat and bivi (bivouac) poles would be carried in the panniers. I had chosen a Vango Banshee 300 three-man tent as it wasn't overly big, but gave me room for all my kit and only weighed 3.5kg. As an alternative, I also had a basher (8 x 6ft nylon tarp) that was quick to erect, ideal in the hotter climates and good for emergencies. I had one full-size roll mat and two sleeping bags; a Vango 200 two-season down bag and a lightweight jungle bag so I could double them up if it was cold when crossing the Andes.

Cooking

All of the cooking equipment and food that I would be carrying was stored in my top box and the water pack fitted on to the front of it (on the pillion seat side). Cooking equipment consisted of a three-piece cook-set, an MSR multi-fuel stove, two 75mil fuel bottles (could also be used for spare motorcycle fuel or cooking fuel), a Camelbak

2ltr water pack, a Rota 3.8ltr water container, plastic cup, plate and cutlery, a tin opener and a multi-tool knife. Food supplies would be bought on arrival in Argentina and replenished as and when necessary.

Test rides

Now that the Tiger and all my equipment were about ready for the trip I decided that I would go on a test ride up to the Scottish highlands for a week to check everything out. I wanted to make sure I was happy with the handling and comfort, and it would also give me the chance to check my riding gear and camping equipment to make sure it was all OK for the trip. With most of the bike prepared and all my gear packed I set off. I checked fuel consumption at motorway speeds and on small back roads, covering nearly 2,000 miles in eight days, and everything was fine. Over the next couple of months I rode the Tiger as much as I could. I also used it for a motorcycle instructor's course and passed the Cardington (Driving Standards Agency) test to become a qualified motorcycle instructor. The Tiger was definitely the right choice, as it was proving to be a great all-rounder and comfortable all day long.

Final day preparation

The last bit of preparation was to carry out a service, oil and filter change etc. I also had a new set of Karoo 3 knobbly tyres to fit. After completing the service I took a trip up to Plymouth Triumph to get them to reset the service schedule on the digital display. Whilst I was talking to the mechanic he informed me that there was new updated engine mapping for my bike and that he could download and instal it whilst I was there for free. So I agreed and he ran the instal programme and, when finished, went to start the bike. To my horror it wouldn't start; we both looked at each other and I was thinking, what the fuck has he done? He looked confused and said this had never happened before. Well it had happened now, I said, and to my bike, and I was departing in a couple of days. I was a little bit worried; however, as he checked it out he quickly found that the download of the new software had been interrupted, so wasn't complete. The problem was soon resolved and after another download the Tiger accepted the instal and all was fine.

Arriving back home I got ready to change the rear tyre. Now over the years I've repaired and/or changed a few motocross tyres, all fairly easy and straightforward. I was about to discover the 17in diameter rim, 150-section stiff tyre that is fitted to the Tiger was not going to be easily removed. Using the tyre levers that I would have on my trip (two 13in and one 10in) it was almost impossible to break the bead. After about an hour (by which time I was stripped to the waist and proper hanging out) with no movement, I almost gave up. But I decided to try WD40 round the tyre and rim. Thankfully, this did the trick and the bead (not me) was broken, but it was still extremely hard to remove. Fitting the new tyre was a lot easier. Lesson learnt; I knew I could remove the rear tyre with a bit of effort if required to repair punctures. Also when renewing tyres I would get changes done at tyre fitters or garages where possible and hopefully I wouldn't get any punctures, which I would have to do myself. I planned to change the front tyre the following day.

First emergency repair

Getting ready to change the front tyre I almost had a disaster and I had to carry out my first emergency repair. I took the front wheel off to fit the new knobbly for the trip and all was going fine (apart from pinching the tubing and then having to patch it). I was just about to refit the wheel when the bike somehow rolled off the centre stand. Luckily it landed on the front forks and the sump guard and stayed upright so there was no damage. I had to call my neighbour to come and assist me with trying to lift it back up on to the stand. It wasn't easy, and in the process we managed to break the front mudguard mounting points on the right-hand side. So a quick botch job was called for with two small metal brackets that I had to fabricate from an old gate lock. All repaired, but it could have been so much worse.

I was now ready to go, bike packed, *adios amigos!*

Departure day

Departure day had finally arrived and after saying goodbye to my wife and a last kiss before donning my helmet, at 9.30am I was off. As I rode down my steep gravel drive, I applied the rear brake, but nothing happened. A combination of the weight of the bike fully loaded and the fact that I hadn't used the back brake since refitting the rear wheel saw me head for the other side of the road. A few panic dabs on the brake lever pushed the pads back and braking was re-established. It was raining and cold as I set off so I had decided to wear full riding suit; quilted liner, waterproof liner and Cordura outer plus another waterproof on the outside to keep all the road grime off and offer another layer of wind protection.

The heated grips were on from the off and the traffic wasn't too bad. I had under half a tank of fuel and decided to ride to Taunton Deane services on the M5, 75 miles away, before refuelling. Whether it was a combination of the weight and the new knobbly tyres my previous fuel consumption tests were not quite right, as I was about to find out. After the reserve symbol flashed on the dashboard display, I calculated that I would make it to the services easily – wrong! About a mile and a half before the services the bike started coughing and spluttering and I had to resort to praying and shaking the bike from side to side to keep it going. As all my spare fuel cans were empty in readiness for the cargo flight the thought of a long walk in all my bike gear to get fuel was at the front of my mind as it looked more and more like I wasn't going to make it.

However, the gods of biking must have been watching over me, because I reached the services slip road still coughing and spluttering but more importantly the pumps were within sight. With around 50 metres to go the bike cut out, so I quickly pulled the clutch in and managed to coast to the pumps – phew, too close for comfort! My 19ltr tank then took 19.1ltr (according to the pump reading) of fuel to fill it. So I had to reassess the range to empty with the bike fully loaded and with the Karoo 3 tyres, and note to self, fill up early!

As I left the services the sun had come out and stayed out for the rest of my journey to London, although it was still bitterly cold. Arriving at James Cargo I was met by one of their staff and shown into the warehouse. After a quick change out of my riding gear, I disconnected the battery, took off the screen and top box and repacked what I was leaving with the bike (everything more or less) and that was it, all pretty straightforward and hassle-free. I then decided to walk to my hotel as the weather was still nice and it was only four miles away, and I had nothing better to do.

I had booked into an easy Hotel for the night as it was the cheapest. First impressions of the inside were that it looked like a ship, with long passageways, and the room was even more ship-like; no frills but clean and cosy and with a TV and an en-suite toilet and shower even though it was very small and not a lot of room to move around in. After sorting my room out I went to the rest area for a coffee and the first person I met was an ex-bootneck called Billy from Plymouth (small world) sitting drinking cans of lager – and it was only just past four o'clock. After spinning a few dits (stories) and getting something to eat, a good night's sleep ensued and the following morning I made my way to terminal four, initially by foot. After realising it was about five miles, I jumped on an Avis car hire courtesy bus at their depot as I didn't fancy another long walk. I would be in Argentina tomorrow (4 March), the bike was due to arrive on Sunday and then my tour and dream trip would begin properly.

2.

Arrival in Argentina

Flight and arrival in Buenos Aires

I flew with Alitalia as it was the cheapest ticket I could get, so the first leg was a two-hour flight to Rome. This was followed by a one-hour-forty-five-minute turnaround before boarding another Alitalia plane for Buenos Aires. I was seated in between two young women, one English, the other Italian, both going on backpacking trips around South America. After chatting about our prospective trips for a while it was time to try and get some sleep. Fourteen sleepless and uncomfortable hours later we arrived at a gloomy, rainy and hot Buenos Aires (EZE) airport.

As the Argentine peso is a closed currency (you can't buy it in the UK) I arrived with no cash so the first priority was to find an ATM. The first couple I tried in the airport had no money so I was beginning to worry a bit; however, I found another and it was third time lucky. So cash in hand and hungry it was off to McDonalds in the airport for breakfast and a coffee. Whilst I was having my coffee two blokes sat down next to me and one of them was English. As we got talking he turned out to be an ex-Para (small world) working here as a security advisor for polo players. He offered me advice on the roads, security and money – anyone coming here should bring plenty of US dollars as this is the preferred currency. He also invited me to the ranch where the polo players do all their training, to meet his boss, who is a retired British Army Colonel, so as it's on my route I might drop in for a few beers.

We exchanged details before I got a taxi into town; this was quite expensive at around £30. Coming off the motorway into the city the taxi was surrounded by beggars and this was to be a regular occurrence at every junction afterwards. First impressions; thus far Buenos Aires did not impress. Most, if not all, hotels have locked gates like prison bars on the entrances, as do the shops. There are burnt-out and wrecked cars on nearly all the streets, one directly opposite my hotel. Dog shit is everywhere and the city just looks run-down and in need of some TLC. As I walked around the streets (and I covered a few miles) it was apparent that there was a lot of poverty. Every corner had either homeless people or prostitutes; however none of them pestered you like in some countries I've been to. There are some nice public parks that are well looked after and just around the corner from my hotel I found a McDonalds to sit in and drink coffee and use the free internet.

My hotel is interesting; I chose it because it was a cheap place to stay whilst I waited for my bike to arrive. Cheap and cheerful is an understatement: no hot water, doors with no handles, bare wires and heaters hanging of the wall, are but some of the faults. On the plus side there is a TV – one of those 1960s models – but it works, and there are a few English-speaking channels. So after walking around all day yesterday I settled down and watched Bruce Willis (Hudson Hawke) on the TV. However, by eight o'clock I was struggling to stay awake after my journey here, so lights out and off to sleep, only to be woken every few minutes by dogs barking, cars revving and general city noise, including the 3am garbage collection truck. There may be a better area in Buenos Aires but I'd yet to find it.

Planes, trains and automobiles

I had a meeting with Dakar Motos in the morning to arrange for my bike (which arrives on Sunday) to clear customs so I can begin my trip proper! Looking at the map, I worked out that the distance to Dakar Motos was about 16 km (10 miles). A bit too far to walk so I decided to get a bus as there was a bus terminus just down from my hotel. I eventually found out which bus I needed to get to take me to Vincente Lopez district. What I didn't know was that you needed coins for the bus and I didn't have any. A debate followed with the bus driver and we clearly didn't understand what each other was saying. Then an official-looking guy turned up and after some sign language I was waved on for free. After two hours slowly driving through the gridlocked city traffic watching the world go by, I reached where I thought I had to be. I got a good look round the city so it wasn't a wasted journey.

I asked some policemen for directions. After a while wandering around and getting nowhere, more questions to police and taxi drivers about the whereabouts of Dakar Motos followed. I found out to my dismay that I was still five or six miles away and decided to get a taxi. Dakar Motos was difficult to find even for the taxi driver; there is no shop sign or any other clues and it is right out in the suburbs. Anyone using Dakar Motos in the future should get a train from the Retiro train station in the town centre, cost about 50p to Florida station, and then it's a five-minute walk. Knocking on the large steel doors I was greeted by Sandra and Javier, who at first didn't know who I was, which was a bit concerning.

I soon found out it was my Scottish accent that they didn't understand. After a chat during which I told them where I was staying, they both looked shocked and told me I was in the roughest part of town, which I had already deduced for myself. They told me not to go out alone at night and filled me with horror stories about the area, so on their advice I was moving hotels. Sandra was going to meet me at the airport on Monday to sort out customs clearance.

After explaining all the additional costs; their fee, customs fees, air way bill, third party insurance (all in about £400), and sorting all the paperwork, it was time to make my way back into the city.

Sandra directed me to the local train station (Florida), which as previously mentioned is a five-minute walk. The first thing I noticed at the train station was that there is no health and safety here; there are women and children crossing the rail lines with prams, people hanging out of windows and sitting in open doors as the train got moving. So I got to see other parts of the city on the way back, and once in the Retiro (centre) I thought I would walk back to my hotel. Some three hours later, after dare I say it becoming slightly geographically disoriented (lost), I soon began seeing clues telling me that I was nearing my hotel. The number of beggars and prostitutes increased as I got ever nearer and I eventually arrived at my hotel exhausted! And more importantly, before nightfall.

A cold shower was followed by another crap movie and another early night. On the plus side, during my walk I managed to get all the things I couldn't bring with me such as; engine oil, WD40, steel epoxy, liquid gasket, sealant, puncture repair glue, etc. None of these were easy to find. Oh, and the small bike garage/lockup opposite my hotel that had been closed since my arrival decided to open and rev the arse of what sounded like a GP bike (but wasn't) for about an hour as I was trying to sleep.

On the advice of Sandra and Javier I had decided to move hotels. I managed to get a last-minute deal on hotelbooking.com in the four-star Bisonte hotel, right in the tourist area in the centre, for less than I paid for the dilapidated building I had been in. Should have planned this bit better; still, it adds to the experience. Kit packed I was off on another walk; passing by sleeping vagrants, dog shit and the odd dead rat, and one and a half hours later I arrived at the hotel, luxury! At this rate I'd be needing new shoe rubber before new tyres. I'm starting to look and feel more like a backpacker – with my bum bag, daypack and grip draped over my shoulders, wandering around town with my map – than an adventure motorcyclist. Roll on Monday!

Still in Buenos Aires

I had now been in Buenos Aires for five days and had just been informed that my bike would not be here until Monday evening and wouldn't clear customs until Tuesday. I have now explored about all there is to see around town and I am glad to say that the hotel move from the previous location was well worthwhile. There are plenty of restaurants, bars and tourists in this area and things to see. Saying that, the city is definitely a city of two extremes; there are clearly affluent people and sadly a lot of impoverished and homeless people and they are living cheek by jowl together.

Good points; steak is cheap and fantastic, as is the beer, but everyone here (men and women) seem to drink from litre bottles, the poor drink them in the streets and the well-off drink them in the bars. Smoking is still socially acceptable and all the bars have that real old-fashioned bar aroma of stale beer and fags – lovely. Trying to get a small beer is difficult and I feel like a wimp asking for a *pequeño* (small) *cerveza*. I have visited many points of interest; Britannica Tower, Argentine Malvinas (Falklands) War Memorial, the Mausoleum/Cemetery (very eerie) where Eva Peron is buried, to name but a few. She was the wife of Juan Peron, former Argentine Presidente, and the musical Evita is based on her life.

Things I noticed; breastfeeding is common in the streets and cafés, Goths and Demi-Goths are numerous, as are tattoo parlours (a whole shopping centre with just tattoo artists). The police wear similar uniforms to British police and are really young or am I just old? There are also red post-boxes, but that is where the similarities end.

And still I hadn't turned a wheel in anger! All in all it had been a good week, and I had met lots of interesting people, but it was time to vamos.

Bad news: the Tiger is delayed

It was Monday morning, only 5am, and I was woken by a phone call from a doctor from the Army war pensions department regarding a medical. I had to tell him I'd rearrange in six months' time or so as I was on a motorcycle holiday, or was I? Still no Tiger. I couldn't sleep anyway with the excitement of my bike arriving, so seeing as I was awake I thought I'd check my emails, and what I saw was not good. I had an email from Giles at James Cargo telling me my bike was still in Toronto, Canada, and there would be a slight delay; my heart sank. I then got another email from Sandra at Dakar Motos in BA telling me that it would not be here until the following weekend, a detail that James Cargo had not mentioned. Two phone calls later I managed to speak to James Cargo, who said they were waiting on an answer from the air company.

I also found out that when the bike was shipped they used Air Canada (hence why it was in Toronto) and it would then go via Chile to Buenos Aires. Two hours later I got another email saying the bike would be here Wednesday; not so bad but still another three days to wait. Now you aren't allowed to take any bags to customs with you when you collect your bike and I didn't fancy riding all the way back into the city to pick up my kit. So I decided I had had enough of the city and I moved hotels again back towards the airport, which is south of the city, so that when the bike arrived I could get on the road south easily and not have to ride in and out of the city. I booked a bed in a ranch only six kilometres from the airport, well that's what it said on the internet, but it was more like 26. It also said it was the last room, which it wasn't.

So a taxi ride to the airport was followed by another taxi ride to find the ranch. And after an hour looking for it using my satnav and the driver asking passing motorists, policemen and cyclists, we found it. It was a couple of miles up a dirt track and looked deserted, and it was. There was no one here except for two farmhands and an old woman called Betty who didn't speak English but thankfully was expecting me. She took my pesos and showed me to my room, which, as there wasn't another single soul there, was in the main farmhouse and not the converted barn with the dormitories.

On the way along the long corridor with immaculately polished wooden floors I thought she was going to die as she struggled for breath and coughed and grunted to me in what I think was Spanish. On the way there we passed a large sitting room where she introduced me to Jack, the owner, who spoke perfect English and was really friendly. Bags unpacked, I decided to go for a walk around the ranch. I had a quick look at the animals on the farm and watched a fat gaucho breaking in a horse and felt sorry for it; he looked too big and it too small.

I then decided to go for a walk around the countryside and see if I could get something to eat. Three hours later, tired, starving and thirsty I returned to the ranch and was reduced to eating some crackers that I had bought earlier and washing them down with tap water – delicious! After a good night's sleep I awoke in the morning to the sound of birds chirping and tweeting and brilliant sunshine streaming through my window, and felt slightly better. Looking out the window I was greeted by blue sky and cattle grazing in the meadow, which was emerald green and sparkling like thousands of diamonds with the early morning dew – not bad.

Breakfast, on the other hand, was disappointing; little quasons, stale bread and lukewarm coffee. More walking followed and I found a small Argentine equivalent to the truck-stop burger van, hallelujah! I had a large chorizo-type sausage on a nice baguette washed down with ice-cold Coke, all for around two pounds, and life just seemed to get a lot better. I sat there for a while, full and contented, watching 18-wheelers go by and the odd bike. On returning to the ranch I found it was all locked up, so after walking around in the sun for a few hours I sat by the dirty pool, which was nice, but I didn't dare swim in it for fear of catching something.

Eventually Betty turned up and let me in; I'd had too much sun so went for a siesta. A while later I was woken by a motorbike purring gently in the background so went to investigate. I found it was Jack and he had a Honda VN500; he had taken out the indicator bulb, which he thought was broken. I had a quick look at it and it looked OK so after a quick bit of fault-finding it turned out to be a loose connection, which I duly fixed for him. I had my hands on a bike, not mine but it made me feel good. Jack then kindly offered me the use of his bike the following day. I politely declined as it's not my sort of bike and anyway mine would be there next day, I hoped.

Arrival of the Tiger and the ride south to Ushuaia

Four days later than expected the Tiger had finally arrived in Buenos Aires. So it was off to the airport like a kid at Christmas all excited, to meet my customs fixer Sandra from Dakar Motos, who I must say did a great job. I paid my pesos (she wasn't cheap) and was then led round different departments where I was fleeced for ever more money to release the beast from its box. In under three hours all the paperwork, money (extortion), airport storage, *aduana* (customs) fees were completed. Then after refitting the bits I had taken off (screen, battery, top box) for the flight, I was off and on the road. Back at the ranch I was itching to get going so a quick repack of kit ensued and I was on the road for one o'clock – and my motorcycle trip had begun properly.

On the road at last, *Ruta* 3 to Ushuaia and it was red hot, I felt like an adventure bike rider, hoorah! After leaving the ranch I rode all day until around seven pm, and then had my first stop by the police at a roadblock near Benito Juarez. I had thoughts of fines or police corruption running through my mind, but they just checked my paperwork and asked where I was from. I said '*Escossia*'; they were all very friendly and asked me lots of questions about where I came from and where I was going, how much was my bike. I asked them where the nearest campsite was and they informed me that it was about 80km away. I asked if it was OK to just camp anywhere and they said no, it is not allowed.

As I waved goodbye to the police at the checkpoint it was already getting dark so after a few kilometres I stopped at a hotel. It was very expensive so I asked if there was anywhere I could pitch my tent. I was led outside by one of the staff and he pointed to a children's play park at the front of the hotel – winner. So my first night out of Buenos Aires was spent in a children's play park where I cooked my first meal. After supper I had a few beers in the hotel bar and I was glad to finally be on the road.

The next day it was a bit damp as I set off on the road south. The weather had changed and the temperature had dropped; as it got really cold, I experienced four seasons in one day. The wind had also started getting stronger as I made my way further south on *Ruta* 3 towards Patagonia.

Now, I had read about the Patagonian winds Viento Fuerte (Strong winds) in books. Here in Patagonia they are also known as the Broom of God, by the locals. Whether or not they are stronger at this time of year with winter approaching I don't know, but I was not prepared for the strength and the consistency of them; it never stops. On the way south the wind was always coming from my right and so was constantly trying to blow me into the path of oncoming traffic. As a result the ride was not relaxing as I had to fight the wind and constantly ride at an angle, just to stay in the right lane. This means you have to concentrate much more and you can never relax, as the wind buffets you and tries to blow you off the road.

Ruta 3 is a very busy road as it is the main artery which runs down the east coast of Argentina. So there was a never-ending stream of 18-wheelers both on my side of the road and coming in the opposite direction, most which were travelling in excess of 80mph. Overtaking them through the spray and with the wind buffeting you is scary, but not as scary as riding towards oncoming trucks. As you ride into the spray and turbulence it is like a massive slap, which causes the bike to veer and wobble. Then the rain got heavier and it got a lot worse with poor visibility. Riding towards the 18-wheelers got even more interesting, like riding into a power washer; one truck was bad enough but if you got two or three together it was an arse-clenching white-knuckle roller coaster ride through, only not as much fun!

So what is there to look at? On the route south from Buenos Aires on *Ruta* 3 you soon realise that the roads are long and straight and the country is vast never-ending flat *pampas* (grasslands) as far as the eye can see, with thousands upon thousands of cattle and horses, but mainly cattle: mile after mile for hundreds of miles, fields full of cattle. After a thousand miles or so the terrain becomes a bit more moor-like, but still flat and then there is a new problem to contend with, wild llamas!

Now you would think that with all the vast pampas they would graze on them but no, they roam the verges. And believe it or not, emus. Well that's what I thought they were until I googled them; they are actually rheas (very similar to emus) and native to South

America. The roads are long and straight with the odd kink in them but obviously very dangerous as roadside memorials to the hundreds of fatalities are everywhere. As are the different types of roadkill littering the verges and the road; cattle, llamas, dogs, rheas, rabbits, and all sorts of other unidentifiable animal corpses.

As I was riding along I noticed that my satnav had stopped working – not good as I'm only a few days into my trip. So I pulled over to investigate. Now my satnav was just the one from my car (Nuvi 250) and was attached by Velcro to a bracket fitted to my windscreen. The power lead plugs into a 12v socket that I had mounted to the bars. I would have to do a bit of fault-finding to try and find out what was wrong. I disconnected the satnav and checked to see if it worked with the internal battery, which it did. So next I checked the plug that fitted into the 12v socket. As I unplugged it from the socket the base securing bolt fell off and all the internal bits fell out and onto the sandy ground. I found most of the bits quite easily but spent the next thirty minutes searching for the small spring. I eventually found it in the sand and reassembled the plug only to find that the satnav was still not working.

I had to get out my map and after a quick check I set off for my destination for the night, Balneario El Condor, where I had been told there were a few campsites. Arriving in the small seaside town I had a look around for the campsites. After riding up and down the seafront a few times I couldn't find any. The town was like a scene from an old western, deserted roads with deep blown sand everywhere. I stopped a police patrol car and asked if they knew where there was a campsite and also for directions. They were very friendly and helpful and offered to guide me to one of the campsites, which I accepted. They took me right to the camp entrance and as I waved them off and turned in to the camp (which was up a slight sandy slope) the bike suddenly slid violently to the left. I tried to correct the bike by

Beginning of the adventure riding south from Buenos Aires on Ruta 3 Argentina.

LEFT *Waiting to cross the Straits of Magellan to Tierra del Fuego.*
RIGHT *Arriving in Ushuaia.*

accelerating but the back end came round and I had my first OFF! I had ridden into deep soft sand, no harm done as it was only a slow off and more importantly my guides had not seen my embarrassing fall. Picking up the fully laden Tiger that weighed roughly 300kg in the sand was a shock to the system, as I only just managed to get her up.

Once in the campsite I had a proper check of my satnav and carried out a full repair of the plug, gluing the nut back on to ensure it didn't fall apart again. After testing all the components and cross-checking other electrical equipment – laptop, phone – nothing worked, so it must have been the actual charging lead or fuse. I had to take off the right-hand side panel to gain access to the fuse and found that it had blown. Now the 12v electrical socket is an aftermarket car accessory and it takes a 10amp car-type fuse, and all my spares were the small bike type. So I knocked on the door of the campsite owner and ask in my best Spanish (sign language) if he has a fuse? He had, it was a 15-amp, but it'd have to do, so I fitted it and the satnav worked, happy days.

Next morning I woke early and went for a walk on the beach and did some stretching whilst I watched the sun rise over the South Atlantic. The final few days riding to Tierra del Fuego were bright and sunny but bitterly cold, around three or four degrees, but no rain and there was considerably less traffic. There were still llamas everywhere but now also sheep in the fields and the terrain was becoming more rolling and hilly.

As I arrived at the Chilean border, which you have to cross to get to Tierra del Fuego, there were no guards and no gate, so I just rode straight through and thought, that was easy, and on to the ferry to cross the Magellan Straits. I rode off the ferry and got up to my cruising speed of around 110kph when all of a sudden the road stopped and I found myself going far too quick for comfort on *a* gravel track. Riding the Tiger on gravel seated is like riding a drunken hippopotamus on ice! On the good bits with not so much loose gravel it's fine and soaks up the bumps and stuff well. However, on loose gravel it's like riding on ball bearings with the bike weaving from side to side and you never feel really in control; maybe I should slow down.

I decided to stand up Dakar-style and it was better, constant throttle letting the Tiger find its way. Two problems; one, I'm still having to ride at an angle in the fierce side wind and two, it is forcing me out of the clear bit of track and into where the loose gravel gathers between the car tracks. Now this can be deep and it sucks you in and the bike weaves and wobbles and fighting the Tiger fully laden is man's work. Still I was keeping a good pace as I'd got over 100km of this to go to the Argentine border and tarmac. Approaching one of the few proper bends on the track I got blown and sucked right into some really deep gravel, the bike lurched to the left, I counter-steered but I was still sliding and weaving ever deeper into the gravel. The Tiger then started bucking and shaking and it was now like riding a rodeo bull at 60 plus kilometres an hour. I thought I'm off, visits to hospital rushed through my head, my heart was pounding, arse clenching. I kept the power on and somehow stayed on and rode out the other side. I told myself, slow down, it's not a moto crosser!

Arriving at the Argentine border on Tierra del Fuego after crossing the small part which belongs to Chile, I had a problem. I hadn't stopped at the Chilean checkpoint so when asked to produce my documents, I had no stamp in my passport or documentation for my motorcycle. I played the dumb tourist as I was asked a lot of questions. After a lot of shoulder-shrugging and me saying 'No entiendo', I was given some paperwork, which I should have got on entering. Relieved and happy to have got through my first border crossing, I left Chile and re-entered Argentina, and was even happier to see that the road was now tarmacked again.

I was absolutely knackered after concentrating intensely and hanging on to the wild, weaving Tiger for over an hour in the gravel and ferocious wind. So I was relieved to find that the last 100km to Ushuaia were going to be a joy with smooth tarmac and beautiful scenery. I had left behind the flat lands of the pampas and it was now more alpine-looking with big jagged snow-capped mountains and green valleys with strange-looking forests, some of which were ravaged and stripped bare of leaves by the Patagonian winds. The road was also more interesting, with sweeping bends that wound their way through the valleys towards Ushuaia. On nearing Ushuaia the road climbs over the Pasó Garibaldi with tight hairpin bends and spectacular views before descending down the other side to the most southerly town in the world, Ushuaia.

After five days' riding averaging about 650km a day, in unbelievably strong side winds, rain and freezing temperatures, I had arrived in Ushuaia (my start point) and I now felt, looked and smelt like an adventure bike rider – bring it on, living the dream, or on some occasions for a few seconds, a scary nightmare.

I found a nice little hostel in the centre of town and spent the next two days doing some touristy things. I took a boat trip out into the Beagle Channel for a few hours and went to see some sea lions and some small islands full of all sorts of seabirds. Next we went to another small island that used to be inhabited by indigenous Indians, who (according to the guide) apparently lived naked in this inhospitable climate. I also got the chance to wander around and take some photos of Ushuaia from the seaward side. Looking back across the Beagle Channel from the island the surrounding mountains reminded me of Norway, with snow-covered peaks sloping down into the icy waters of the channel. The scenery is fantastic and the boat cruise was a great way to see the area and was a nice relaxing change from the bike.

As an ex-soldier I also took time to visit the Argentine memorial to the Falklands War (or Malvinas as they call it). The Falklands were and still are a contentious issue with the Argentinians, who believe that they belong to them. On the way south I had noticed that there are road signs everywhere that say 'Las Malvinas son Argentinas'. Nearly every town has a memorial to commemorate the conflict. This one in Ushuaia is different in the fact that, surrounding the main memorial in a large semicircle, there are dozens of large photographs depicting scenes from the war. But more interesting are the ones of families; mothers, wives and children greeting soldiers returning. All the narratives accompanying the photos are from an Argentine perspective, and very interesting.

3.

North through Argentina and Chile

Ushuaia to Puerto Natales, Chile

After a couple of relaxing days I was up early on the Tuesday morning to start heading north. It was windy, raining, freezing, dark and gloomy with menacing clouds in the mountains behind Ushuaia. So right from the off, I was fighting the strong winds as I climbed back up towards the Pasó Garibaldi. Nearing the top visibility was almost reduced to zero with the clouds and mist, but cleared as I dropped down the other side and a bit of sun appeared if only for a brief period. After a few hours I reached the border piss-wet through and again wearing seven layers of clothing. Passport stamped, paperwork signed and off I went en route to the Chilean town of Porvenir, which sits on the northwest coast of Tierra del Fuego, to catch the ferry across the Magellan Straits.

From the border it's just over 100km on route Y71, a gravel track; the rain had now stopped and the track was bone-dry with virtually no traffic bar the odd car or truck. But unlike the main route to Tierra Del Fuego the gravel was mostly hard-packed with few ruts and not too bad to ride on. Only problem is it follows the coast west and then north around the island to the town and the wind was unbelievable.

The track was also narrower so I had to concentrate and fight the wind to stay on the track as I was buffeted constantly by the ferocious wind, straining my neck and shoulders.

After a brief stop for a map check, I set off and was caught by an exceptionally strong blast of wind that blew me right off the track and over the verge. I had no option but to point the Tiger downhill, hang on and ride down the grassy slope through the gutter and berms of earth at the bottom. It wasn't that steep but it was rough and very bumpy with rocks and boulders everywhere, but the Tiger ploughed right over and through without a problem. Heart racing and slightly shaken, but thankfully I hadn't come off or suffered any damages, I turned around and headed back up on to the track.

On arriving at Porvenir at around 5pm, I found out that there was no ferry until the following morning at 7am. I was exhausted anyway, so found the cheapest, dirtiest hotel in town and then looked for somewhere to eat. I went for a wander around but there wasn't a lot to see or do; Porvenir is a small quiet town and most of the buildings are made of corrugated steel. I couldn't find a restaurant anywhere and didn't fancy eating in my hotel, as the kitchen (which I had entered through after parking my bike at the rear of the hotel) was the most disgusting place I have ever seen. So I was reduced to eating crisps and nuts washed down with Coca Cola before getting my head down for the night.

I got up early the following morning and it was freezing and raining again but I only had five kilometres to the ferry. Once on board I could get something to eat and drink and relax during the three-hour crossing across the Straits of Magellan to Punta Arenas. Getting off the ferry it was time for seven layers again as the weather was a mixture of heavy rain, hailstones and the ever-constant wind, damn it. I set off from the ferry and stopped at a fuel station a few hundred metres up the road. After refuelling I realised that I had left my Camelbak on the ferry, so I returned to find one of the crew members standing on the ramp with it and in perfect English, he asked 'Is this yours?' I thanked him and after a long chat said my goodbyes and I was back on the road.

A few kilometres outside the town I pulled over to adjust my neck warmer as cold air was getting in. As I was trying to put the side stand down both me and the bike were blown over. The bike fell on the right-hand side and I tumbled down the verge – nightmare.

I now had to try and pick the bike up with the tank on the downward side of the slope. There was also the wind to contend with pushing against the bike as I tried to lift it – double nightmare. Using every ounce of strength I somehow managed to upright it but I was now stuck on the right side of the bike pushing against it to stop the wind blowing it over again. Now, I couldn't get on from this side as it's too high, but how do I get around the other side without dropping the bike? Not bloody easy that's for sure. I had to edge my way round constantly pushing, pulling and leaning into the relentless wind. Once on the other side I then had to pull and lean backwards in an effort to keep the bike from going over again, still unable to get on as the wind was so powerful. I was exhausted and sweating from my efforts and was just about to give in when I felt a little decrease in wind pressure. So I took my chance and leapt on board, managing to plant my right foot on the other side to gain control at last. I had fought the wind and won, well this round at least! Living the dream.

After another few hours riding, straining and fighting to stay on the road the constant hammering from wind was tiring me out. As was the ever-changing weather; rain on, rain off, hail on, hail off, sun out, sun in, rain on etc. The only constant was the relentless wind! Fifty kilometres in the wrong direction on a gravel track didn't help either, caused due to concentrating on the road and missing my turning. I only realised I was going the wrong way when the sun made an appearance on my left, but should have been in front of me as I should have been heading north.

I had originally planned to get to El Calafate but it was still 300km away so I decided to call it a day after only 300km (shortest day yet) in Puerto Natales. The usual routine of refuelling before finding somewhere to stay followed. I was just putting my helmet back on at the service station when I heard a crash as the Tiger got blown over at the pump – nightmare. Two pump attendants helped me lift it and as it was on flat concrete it was easy. Twice in one day not good; however, the crash bars and panniers and the other protective parts are doing their job, so no damage done at all.

Two days riding in the pissing rain, hail and wind, windswept, freezing, tired and aching, adventure riding, living the dream?

Puerto Natales to El Chaltén and Mt Fitz Roy

Puerto Natales at first glance seemed quiet and looked as if there wasn't much to it as I rode up and down the street looking for somewhere to stay. But it turned out to be a very nice chic little town with lots of rustic cafés and restaurants. After what was a gruelling day, I found a cheap hostel and then went for a good meal in one of the many lovely restaurants. The chef came out personally and recommended the *Lomo de Liebre* (back of the hare) so who was I to disagree? When the meal came I was surprised at the size of the hare steaks (8 x 2in) of which there were two, washed down with a nice Chilean red. And I must say they were succulent, tender and absolutely delicious.

I was awoken the following morning by the sound of the wind howling and dogs barking and feared the worst for the day. However, after breakfast as I set off there was surprisingly no wind and the sun was out. It was still bitterly cold and I had my usual six layers of clothing on for the short journey back to the border with Argentina. It took half an hour to get through the checkpoint, which is the longest so far but I've been told I can expect longer the further up country I get. On leaving the border I joined the famous *Ruta* 40, smooth tarmac with long sweeping bends and still no wind so I was able to relax and enjoy the ride. After 80km the road does a big 160km loop around *Rutas* 5 and 7 before rejoining *Ruta* 40.

There is, however, a 70km gravel track that cuts directly across country and as there was no wind I decided to take the track, I was on an adventure after all. Best decision so far as I got the chance to really see what the Tiger was capable of on the tracks without being blown around. So it was up on the pegs and give it some gas. The track was rough and rutted in areas but not a lot of loose stuff and the difference without the wind was remarkable. Fully loaded, I reached speeds of 90kph and the Tiger took it all in its stride. It was very stable, agile, responsive, going where I wanted it to go and changing direction with ease. The only negative was when stood up it was a bit wide and the bit just below the tank dug into my knees and splayed my legs at an awkward angle. I also saw lots more rheas more than usual running around the valley. Rejoining the paved part of *Ruta* 40 I was on an adrenalin high and it didn't stop there as the route into El Calafate was superb; long fast sweepers with spectacular views of the mountains. So it was a short day's riding – only 277km – but by far the best, most enjoyable day yet.

I arrived in El Calafate hungry so decided to eat first before finding somewhere to stay. As I was sitting in a café eating pizza a guy walked in and introduced himself as Jeremy; he was also an adventure bike rider, the first I had met on the trip. He has been on the road for seven months riding down from Canada through the Americas. We had a chat and agreed to meet for a few beers later and swap route information and advice. That evening and some considerable amount of beers later, and good dits from Jeremy about Central America, we called it a night. He has a website (mylucinda.com) which is very good and informative for anyone thinking of doing the north-to-south route.

The following day I had a good wander around town before meeting Jeremy again for a bit of lunch and a look at his bike. He is riding a BMW HP2 with the smallest panniers I have ever seen, no camping gear (as he uses hotels all the time), just a few bits and pieces and a spare fuel can, very lightweight. I spent two evenings with Jeremy gleaning information about routes, problems, where to get tyres and all sorts of other bike-related things. He also introduced me to Fernet Branca; no, it's not a person but a 75% proof alcoholic drink favoured by the locals. I might as well have drunk my spare petrol as that's what it tasted like, awful! Jeremy stays in the best hotels available and plans his next day's riding to the minutest detail. He spends more time in each location and is travelling at a more relaxed pace that I am. I would find out later that he was a millionaire, hence his lack of equipment, he just bought what he needed. I didn't get the chance to ride with Jeremy as we were going in different directions, but he was good company and it was a great couple of days. Some weeks later I got an email from Jeremy, he was concerned about how much distance I was covering and how fast I was travelling. It was like getting a letter from my dad, even though we were the same age. I replied to him jokingly and said, that's why my blog is called 'Steve and the Tiger RIDING THE AMERICAS', not sitting around in hotels!

The following morning (Sunday) I set off for the shortest leg so far, 227km around Lago Viedma on *Ruta* 40 and *Ruta* 23 to the small town of El Chaltén at the foot of Mt Fitz Roy. The sun was out, it was still cold, but no wind and I was down to only five layers of clothing – winner. On arrival in El Chaltén I couldn't find the fuel station and had to ask some locals. Eventually I found it in a blue twenty-foot container on the edge of town but it was closed due to it being Sunday. I was staying the night anyway so I found a hostel, had a quick bit of lunch, then set off for the viewing area in the national park to see Mt Fitz Roy and the ice fields. There are several walks that you can do here but I chose to do the short one. It took just over an hour's walking at a fair pace up the mountain and the views were spectacular. It was well worth the walk and it gave my legs a good workout after having been sat on the bike for over a week.

El Chaltén, Argentina *Ruta* 40, Carretera Austral (*Ruta* 7) to Puerto Montt, Chile

After having a nice day in the national park it was time to start heading north again. It was another bright crisp day and the sun was out, very little wind but still a bit cold. My route today would take me 80km along *Ruta* 23 before rejoining the famous *Ruta* 40 for the roughly 600km ride to Perito Morino. The first leg was mostly fast sweeping roads on tarmac all the way to a small one-horse town called Tres Lagos, where the road forks north. Just before Tres Lagos there were the now familiar *Devisio* (diversion) signs of roadworks ahead. The way these work is they detour you to the side of the road and onto a gravel track which follows the main route. Most of the time there is no one working on it and annoyingly you can see perfectly good road but can't get on to it. I did try going on it at one point but every so often there are big berms of earth blocking the road. You can't ride over them and the banks are too steep to ride down the side, so I had to turn around and ride back to where I had joined the tarmac and rejoin the gravel track.

Because of the roadworks I had somehow missed the turning on *Ruta* 40 and ended up going right into Tres Lagos, which has a main street roughly one kilometre long. The road is made of cricket ball-sized gravel, if you can call it that, more of a boulder field. There was also supposed to be a fuel station here but after four trips up and down the street (just to test my riding skills) looking for it, I couldn't find it. I also couldn't find the way on to *Ruta* 40, so it was out with the compass for a general direction check before heading off in search of *Ruta* 40. After much riding up and down looking around I eventually found the turning and soon afterwards also the gas station, which I must have somehow missed on the way in (again) as it was just outside town. The next 200km were on gravel track running beside a mostly complete and perfectly good-looking bit of tarmac with no work going on, very frustrating.

I refuelled at Gobernador Gregores where I met and had a chat with a German couple who were travelling from Alaska to Ushuaia in a VW truck. I was now back on tarmac and the temperature had risen quite a bit so I had to stop and take out the waterproof liners from my riding suit. The journey was taking longer than I expected so I decided to stop for the night in the small town of Baja Caracoles, but it wasn't a town, it was just a petrol pump, a couple wooden shacks and a closed hostel. So after a quick refuel, it was throttle to the stops and I made best speed for Perito Morino so as to get there before nightfall. The road was superb – fast flowing corners and perfectly smooth tarmac. The total trip distance for the day was 671km and it was also some of the remotest riding I had done, I only saw a handful of vehicles all day.

The following morning after a good night's rest in a nice hotel, I set off for the border town of Chile Chico which would take lead me on to a fantastic single track towards the Carretera Austral. The border crossing took about an hour as the environmental police wanted to check all my panniers and I also had to put my grip and tent through a scanner. The Chile Chico track (*Ruta* 265) runs from the border west for some 100km towards the town of El Maiten with Lago (lake)

General Carrera on the right and the Jeinemeni Mountain and national park on the left. The first half is desert-like, dry, barren and rocky with the track twisting and winding up and down through some fantastic gorges and with some scary drops down into the lake. The track was mostly hard-packed with some loose gravel but very enjoyable to ride. At the end of Lago General Carrera it joins the Carretera Austral (*Ruta* 7) a famous route that runs north through southern Chile.

Halfway along the scenery started to change and there was more greenery with deciduous forests, green fields and some farm land. The track was now mostly hard-packed dirt, but still very enjoyable as it twisted and wound its way up and down hillsides through the forests and along the edge of the lake. And if I thought the previous days had been long and lonely this was even lonelier; maybe one or two cars and trucks all day and bizarrely two young Germans backpackers. One a 19-year-old lad sitting by a small village where he had been all day, and a bit further along after I had taken yet another wrong turn I met a young German girl sat in the track junction. After a quick chat I wished them both luck and went on my way.

On reaching the Carretera Austral nothing changed (scenery-wise) except the track direction, which runs south to north up through the Cerro Castillo National park. The track was still the same; gravel, dirt, beautiful mountain vistas, twisting, winding and snaking its way up and down valleys and on through the mountains ever northwards. After having ridden for some 278km, all of which were on demanding gnarly dirt tracks, I was tired. I decided to stop at the little village of Punto Rio Tranquila. I checked into a nice hotel on the lake side and after changing I went for a walk on the beach. There were three young Chileans sat on a bench drinking beer. I must have looked like I needed one as they offered me a beer, which I accepted of course. We then sat for the next half-hour chatting, and despite the language difficulties, had a laugh and drank a lot of beer, living the dream!

Ruta *265, Chile Chico Track.*

ABOVE LEFT Ruta *7, Carretera Austral.*
ABOVE RIGHT Ruta *40, Argentina.*
RIGHT *Carrying out a service on Ave Las Heras in Mendoza.*

The next day I set off with no real aim except to ride north until I got tired. However, after covering 223km I took the opportunity to refuel in the town of Coyhaique, where I met a Canadian biker called Marc, who was travelling with his wife Nadia, on a BMW R1200 GS adventure. They were staying in a little hostel so I decided to call it a day and spend the night with them. Marc had just been to the service station to wash his bike and I decided to do likewise as the Tiger was looking the worse for wear after 4,000 miles in the dust and dirt. I got the hostel address and arranged to meet them after washing the Tiger. I decided to leave all the luggage and panniers on and wash them down as well, roughly 315kg total weight. Not the best idea I have ever had; as I attempted to lift the Tiger on to the centre stand it wouldn't go, so I tried again and gave it an almighty heave. At the same time I pushed as hard as I could on the centre stand with my right foot. I felt a snapping sensation in my right calf and searing pain immediately coursed through my leg.

I knew immediately that I had torn part of my calf muscle and I was in excruciating pain, unable to bear weight or walk – nightmare! I hobbled to the garage in some considerable pain fearing the worst and wondering how bad it was. I got some tokens and washed the bike down hoping that the pain would subside and wondering what I was going to do. How bad was it, would I need to go to a hospital, was it going to affect my trip? Thankfully despite the pain I was still able to ride the bike back to the hostel. By the time I got there, which was only a few minutes away, and had a look at my right calf it had swollen to twice the size of my left calf; not good, and now I couldn't walk at all.

Some painkillers were called for so it was into my first aid pack, took a couple of painkillers and anti-inflammatories, applied a couple of bandages and hoped it would be OK in the morning. That night I could barely put weight on it but I hobbled (slightly embarrassed) to a restaurant with my new companions for some supper. It was very painful and I was still wondering exactly how bad it was and how it was going to affect me. On waking the following morning I had a nice purple bruise running along the middle of my calf muscle, I could bear weight on it but still had difficulty walking. Marc asked me to ride with them as they were also heading north. It seemed like a good idea as they could assist me with the bike if I needed to push it around or lift it. They also both spoke Spanish, Nadia fluently as she's Mexican.

We decided to ride all the way to Chaiten, which is right at the northern end of the Carretera Austral, a good 427km away. Leaving Coyhaique the first 186km were on super-fast sweeping roads with immaculately smooth tarmac as it wound its way north. The views of the mountains Sancho, Bayo and Colorado were absolutely stunning. After the tarmac ended we entered the national park area of Lago Rosseloto, which heralded the start of a 200km plus gravel and dirt track. It began with a steep climb up a single track through a forest on a loose dirt road with tight hairpin bends. As we climbed higher into the mountain the temperature dropped and the rain started and as a result visibility decreased. Dropping down the other side was tricky due to the conditions but overall the track wasn't too rough and not a lot of loose stuff, but still demanding. It then changed to really loose gravel but the track was a little bit wider, more flowing and not as twisty. So we upped the pace and were doing around 80kph with the Tiger moving around freely under me on the gravel. Without the Patagonian wind interfering, the Tiger was now like a figure skater, poised and graceful.

Due to my injured calf I was unable to stand on the pegs so had to ride the full day including the whole off-road stint of over 200km seated, which actually wasn't too bad. That is, except for one section of gravel (that thankfully wasn't too long), which was again like a boulder field, only this time the rocks were bowling ball-sized like obstacles on an enduro course, both on the uphills and the downhills. But keeping a steady throttle and in fourth gear doing about 40kph the Tiger just skimmed across, over-revving, roaring and growling. The rear skipped and bounced over the rocks, repeatedly losing and regaining traction –very scary but exciting and rewarding. Coming out the other end still on board I was becoming ever more confident of the Tiger's abilities. The last 40km into Chaiten were on more super-fast winding tarmac, all in all another great day's riding.

Once settled in to the hostel we looked at the options for the following day. I had originally planned on re-entering Argentina 300km up the Carretera Austral by *Ruta* 231 at the border crossing at Futaleufu. However, now I was riding with Marc and Nadia who wanted to get a ferry northwards across to Puerto Montt. I had a change of plan due to various factors; one, my injury; two, the fact I needed a new set of tyres (as after 7,200km the Karoo 3s were done); and three, the weather forecast for the next day was torrential rain and the locals said the track would be too dangerous. So I decided to go with them. It would be a 10-hour 100-mile ferry ride up through the *Golfo de Ancud* (Gulf of Ancud) to Puerto Montt and then it was only a short paved road ride of 120km to the town of Osorno where I could get new tyres.

Even though I had been able to ride the bike relatively OK, this would also give my calf muscle a rest and hopefully time to heal a bit. The ferry was very relaxing and at a cost of only £30 for a 100-mile trip, why does it cost £200-ish to go to France from England only across the Channel? In the morning, as predicted by the locals the weather outside was horrendous, so I think I made the right choice.

On arrival in Puerto Montt we booked into a small hostel opposite the docks and to keep the cost down we shared a four- person room.

Puerto Montt, Chile to Malargüe, Argentina
(Snow, rain, sunshine, ferocious winds and flying canoes)

After spending the night in Puerto Montt, I set off with Marc and Nadia for Osorno; it was another cold, wet, rainy day and after about an hour we reached the bike shop there. The manager told me that they had a shop in Santiago some 1,700km away on tarmac roads. So I decided to use every last bit of tread on my tyres and get them changed in Santiago. After getting directions to the Santiago shop we set off, heading for the town of La Angostura just over the border in Argentina. After the Chilean checkpoint it was around 40km through no man's land over a mountain pass before reaching the Argentine checkpoint. The road was sublime; switchback corners, perfect tarmac and virtually no traffic. It was still raining but the tarmac was grippy and it was a joy throwing the bike into the fast sweepers and driving hard out of them as the Karoo 3s were performing well for off-road biased tyres which were already past their best.

Once in La Angostura we found a little boutique hostel. That evening Nadia had decided to stay in the hostel and relax. Mark and I went for something to eat and I had the biggest *bife de chorizo* (steak) ever and washed it down with a bottle of Malbec, an Argentinian red wine. We spent the evening chatting and getting to know each other a little bit better. Marc told me all about himself, how he had met Nadia and that they weren't long married. He also asked if I'd noticed the age difference, as he's 53 and she is 21. I laughed as I said no I hadn't; Marc saw that I was being sarcastic and laughed too. Mark and Nadia had decided to stay for two nights as the weather forecast was not good. Not wanting to hang around with the newlyweds (two's company, three's a crowd) I decided to head north regardless.

On leaving Angostura in the morning the temperature was around 2 degrees and it was snowing. So it was back on with the quilted liners and all seven layers of clothing. The snow wasn't too heavy and as I headed East along *Ruta* 23 the snow turned to rain and the dreaded wind was back! After 80km I reached the junction for *Ruta* 40 and the winds were now severe but the gods of motorcycling had brought out the sun. The temperature rose quickly and I was beginning to overheat with all my layers of clothing on, so I pulled over at a viewing point overlooking the Rio (river) Limay to take some off. After changing and taking a few photos of rafters floating by I headed off down *Ruta* 40 with the road following every curve of the river as it flowed down the Valle (valley) Encantado. Again the road was a perfectly smooth, never-ending tarmac dream with corner after corner of motorcycling delight.

However, I could see ahead of me what looked like rain clouds, but as I was about to find out I was riding right into a sandstorm with the *Viento Fuerte* whipping up the sand and dust. For the next 100km or so it was another white-knuckle ride as I fought to stay on the road and see where I was going. I was battered and blown from side to side as I weaved my way down the valley and up over a pass. A few weeks earlier it had been like riding in a power washer as I headed south to Ushuaia, now it was like riding in a sandblaster. The scariest thing now was I could see how fast the wind was blowing as the sand flew past and around me. Visibility was at some points reduced to zero as the storm got worse, my eyes were full of grit and watering as I tried to look through my visor and see where I was going. All the way through the Pasó Chacabuco and along the side of the Rio Collon Cura river and lake, I was hammered almost into submission. The conditions were testing my riding and sense of humour. Eventually I came out the other side and could see the dust clouds behind me, still extremely windy but no sand blowing around.

As I rode over the Sierra de Catan Lil and up past Mt Negro, roughly 1,400 metres, the constant side wind (which was coming from my left) was again hammering me and trying to blow me off the road. No time for relaxing, but concentrating on the road and reacting to the even stronger blasts that would occasionally try and catch me out. As I battled on across the sierra, up ahead I could see a woman on the road beside a car. She was on the verge gesturing for me to pull over. My first thought was, I'm not stopping, as momentum is as your friend. Like a boxer who is getting out-boxed and out-punched, you have to keep moving or you will get caught, pummelled and knocked to the ground.

The wind is similar; moving keeps you upright, keeps you safe, stopping is like getting caught in the corner and the wind takes advantage as it tries to deliver a knockout blow. However, seeing a damsel in distress the officer and gentleman in me overrode my sense of self-preservation and I slowed and stopped. As I tried to turn the Tiger into the wind at the other side of the road to stop it blowing over, the inevitable happened; the wind saw I was vulnerable and delivered a knockout blow. Both the Tiger and I bit the dust. However, I was up before the ten count and so was the Tiger. The women who had flagged me down didn't even come over to help. Anyhow, I managed to get the Tiger side-on to the wind with the side stand down but the wind continued to pummel it and it flexed and shook with the force.

I then crossed the road to see what was wrong with the distressed woman. As I crossed the road I immediately saw what the problem was. Lying in the ditch below was a 15ft lime-green canoe attached to a bent and broken roof rack. It had been ripped off, along with her roof rack and was now lying 20 metres away down in the ditch. She did not speak any English but I knew what was wrong and how it had happened, no need for an explanation. First, I straightened her bent roof rack and re-fixed it to the roof of the car. Then the difficult part was how to get the 15ft canoe back on the roof with a raging wind trying to blow it and us away. The first attempt didn't go well; as we lifted the canoe and tried to get it on the roof it took off flying through the air like a big green flying banana. Time for a rethink; we put some straps on the roof and slid the canoe under them and then tightened them up. We also had to put some of the straps in through the doors and close the doors on them to make sure the roof rack wasn't ripped off again. Job done, I bid farewell and off I went once more into the teeth of the ferocious winds.

Then the next problem. I had had to use some of my extra fuel cans twice already due to the distance between stations, but not all of them. I was carrying eight and a half litres extra, spread over five cans; one 3ltr, two 2ltr and two 75ml bottles mainly used for my MSR stove. I had been averaging roughly 15km to the litre, but the wind had affected the Tiger's fuel consumption. I had used almost all my spare fuel when the bike cut out with 20km to go to Zapala, the next town. All I had left were the two 75ml bottles, one of which was half empty; this should have given me roughly 15km riding, but I might not make it. So in it went and off I set for Zapala, which thankfully was mostly downhill. I coasted downhill when I could to preserve fuel and pottered along slowly when I had to use the engine in the hope of reaching Zapala. And by the grace of the gods of motorcycling, I somehow made it without a drop to spare.

Refuelled, I set off for the town of Las Lahas 50km north, where I hoped to find a hostel. Well there was no hope, I rode round and round, up and down asking around and could not find anywhere at all. I was now faced with the decision of riding another 160km north in the dark with all the dangers of the South American roads; rheas, llamas, rabbits dogs, sheep etc., or going back 50km to Zapala. Zapala won and I only had to ride for about twenty minutes in the dark before finding a nice cheap hotel.

The old lady in the hotel gestured for me to bring my bike into the restaurant and started moving tables and chairs out of the way. The only problem was that there were three big steps leading into the hotel, and I'm not Dougie Lampkin (former world trials champion) and the Tiger's no trials bike. So I told her it was not possible. She disappeared and on returning gestured again for me to follow her and I secured the Tiger in the owner's garage, which was the other side of the road. Exhausted after 570km in all conditions, I fell into bed and slept like a baby.

On waking in the morning there was no wind, the temperature was up and I was off towards the town of Malargüe some 555km north. A mostly enjoyable day, no wind to speak of, really hot, and I was actually able to enjoy the road and scenery. The only thing of note was meeting an old Spanish rider called Pedro, on a Honda XR250 out here visiting friends and doing a little bit of touring. The roads between Zapala and Malargüe were biking heaven; smooth tarmac, continuous radius bends, hairpin bends, fast flowing bends, more bends than anyone could dream of, biking nirvana. There was only one stretch of *ripio* (gravel) of around 60km and even that was brilliant!

Malargüe to Mendoza (Maintenance)

I spent the night in a little hostel in Malargüe and updated my blog. I also managed to find a *Farmacia* and bought an elastic bandage to try and stop my lower right leg from swelling any more. It was still very painful and black and blue from the top of calf down to the ankle joint. I was just able to bear weight and walk with a slight limp but more importantly still able to ride the bike. The following morning I woke to dark ominous clouds and more rain so it was back on with the waterproofs. The ride from Malargüe to Mendoza was fairly uninteresting, long straight roads with not much to look at and it rained all the way so I covered the 430km pretty rapidly.

For the past couple of days the Tiger had not been starting properly, cutting out at junctions when I pulled in the clutch, and not idling properly. At idle it had been pulsing between 500 and 1,200rpm, 1,200rpm being what it should idle at. It was going OK at speed so I suspected the air filter might be clogged up (after all the off-roading that we had done) and not allowing the Tiger to breath properly. Just for peace of mind before I changed the filter, I rang my mate Graham (mechanic at Plymouth Triumph) for some advice and asked whether or not it could be anything else. He told me to check a couple of other bits and pieces whilst I had the tank and air box off, but agreed it was most probably the filter.

I was going to spend a few days in Mendoza having a look round so booked into a nice hotel in the town centre and also planned a day of maintenance on the bike. I carried out the maintenance on the main street of *Ave Las Heras* outside my hotel next to a restaurant and little café. This caused some strange looks and lots of questions from passers-by but otherwise no one was bothered. On taking out the filter it was obvious that the Tiger's difficulty breathing was down to the air filter. It was absolutely filthy and full of sand and dirt. So I thought in future I would have to change it more regularly. After servicing and putting in the new filter the Tiger started first time and seemed to be ticking over nicely, purring like a big cat (pun intended), so hopefully that had cured her breathing problem. I was riding to Santiago in the morning so I would see if she ran OK. Once there I would take the opportunity to drop the oil and change the oil filter whilst my new tyres were being fitted.

Mendoza to Santiago, Chile

My last day in Mendoza and I was up early and packed the bike ready for the ride over to Santiago. But first of all I wanted to go and have a look at the monument on the *Cerro De Gloria* (Hill of Glory), built to commemorate General San Martin and the Army of the Andes, and their victory over the Spanish Royalists in 1814 in the war for liberation. I had been unable to walk to it the day before because of my injured leg. It was a bit overcast and it wasn't too warm as I set off, so I had my riding suit on and the waterproof liners inside as well. The monument was only 8km away at the top end of the city and the roads were quiet as it was only 8am. I parked the bike at the bottom of the hill and began the long walk up to the top, which sits at 960 metres above sea level.

After only a few metres I was beginning to sweat due to all my clothing and my leg was hurting; however, I continued upwards to the summit. Arriving at the top I was sweating like an overweight chip fryer and in some considerable pain. The walk was definitely worth the sweat and pain, however. The monument is one of the most impressive I have seen anywhere in the world and the views across Mendoza were spectacular in the early morning light. The monument is carved out of the top of the hill and has 14 tons of bronze sculpted into it. It is topped by bronze statues of Liberty and a mounted General San Martin at the front. The sides are surrounded with very detailed bronze friezes depicting the campaign; very, very impressive. After taking a few photos I made my way down, which was just as painful as now my arthritic right knee was hurting as well as my torn calf muscle. Time for more naproxen.

The sun was now up as I made my way out of the city (glad I had my satnav) and onto *Ruta* 7 towards the Andes. The road was fairly straight to begin with but in then started to weave and wind its way ever closer to the mountains. At first I could only see the foothills due to low cloud but the clouds started to part and eventually disappeared. I could now see glimpses of snow-covered peaks towering above the foothills like giant sharks' teeth. The road was now getting twistier as it climbed ever higher with the mountains now looming over me on both sides. The road continued to twist and turn as it followed the Rio Mendoza, climbing gently ever upwards between the Cordillera del Tigre and Cordillera del Plato mountain ranges. The thing that struck me most about the Andes was not their size but the vivid colours of sand, orange, greys, blues and purples, which reminded me of the bruising on my calf.

On reaching the pass at the top the Tiger again started coughing and spluttering and cutting out, even though I had changed the air filter the previous day, so something was still not right. Going over the top at the border crossing the road passes between Mounts Aconcagua (6,959m) and Juncal (5,190m) so I thought the Tiger's problems might have been due to the altitude. Christo Redentor border checkpoint is one of the main routes across the Andes between Argentina and Chile and it was very busy with tourist coaches and other vehicles. Getting through, though, was fairly straightforward as all the departments – immigration, and *aduana,* both Argentine and Chilean – are in one building. As I left the border the temperature had risen quite a bit so it was off with the waterproofs and for the first time since leaving Buenos Aires over three weeks ago I only had a T-shirt on under my riding suit.

The climb up had been long and gradual and I didn't notice how high I had climbed. But coming over the top I was greeted with an amazing awe-inspiring sight. The road down the other side was virtually carved right into the rock face and was an almost vertical series of around thirty hairpin bends dropping down into the valley below. It gave me butterflies in my stomach as I rode the Tiger down, occasionally peering over the edge of the barrier-less roads. The road then began to descend more gradually with bend after bend of motorcycling heaven as it followed the Rios (Rivers) Blanco and Colorado towards Santiago.

Arriving in Santiago I went directly to the Triumph Chile motorcycle shop to see if I could get the Tiger's breathing and coughing sorted. The staff there were very helpful, but I was originally told they couldn't look at it until the following Tuesday, five days away. However, Christina the servicing manager told me to bring the bike back in the morning. I spoke with the mechanic and explained the problems that I was having. Thankfully he understood and spoke very good English (as did most of the staff) and said the injectors probably needed cleaning as well due to all the riding on the *ripio*. I decided to have the bike serviced as well as having the new tyres fitted.

I then had an interesting hair-raising 8km ride through the extremely busy city to my hostel. It was like *Death Race 2,000* and *Wacky Races* combined as I made my way across the city. There did not seem to be any lane discipline or speed limit, with the maniac car, bus, and taxi drivers, motorcyclists and cyclists all fighting for a bit of road with pedestrians getting in the way. As I sped off from one set of traffic lights five abreast with other bikers and cars hotly on our tails it nearly ended in pain and tears. An old man who had not cleared the crossing quickly enough ran directly into my path. I had to swerve to miss him, forcing the biker on my right to swerve as well. Tragedy averted I ducked and weaved through the gridlocked madness and eventually arrived in one piece at my hostel. And I had it all to look forward to again in the morning.

I dropped the bike off at 10am the next day and went for a walk around the city whilst I waited. New tyres were put on the bike, I had the injectors cleaned and the oil and filter were changed, as well as a full diagnostic and engine mapping check done. They also gave the bike a good wash and when I picked her up not only was she looking good with her new rubber on and all sparkly, but was sounding and running better too. So definitely worth the trip here to Triumph Chile. A few photos were taken and I exchanged details with some of the staff before riding off, on a healthier, responsive and growling Tiger.

Santiago was the most modern place I had visited so far; very cosmopolitan, lots of nice building and statues. It has a massive café culture and there are lots of cafés and bars (proper bars) full of people and entertainment. I had a great night out with some American guys; Brett (techno guy), Aaron and AJ, (good all-American names) and Paul, a mad Irish accountant. It was so good we never heard or felt the earthquake that hit the city that night. So after my first real good late night out, I wasn't best pleased to be woken early the next morning by the Indian bloke on the bed opposite. He was sitting cross-legged on his bed with his hands in a prayer-like fashion, chanting over and over again, sounded like a cow mooing! The day was spent wandering around and I took a trip to the statue of the Immaculate Conception, which sits on top of a mountain in the centre of Santiago with spectacular views over the city. And thankfully I didn't need to walk up, as there is a tram car (Funicular) which transports the fat, lazy and injured (me) to the top and back down again.

After a few days doing the touristy things and resting here in Santiago I was ready for the Atacama Desert, which I would be riding through in the next week or so. Great city, but the bike's ready to go so it's ever northwards to Alaska.

Santiago to Vin del Mar

I got up early in the morning to get packed and out of the city before the traffic got too busy. As I was packing the bike I noticed a man lying on the ground a few metres away and at first I thought he was a vagrant. But looking at his clothes and the fact he had nice shoes on I then thought, he's not a vagrant but he looks dead. So I went across and gently prodded him with my foot and he grunted and I could smell an overwhelming stench of stale alcohol. So he wasn't dead, just dead drunk and sleeping it off on the pavement.

Just as I was finishing packing and about to set off I saw what looked like another vagrant shouting and running across the road towards me. He was over six foot tall wearing a Peruvian-style hat but it had a tiger pattern, he had long hair and an even longer unkempt beard. His clothes were also looking a bit the worse for wear. As he started talking to me in English I could also smell alcohol and wasn't exactly sure what he was saying, as he seemed very excited. As it turned out his name was Phil and he had just finished a 20-month motorcycle trip down from Canada. He hadn't shaved or had a haircut since he started his trip. He had also been out all night drinking and was flying back to Canada later that day. I had a good but brief chat and he gave me his card and wished me well and told me to get in touch as he had got lots of contacts from his trip.

As I set off I wondered why there were lots of police around and soon found out it was because the Santiago marathon was on. So it took a while to get out of the city as I was turned around at junction after junction trying to find my way out. Thankfully I had my satnav, which just kept recalculating the route out. Once clear of the city it still took quite a while to eventually clear the suburbs. I had programmed the satnav to avoid the toll roads and I followed the old road to Valparaiso.

The road wound its way up and down through some fantastic mountains as it headed west towards the Pacific coast. The tarmac was as smooth as velvet with corner after corner of perfect radius cambered bends of joy. However, after crossing the top of one mountain and passing a sign that said Welcome to Valparaiso Province (they must have no money), the road turned into a pot-holed nightmare, they were huge and deep and on every hairpin bend. So I had to slow down and pick and weave my way through to stop us being swallowed up in the vast bottomless pits, as that is what some of them looked like.

Arriving in Valparaiso, which is a Chilean Naval and cargo port, it didn't look like much so I rode along the coast to the resort town of Vin Del Mar. I found a lovely little hostel which was more like a guest house and the two owners spoke English. I only booked in for one night but after speaking to some other guests who all raved about Valparaiso I decided to stay another day. There is a very modern metro that would take me right into town and I planned to get it the morning. The metro was cheap – £2.50 for a return ticket – and only took 10 minutes to get there. I must say I am glad I did as the weather had warmed up and I had my shorts and flip-flops on for the first time in over a month. Away from the container port on the seafront, the town is very characterful with interesting architecture and old wooden buildings. The buildings are all painted in bright vibrant colours and most have some form of artwork on them as well.

Valparaiso is also home to the Chilean Naval Headquarters, which are housed in a lovely-looking blue building. Because the town is built in to the steep hillsides there are lots of funiculars that take you up or down to the next street level. Most of the cafés and restaurants are on rooftops with wonderful views across the town and the bay.

I had lunch in one and had my first taste of *pisco* sour, a favourite aperitif of Chile, very strong. I arrived back in Vin Del Mar in late afternoon and as it was still hot I decided to go for a walk on the beach and dip my feet in the Pacific, which was bloody freezing so no chance of a swim.

As I said there were no backpackers in this hostel, which made a nice change. My fellow guests, of whom there were five (more of them later), were here in Vin Del Mar along with 800 others from around the world, attending an Environmental Impact Assessment Conference. There were three environmentalists that I got to know and they were not your typical tree-hugging lentil-munching types. Firstly, there was Alan, from Canada who was loud and brash, almost like an American. Then there was Patricia, from Peru, and Birgit, from Austria. All three of them had speaking parts and were giving presentations to the conference. The other guest I got to know was Felix, from Columbia, a professor in traffic management who lectures/works at the university here in Vin Del Mar. Great guy, very softly spoken and clearly very intelligent and nice to talk to.

That night in the hostel the environmentalists were preparing to deliver their respective 10-minute presentations to each other as a rehearsal for the conference. Having taught, instructed and lectured at various times throughout my Army career and given I had nothing better to do, I thought I would listen in and offer my opinion and constructive criticism if required. Bearing in mind these were all complete strangers from different parts of the world who had just met and were presenting in English, the following is how my evening went:

Up first was Birgit who gave a presentation on Citizen Science (gathering information from locals about changes they have noticed) and the environmental management of the Danube river basin now and in the future. All very well presented and interesting, I thought. We then all offered a few suggestions on how to improve the presentation. However, Alan was very critical and told her how to stand, how to hold her hands, what to say, what slides to get rid of and what to change and he went on and on. Some of what he said was right but he just overdid the criticism. Birgit smiled, listened and was happy to change and modify a fair bit of her presentation.

Next up was Patricia, who gave a presentation on the impact of deforestation of the Amazon district of Loretto in Peru due to oil drilling, road building and palm-oil tree plantations. Again all very interesting, informative and on the whole well presented. Again we all offered a few words of constructive criticism, and again Alan went on and on about how to stand, what to say, where to look, get rid of this, change that, don't say that say this etc. Patricia duly changed and amended different parts of her presentation.

Now it was Alan's turn and he presented on the problems and plans for keeping safe the MacKenzie province in Canada. This is where the world's largest underground deposits of arsenic (the leftover results of industrial gold mining) are stored. There are billions of tons, enough to fill over 50 football fields, and kill the world's population 16 times over. All scary stuff and very interesting and as a whole, also well presented, if a bit long at 20 minutes. As we started to offer our constructive criticism it quickly became clear that Alan loved giving it out, but was not keen on receiving it. For every suggested change we gave him on how to make it better, clearer or simpler for the non-English speaking audience, he simply dismissed it out of hand. He just said it didn't need changing or made excuses as to why it was in there and didn't change a single thing in his presentation. What a guy!

It was a great if unusual and interesting evening and got better when Felix (the professor) turned up along with some other environmentalist and we drank red wine and got round to talking politics. Who'd have thought me in the same room with environmentalists and a professor, all very high-brow but good fun all the same?

The following day I went to the beach and spent the day lying around sunbathing. Later on I checked the bike over for the ride back into Argentina. I was going to ride back over the same pass I had come here on before turning north for 400km to the next pass, the Paso de Agua Negra, and back into Chile.

Vin del Mar, Chile to Las Flores

It was another early start to get a quick getaway from Vin Del Mar where I had just spent three days loafing around sunbathing. I set the satnav to avoid the toll roads and off I went following the coast north before swinging east. After some 40km in fairly busy traffic I realised that I had left my head torch attached to the bunk above where I had been sleeping. I briefly considered leaving it but as it was a Christmas present and I'm Scottish I decided to turn around and go back for it. The landlady thought I had liked it so much I was back for another day but laughed when I told her it wasn't that good, I had just left something.

Torch recovered I reset the satnav for the tolls to make up time. And I must say I am glad I did, because for a couple of pounds, I was treated to a very quiet, super-smooth, super-fast constantly sweeping, motorcycling road of delight. After the tolls it was on to *Ruta* 60, which follows the rivers Colorado and Blanco back up towards the pass and border crossing at Christo Redentor. This is the same pass I had come across on so I had the vertical series of hairpins to look forward to on the way up. And they didn't disappoint; this time I had the added excitement of trying to overtake the slow-moving 18-wheelers as they climbed the steep mountain.

Not as easy as it sounds as the distance between the corners wasn't that great so it involved a quick glance up the next level and then a mad dash with hard acceleration past before jamming on the brakes and throwing the Tiger into the hairpin. I must say the new road-biased Full Bore tyres that were fitted in Santiago were great, very grippy. We were through the border checkpoint again quite quickly with no problems and back into Argentina and onto *Ruta* 7. I cruised down the other side occasionally stopping to take photos along the way.

On reaching the small town of Uspallata I found a little campsite and so for the first time in over three weeks I managed to get my tent up. It's not a real adventure unless you're camping! It was also nice to use my camping gear that I have been hauling around with me. I was the only camper so had the whole site to myself. After cooking some pasta I took a quick walk into the little village to get something for breakfast. Not a lot to look at in Uspallata but it sits at the foot of the Andes, so I watched the sun go down before getting into my sleeping bag. After a cold night (Uspallata sits at around 3,000 metres) I woke to the sounds of the birds chirping and the sun streaming in through the tall slim trees that surround the campsite, glorious! For breakfast I had fried sausage and eggs and I then set off for *Ruta* 149, which runs directly north through the El Leoncito National Park.

A few kilometres out of Uspallata the road ends and there is then a 40km section of *ripio* track. I have come to enjoy the *ripio* and this bit was fairly easy, not too rough and devoid of any other traffic. Once back on the tarmac the road was pretty straight all the way into the small town of Barreal, where I stopped for a coffee. Leaving Barreal the road follows the Rio Los Patos as it snakes and weaves it way along the Valle de Calingasta. It then swings right around the Sierra Del Tigre mountains and follows the Rio San Juan east for some 60km through the gnarliest, testiest road imaginable.

The mountains jut out on the right-hand side, all ragged and rough where the road has been carved into it. With the Rio San Juan down in the valley below the road follows every curve of the mountain. No sooner have you picked the bike up you are dropping it into the next corner so the tyre edges were getting put to good use. It was a never-ending series of short lefts and rights; the only thing irritating was the wind, not the *Viento Fuerte* of Patagonia, but the 'I'm a bit angry' wind that came from different directions as you rounded each corner.

On reaching the bottom of the valley the road then forks left (north) and begins to climb up over the Sierra Del Tigre Mountains in a long series of super-fast smooth bends on billiard-table-smooth tarmac. On reaching the top I had my first experience of Andes fog. Not too bad at first but as I rode into the clouds visibility was down to just a few metres. Thankfully it didn't last too long and as I started to descend on the other side I left the fog behind me and rode down into sunshine and warmth. *Ruta* 149 is a must for adventure motorcyclists; great scenery, great roads and absolutely no other traffic – biking nirvana!

On reaching the village of Las Flores there was only one hotel and it was very expensive so I rode on only to find the border crossing was just a few kilometres up the road. This was some way short of the border marked on the map, by at least 60km. The guard told me there was no accommodation until well into Chile a few hundred kilometres away, so I decided to go back to Las Flores and use my last Argentine pesos for the hotel.

Finally saying goodbye to Argentina after a month riding around (including a few trips over into southern Chile) and about; beautiful countryside, vast open empty expanses, unbelievable mountains, great country, great roads, scary winds, exciting gnarly tracks, *adios*.

Las Flores to Patquia (Day of closures)

All packed after a comfortable night's sleep, I set off for the border checkpoint 2km up the road. It was a glorious day with brilliant sunshine, red hot and it was only 9am. On arriving the border official told me that the pass was closed due to a heavy snowstorm up in the mountains but it might open in an hour or two. It looked lovely from where I was stood, not a cloud in sight, so I took a few photos, made a cup of coffee and waited. I thought I was being wound up when a car arrived in the checkpoint coming from the Chilean side.

However, when I spoke to the old couple who were in the 4x4 they told me that they had left this checkpoint a few hours earlier and had had to turn back due to heavy snow 50km into the pass. After hanging around for over two hours the official informed me that the pass would not be opening today and might reopen tomorrow. I wondered, what if it doesn't reopen? So I decided to move on and ride further north to another pass.

So after bidding farewell to Argentina I found myself saying hello again as I turned around from the border. I had decided to ride another 560km further north (as the crow flies), over 960km by road to the Pasó San Francisco; that's the good thing about not having a plan or schedule. The only problem was I had used my last Argentine pesos for the hotel and there were no banks around. I did, however, have a full tank of fuel so I set off towards *Ruta* 40.

At first I followed *Ruta* 150, which runs east through a small pass following the Rio Jachal. Beautiful scenery but I couldn't look at it too much as it's a single-track road most of the time with jagged rocks sticking out on the right and drops down into the river on the left. After about 60km I rejoined *Ruta* 40 and started heading north. It runs up through the De La Luna National Park with the Andes on the left and a vast valley stretching out as far as the eye can see to the right and more mountains. It's a long straight road, not a lot to look at, desert-like terrain and some 100km long with hardly a kink in it. It does, however, have a different type of bend – up-and-down ones.

The road follows the contours of the valley, which has hundreds of *badenes* (water courses) running through it where the water runs of the mountains. It is like a giant roller coaster ride as the road continually rises up over blind crests and then drops into the dips every hundred or so metres up and down, up and down. The dips in the road are concreted for about 50 metres or so (probably erodes less than tarmac when the water is running through them) and the crests are tarmac, and thankfully the bottoms were all dry as it was summer, or so I thought.

I was about to get my first of three river crossings of the trip. Bombing along at about 80mph, I came over a crest and there was a river running through the dip ahead. There was no time to brake so I gripped the tank tightly with my knees and leant back and hoped I'd get through OK. Heart in mouth, arse twitching, I rode the *badenes* and the Tiger was like a torpedo as it cut a swathe through, creating a massive plume of water on either side. It was only about 5 metres wide and less than a foot deep but it caused the Tiger to shake its head a little, but I got through safely.

It was still red-hot and for the first time this trip I had drunk my Camelbak dry and I was also becoming a bit queasy. After 60km of riding the *badenes*, all the upping and downing had my stomach in turmoil as there was a second of weightlessness going over the crests. My insides floated up into my mouth going over the top and then sank to the bottom of my stomach in the dips as the suspension bottomed out. So I pulled over for a rest and to top up my Camelbak from my water jerry can.

Just after setting off I was about to get my second river crossing, only this time there was a warning sign saying river ahead. So I slowed down and what greeted me was a bit daunting, all brown and sludgy-looking, 10 metres wide and I can't tell how deep. Second gear, feet dangling by the side like a novice rider (I definitely didn't want to fall over and have to pick it up in here), I pushed through. There were a few wobbles but I made it through safely, with only wet muddy feet and trouser bottoms. The third was again signposted and it was considerably wider than the previous two, but it was clear water a few inches deep and I could see the bottom and the concrete, so I rode through at full speed ahead creating big plumes of water, great fun.

When I reached the town of Villa Union the garage was closed, as was the road ahead through the pass on *Ruta* 40, which was all blocked off. This meant another detour of around 330km south and then back up north around the mountain that the pass should have taken me through. Running low on petrol and still with no money I headed off down the road only to find the next garage was also closed, bummer. I was now starting to worry a bit, but a bloke at the garage told me there was a bank and another petrol station at Villa Union where I'd just come from. So I turned around, rode back and thankfully there was a bank and an open gas station, phew!

Happy that I now had money and fuel I set off on yet another long straight road through the Talampaya National Park, where there wasn't much to look at except sand and cactus trees. I arrived at around 7pm in a small one-horse town called Patquia, which sits on a crossroads of three major routes and has a bus terminal, (well a sandy dusty area with buses coming and going) ticket office and café. You would think it would have had a lot of hotels and restaurants but no, only one flea-ridden hotel. No problem I thought as I checked in before heading off to the restaurant at the bus terminal for supper. Living the dream!

Patquia to La Gruta
(Border checkpoint at Paso San Francisco)

I got out of the flea-ridden one-horse town of Patquia early in the morning and straight onto *Ruta* 7, which would take me north to Nonogasta and *Ruta* 40. This is where I should have been, if not for the closed pass and the 300km plus detour. Another long straight road up through another desert-like valley and not much to look at.

Whilst refuelling at Nonogasta I am approached by an old man who tells me he is a professor (that's two this trip) and is driving a 1924 Model T Ford, of which he has four. We have a good chat and he recommends *Ruta* 78 to me and tells me that it's paved for part of the way but then it's *ripio* for the last 40km.

I took a wrong turn on a single track at the village of Companas and in the process of trying to do a multiple-point turn I dropped the Tiger. I lost my footing whilst manoeuvring and tried to save it but when the Tiger wants to lie down it is going down, so I had to bale. As a result the front left indicator lens had become the first casualty of the trip, broken into four pieces. I spent the next half-hour with glue and electrical tape putting it back together and it looked good as new! I also had a small hairline crack in my left fog lamp that I didn't notice until later.

Botch job done I set off and soon arrived at the section of *ripio*. It was similar to the roller coaster tarmac road I was on yesterday straight with wave after wave of humps. However, the humps were closer together and the dips and crests were deeper and higher and it was gravel, like a giant rhythm section on a motocross track. So I was up on the pegs and wound on the gas – yee ha, let the fun begin! It turned out to be only about 20 km but great fun.

I soon reached *Ruta* 60, the road that would take me all the way to the Paso San Francisco. On reaching the town of Flambala I had been riding for over five hours and decided to call it a day. Only problem was there are only a couple of hotels and they were fully booked, so I checked the map and decided to ride on to the next town, Cortaderas, about 100km up the road. I had something to eat and refuelled before setting off up through the mountains. From Flambala it is a steady climb upwards through stunning red sandstone mountains with the road carving its way through gorges and canyons. It then reaches the valley of Chaschuil, which runs for over 160km due north at a height of around 4,000 metres above sea level. It is surrounded on all sides by mountains of all colours; reds, sand, granite, yellow and every shade of grey.

As I reached Cortaderas, I discovered there was no town, just a massive single-storey hotel smack bang in the middle of nowhere. The car park was empty and there was not a single guest to be seen anywhere. Inside there was a receptionist and a maid, it was also very expensive and had no Wi-Fi, bummer. The receptionist told me there was a hostel and Wi-Fi at La Gruta, the border crossing; well I am sure that's what she said. With the information she had given me I decided to ride on to La Gruta, but when I arrived at the border checkpoint there was nobody around; it was all locked up and the barriers were down. There are only two buildings up here; the border checkpoint office, which is like an old scout hut, and an old dome-shaped building with a corrugated steel roof a bit further on. I wandered around knocking on the doors and looking in windows when suddenly a border official appeared. I was taken inside where I sorted out my immigration and import paperwork and I asked him if there was a hostel here. He pointed at the little dome-shaped building about 100 metres past the checkpoint. Paperwork sorted for the bike, the barriers were lifted and I rode over to the other building.

Again there was no one around and again I was wandering around knocking on doors and looking in the windows. An old man appeared and I asked if this was a hostel and how much it was. Well it was a hostel of sorts but I'd no choice. It was 7pm and the nearest town was back down the mountain 210km away, where I'd just come from, and there was no accommodation there anyway. I was shown around inside and it was like an old Army Nissen hut, corrugated metal roof, 12 bunk beds all with a mattresses each one more minging than the next. The kitchen was even worse – disgusting, with a giant half-empty pot of what looks like pea soup or something. Well I'd been in worse places but really couldn't remember when. I'd been riding all day, hadn't passed or seen another car, and all there was here were two border officials and a soldier in the other building. And me, an old man, a cat, a dog and it was a Saturday night, living the dream!

Well, things weren't that bad, I was self-sufficient, I'd got rations and wine so I sorted out my bed space, a choice of 12 minging bunks and got my sleeping bag out as there were no sheets, thankfully. I then went to the kitchen to prepare myself some pasta and tuna. I put the pasta on, opened a tin of tuna and whilst waiting for the pasta to boil I went outside to watch the sun set over the Andes. Back inside the pasta was boiling away and I went to get my tin of tuna which I thought I'd left on the table. It wasn't there, maybe it was over by the cooker; no it's wasn't there either. Now I have been in this position before (no I don't have Alzheimer's) when entertaining guests at home and my old retriever Millie ate all the starters, but I thought, surely not. I went outside and there licking out the last bits of my tin of tuna was the resident dog and tuna thief.

It was Saturday night in the Andes, I was 4,000 metres plus above sea level, had a bit of an altitude headache (or is it the wine?), no one to talk to, no TV, no sheets, no electricity (generator had just been turned off), no phone signal, no Wi-Fi, and no tuna for my pasta. Pasta and tomato sauce yummy, but thankfully a bottle of Casillero del Diablo to wash it down. Life doesn't get much better.

Never mind, tomorrow I had 120 miles of *ripio* to look forward to as the road ends here.

Paso San Francisco (The longest pass)

Waking up in the morning I could hear the wind whistling around the hostel and feared the worst. However, on looking outside I was greeted with a glorious day with brilliant sunshine, clear blue skies, very little wind but very, very cold. I had breakfast of sausages and an egg (made sure the dog was outside) that I had left over from Uspallata before setting off. There is a single petrol pump at La Gruta but like everything else here there was no one to be found. So I calculated that I could make it to the next station with what fuel I had plus my spare if necessary, even though I didn't know where it was, it can't be more than 330km away, surely.

As I climbed up and away from the checkpoint, *Cerro* (Mount) Incahuasi appeared on my left with another mountain behind it; both are just short of 7,000 metres above sea level and they were bathed in brilliant sunshine – awe-inspiring. The road continued upwards for about 30km on switchback corners with smooth tarmac until it reached the actual border marked on the map. At this point the tarmac ended and the *ripio* began. The pass runs for about 130km and sits at around 4,800 metres above sea level.

I stopped to reduce my tyre pressures before going on the *ripio* and I was amazed at how high they were just with the change in altitude. That's something I had also noticed with my spare fuel cans; sometimes they looked fit to burst going up and down the mountains. It was also freezing even though it was sunny, and the water in my Camelbak hose froze, and for the first time on this trip my toes were freezing too. The *ripio* was fairly smooth, no really deep areas or large boulder fields, nothing too technical just long and straight but I was still having to concentrate as the Tiger moved around on the gravel.

The pass is surrounded by mountains and I passed the Laguna Verde on my right, which looked frozen. It has now been two days since I started the climb up here and I haven't seen or passed any other traffic or seen a single person, except for those at the checkpoint. I don't know why it is this deserted as it is an absolutely stunning pass and great for riding. I continued on, wondering where the Chilean checkpoint was. Some of the distances between border checkpoints

I've been through vary. At one they were both in the same building and others were a few miles apart and even as far as 50km. However, I was now finding out that this one was even farther. The Chilean checkpoint sits right at the end of the pass, that's nearly 160km of *ripio* between the two checkpoints.

As I arrived at the Chilean checkpoint again there was no one about except a couple of foxes wandering around outside. There was a sign saying ring the bell, which I did and two officials appeared from another building. Paperwork all done I ask where the next petrol station, food and tarmac road was and the answer was the same for all three, about 200km away! I put all my spare fuel into the Tiger and was confident I could make it. As I was refuelling a guard shouted, 'Hey, mister.' I wondered what he wanted. He came across and gave me a chocolate biscuit – I must look hungry. Another guy appeared and asked if I needed money which I did, so I exchanged some dollars for Chilean pesos.

Leaving the border checkpoint the track changed from gravel to hard-packed dirt, which is a joy to ride on, almost like tarmac. It then dropped over the mountain and started descending quite steeply with hairpin after hairpin carved into the dirt. As I dropped further and further out of the mountains the temperature started rising and I had to stop and take off some kit. Reaching the valley below I entered the desert region, the terrain changed and was now all sand and rocks. The temperature had also changed and it was now red-hot! I eventually reached tarmac and civilisation after riding for over 560km without passing or seeing another vehicle, around 330km of it on gravel and dirt, utterly amazing!

Over the last five days I had ridden over 2,000km in all kinds of terrain from desert valleys to mountain passes and high plains, on gravel and tarmac; some roads straighter and longer than you would think possible and others with more bends than I had ever imagined or dreamt of. And the vistas are out of this world, my limited vocabulary doesn't do them justice.

Arriving in Caldera later that day I found a nice cheap hotel and went for a meal in a lovely little restaurant by the harbour. There were massive pelicans right outside and every few minutes a seal popped his head up out the sea for a look as well. I was going to have a couple of days rest here in Caldera before riding up into the Atacama Desert. And the Tiger was parked in the hotel lobby all dirty and grimy but looking good just the same.

Taltal, Antofagasta to San Pedro De Atacama
(Stuck in the Atacama)

After two nights in Caldera I set off up the coast road with the intention of doing a couple of short hops of around 200-ish kilometres each day and taking it easy as I was still tired from my five-day epic.

Now as an avid Moto GP fan I knew the series was coming to Argentina for the first time since 1999. I hadn't originally intended on going to it as I thought I would be in Bolivia or Peru by this time. As I said at the beginning, over the years I had been to every circuit in Europe, some more than once, so I thought it would be a shame to miss the opportunity. Seeing as I was still in the south of South America and still near Argentina, I thought I would check and see exactly where it was being held. I was surprised to see it was only 640km away as the crow flies but as usual I would have to go round a few mountains to get there, so about 1,624km, not that far in the big scheme of things. So I decided to get tickets, only problem being that the ticket website was all in Spanish.

Anyway I headed off for the small coastal town of Taltal and on arriving found a hostel right on the beach. I then went for a coffee and as I got talking to the woman serving, she told me her friend was

78

Starting the crossing of the Passo San Francisco.

Laguna Verde, Passo San Francisco.   *Crossing the Atacama Desert, Chile.*

ABOVE LEFT *Argentine Moto GP, Adventure Riders, left to right: Dan Pederson, Trevor Angel, Andi and Ellen Dellis, me, Mike Waterman, Clive Rayman, Sara Pederson.* ABOVE RIGHT *Flying the flag at the Moto GP.*

an English teacher and he would be here later. We were introduced, his name was Javier; well, that's what he said. I told him of my predicament trying to get tickets and he kindly offered to help me the following day. The next day I turned up at his little school and asked for Javier and the woman on reception just looked at me blankly, was it the language problem? Thankfully Javier had seen me arrive and came out, turned out his name was Hector Javier. What a nice guy, very helpful, and we got the tickets for the Moto GP sorted, one for camping and the other for the racing.

I set off from Taltal – which I must say was a beautiful little town and in hindsight I should have spent longer there – to head up the coast road. Riding along I could smell the salt in the air and feel the cool breeze coming off the Pacific. It was red-hot under the baking sun but the breeze from the sea was keeping my temperature comfortable. There were lots of little tracks running down to the numerous beaches that I passed, so I decided as I wasn't in a hurry that I would find a nice secluded one and go down and relax for an hour or two.

Relaxing is the last thing I did. As I rode down to the beach on a nice firm sandy track all was going well until it suddenly became all soft and before I knew it I was stuck. The Tiger had dug herself right into the sand. It was up over the rear axle and touching the panniers and I was not going anywhere. It was now a recovery operation. First the luggage came off and I tried to get the Tiger going as I paddled and pushed with my feet, but no joy. I did initially have a small Army issue shovel but hadn't needed or used it so had thrown it away some weeks earlier. Now I as I tried digging sand out from under the bike with my bare hands it seemed like a bad decision. Next off came my kit as I was overheating trying to lift and push the Tiger from side to side to lift her up a bit out of the deep sand, which was sucking it deeper and deeper in. I tried again to get it going but still no joy. I was then on my hands and knees again digging with my hands; I also tried filling the hole with the few rocks that I could find and tried again to get going. I got going but as soon as I cleared the rocks I was stuck again, as the Tiger just dug itself right back in. I was now back to where I had started; after an hour of trying everything I could think of, I was still stuck.

I had no choice but to go and look for help, so I walked back up the track towards the road, which was only a kilometre away. And I didn't have to wait long, as what I thought was a 4x4 came by and stopped. It wasn't a 4x4 but it did have two young men and a girl in it. I explained in my best Spanish (sign language) and pointing to the Tiger sat upright on the beach that I needed help. They didn't want to take their car so we walked back and with them pushing and me riding it only took a few minutes and I was out of the deep sand and back on the firm stuff. I thanked them and took a few photos before they left. I set off soon afterwards utterly exhausted from my relaxing hour on the beach!

It took me another two hours riding through the Atacama desert to get to Antofagasta and I was shattered so I booked into first hotel and collapsed into bed – what a day. Antofagasta didn't appeal to me from what I had seen riding in; too big, too busy, and too expensive. So I was up early next morning for the relatively short ride to San Pedro de Atacama (SPDA). I had tried to book a hostel on the internet but they were all full and it hadn't occurred to me why. I was going that way anyway so I would chance it.

San Pedro de Atacama (SPDA) (Backpacker central)

I arrived in SPDA on a Thursday after riding the most boring piece of road so far. I rode up from Antofagasta to SPDA through the Atacama Desert on a tarmac road and there was not much to look at and it was, well, boring. I had forgotten what time of year it was – it was Easter and a holiday weekend, so when I arrived I had problems finding somewhere to stay as everywhere was booked up. After riding around for an hour or so I eventually found a room but it was costly and I could only get two nights; I had wanted four for a proper rest, but it would have to do.

My first impressions of San Pedro de Atacama were good; it's a nice little town, very small, dusty, no paved streets, very western-looking (like in the movies) and is obviously the Mecca for backpackers, they were everywhere. But I was going to be here for two days now and I planned to visit the salt flats and do some touristy things whilst trying not to look like a backpacker. I had a quick walk around to find a bank, got some money and then went back to do some maintenance on the bike. Back at the hostel I changed the rear brake pads but decided there were still a few more miles in the ones that were in there so refitted them. Next I checked all the bolts and fasteners and was amazed to find that there were two bolts missing from the left fork top clamp, which could have been disastrous. The other two on the right were loose so I tightened everything up and had to replace the two missing ones with two sprocket bolts, which weren't quite long enough but would do for now.

After completing the maintenance on the bike I had a shower and got changed to go and eat. It was then that I discovered that I had left my travel card in the ATM – nightmare. I ran up to the bank, which was only just up the road, in the vain hope that it might still be there, but no. I then had to ring my bank to put a block on it and thankfully it had not been used, so I thought it must still be in the bank. My bank told me it had not been used since I used it earlier, so it must have been in the ATM machine. Worst case, I would lose £200, as that was all that was left on the card, which thankfully I hadn't topped up. I still had three other cards so losing one wasn't the end of the world. But I didn't want to leave it behind and as it was Easter, I decided to wait until Monday for the banks to open to check if it was still there. My bank agreed to just put a temporary block on it.

So I was now stuck in Backpacker Mecca for five days with thousands of other tourists (backpackers) and Chileanos who were here for the Easter holiday. So I had to look around and find another hostel with a bed available for an extra three more days. Flip-flops and shorts on, I tried to blend in, and booked myself on a day trip to see some of the sights. I chose the salt Laguna and the salt flats and boarded a bus with the other tourists. It was then a case of on the bus off the bus as we were herded round the various attractions (salt lake, meteor sinkholes and salt flats). Too many people, too organised, but nice just the same.

When I wasn't doing the tourist thing I spent the weekend drinking in my favourite place so far, a proper bar and the only one in SPDA. It was a proper man's bar with sports on the TV and full of great characters, both tourists and Chileanos. First I met Alan, a retired surgeon from Cardiff with his three sons. We watched the Cardiff game on TV and we drank and chatted from 2pm until ? Really nice guys and a great day. The next day I spent drinking with Chileano miners from the nearby mining town of Calama – great guys and great drinkers.

In the evening I chatted and drank with my fellow guests at the hostel, who were from all over; Chileanos, Germans, English, French, Canadians, Chinese, South African and Poles. I forgot all of their names five minutes after meeting them. But the one that made me laugh and embarrassed was the Polish girl, whose name was Dorita. She had just explained to me that Dorita was Dorothy (my mother's name) in English so you would have thought I would have remembered that, but no! A few minutes later whilst sitting chatting away, and checking my blog, I had a new follower that I didn't recognise. Without thinking, I said out loud 'Who the fuck is Dorita?' I was only slightly embarrassed when Dorita, who was sat opposite me, said, 'I'm fucking Dorita', and everyone laughed as it was really funny. I then tried to explain the rude version from the chorus of the song, 'Living next door to Alice'; Alice, who the fuck is Alice? but it was lost in translation.

This brings me on to Joanne, a Peruvian woman on holiday with her husband. She had worked in Berlin so she was fluent in German, English and Spanish and spent the night translating for the less educated, i.e. me! There were of course many others but I will only mention the two Joes, both from London, nice young guys, and Joe number one's father was editor of *Motorcycle News* (small world) and knew a bit about motorcycles. Eventually Monday arrived and my kidneys were thankful. I went to the bank at 9am when it opened and asked if my card was there. The security guy asked for my passport, opened a drawer, and thankfully it was, so I was reunited with my bank card, happy days.

After five days looking like a backpacker I was itching to get back on the road and I set off for the city of Salta. I was again a motorcycle adventurer. The ride up over the Paso Jamo was superb, really high altitude – around 5,000 metres – and very cold; hands were numb even with the heated grips on. My Camelbak had frozen again and the drop down into Argentina was the most awesome pass I had been over so far this trip; hairpin bend after hairpin bend, unbelievable.

I had 640km to ride to the town of Salta, where I was going to meet up with Marc and Nadia, the Canadian couple I had met a month ago. From there we would ride to the Moto GP at Termas de Rio Hondo. My route would take me over *Ruta* 9, which is quite a narrow road and it cuts through the densely forested jungle-like mountains. By the time I reached *Ruta* 9 it had started raining and riding conditions were quite bad. Crossing back in to Argentina at the border crossing service station I met a tour truck (bus) full of tourists. The tour guide, Jo, was from Falkirk, first Scot I've met this trip. Arriving in the hostel some hours later I was surprised to find Jo and the tour bus there as well by sheer coincidence (small world).

Salta, Moto GP Termas de Rio Hondo
(Night-time riding and crashing)

Loki hostel was free as they had a promotion on, so I spent a couple of days there as I only had to pay for food and drink. I took the opportunity to visit the city of Salta and whilst there I tried to find a new tyre-pressure gauge to replace the one I had lost. This proved more difficult than I thought. Loki hostel is part of a chain of hostels throughout South America and had a mixed bunch of guests, but mostly they are young backpackers as it's a bit of a party hostel. During my stay I met and got to know Stephanie and Marcel (boyfriend and girlfriend), both nineteen and from France, a nice young couple who were both working in the hostel as they had run out of money.

My first night in the hostel was spent watching all the younger guests playing drinking games (which reminded me of Army mess functions) and getting really drunk. Thankfully the accommodation cabins were some way off from the bar and games area so once in bed the ongoing noise and partying did not disturb my night's sleep. Marc and Nadia wanted to leave really early in the morning but I decided to stay for breakfast and leave a bit later in the day due to having a slight hangover.

At breakfast I met Stephanie and Marcel and noticed that Marcel had an injured right hand. I enquired what he had done and asked if he had fallen over as a result of drinking too much. At this point they both looked at me sheepishly and I could see there was something wrong. I also noticed that Stephanie had some bruising around her right eye. They then started to tell me that they had been fighting with each other; Marcel was apologetic as he explained that he had hit her, and Stephanie was making excuses for him. Now, as a father of a grown-up daughter (coincidentally also called Stephanie), I was rather upset and angry. So I felt it only right to dispense some advice (I wanted to dispense some old-fashioned discipline) and gave Marcel a few choice words of disapproval. And then gave Stephanie some fatherly advice regarding her relationship and where I thought it should go.

Relate counselling was the last thing I expected to be doing on my trip; as I spoke with Stephanie I wondered what if this was my daughter in a foreign land with no money and an abusive partner? So I spent some time listening to her as she poured out all her fears and worries to me and tried to advise her as best I could. This meant I left the hostel even later than I had planned. It also meant that I would now need to ride for maybe one or two hours in the dark to make it to Termas de Rio Hondo. Riding in the dark is not a good idea due to the added dangers and most Adv riders don't recommend it.

The route down was OK, still following *Ruta* 9, which had now widened with fast, long sweeping bends and fairly easy going. On reaching the city of San Miguel de Tucuman, I had a slight detour through the city due to a bridge being out. It was also now starting to get dark and there were no lights on any of the roads. The road was now straight and as dark as the black hole of Calcutta. There were cars and bikes on both sides of the road, some with lights blazing and blinding me, and others with one light or none at all.

One of the things I had noticed here in South America is that when riding on the straight roads it was sometimes difficult to judge distance due to the heat haze or the fact that there were no reference points. So cars overtaking coming towards you would sometimes cut it a bit fine. I was now realising that this was ten times more difficult at night. I constantly had to flash my lights at oncoming cars and trucks as they tried to overtake other vehicles. Sometimes I had to brake and pull over to the right-hand side of the road and even the gravel verge if it was too close for comfort. All pretty nerve-racking stuff and I was having to concentrate intensely. So I was relieved to see a sign saying Moto GP camping a few kilometres up the road; I had made it, or so I thought.

With only a couple of kilometres to go there was a line of cars coming towards me when suddenly one pulled out virtually right in front of me. I thought a head-on collision was certain and I was going to die! As thoughts of death or at best a trip to an Argentine hospital flashed through my mind, I took the only option available to me and swerved towards the right-hand verge. The car flashed past my left-hand side, narrowly missing me as I careered across the gravel verge and plunged into the darkness. Hard on the brakes I tried to scrub off as much speed as possible before what I thought was the inevitable collision with roadside furniture. The back end skidded and then came completely round on me due to the slope and I was down and sliding along the verge on my left-hand side.

A thousand thoughts rushed through my mind, was I going to become just another one of the hundreds of roadside shrines? I held on to the Tiger and prayed as I slid along in the darkness listening to the sound of metal ploughing its way through the gravel and dirt, hoping that it didn't start tumbling or smashing into anything. It seemed to last forever but I came to a halt and it all went quiet. I was trapped with my left leg under the Tiger looking up into the dark of the night but thanks to the gods of motorcycling, uninjured.

Out of the darkness came a whole family; Dad, Mum, teenagers and toddlers of all ages stared down at me with a look of shock. I asked for help and they then lifted the Tiger off my leg and put her upright. Now, I'm no stranger to crashing and being injured as anyone who knows me will testify, but I can't ever remember being so shaken; maybe it was the darkness or the fact I was in a foreign country that made it seem more scary. My hands were visibly shaking and my heart was beating so fast and furiously pounding in my chest that I thought I was going to have a heart attack! My rescuers were looking at me as if I had arrived from outer space, with incredulity written all over their faces. I could not speak and even if I could have they wouldn't have understood. They did not speak English so I just patted my chest to demonstrate it was beating furiously and held out my hands (which were shaking violently) for them to see. I then sat by the road in the dark thanking my lucky stars and trying to compose myself.

After ten minutes I thought I should check out the bike so I got out my head torch and looked it over. My left-hand pannier was gone but otherwise I could not see any other damage. Some of the kids went up the road looking for my missing pannier and returned with it a few minutes later. Remarkably it was still intact with no visible damage, and believe it or not, went right back onto the frame. They also found my side-stand foot plate, which had come off as well. I then started the bike, checked the handlebars, controls and all seemed OK. I thanked my rescuers with handshakes all round and then I was off, still shaking and heart pounding but uninjured.

I arrived at the campsite a few minutes later, got my camp pass and race tickets from the office, found a spot to erect my tent and got straight into my sleeping bag. I was asleep within minutes and had a surprisingly sound night's sleep after my close shave. The next morning I checked the bike over again for damage. The crash bars obviously did their job as they were all scratched, the left pannier locking mechanism needed a little tweaking, I refitted the side-stand base plate after some reshaping, and the side-stand protector was slightly bent and scraped but again had done its job. So I was very fortunate to have walked away uninjured and have a bike with no damage.

Whilst eating breakfast I was approached by a grey-haired Englishman who introduced himself as Mike. Mike was from Kent and had read on *Horizons Unlimited* (bike web) that I would be here. Mike had been in South America for four months and was riding a Triumph Explorer. Next along came Andy and Ellen, a husband and wife team from New Zealand (two Moto Kiwis) who have been on the road for over a year; they had seen me coming in to the campsite the night before and had tried to attract my attention to no avail, so they had come to find me. They were with some other adventure bike riders so I pulled pole (packed up) and moved over beside them. I then met Clive, from Canada, Trevor, from Australia, Sara and Daniel, also Canadians (worldwideride.ca) and also husband and wife. All of them except for Mike had been on the road for some considerable time.

I spent the weekend watching the racing and wandering around the circuit with my Union Flag. I only had a couple of comments about the Falklands (*Malvinas*); most people were just interested in where I came from. As we (the Adv riders) all had different tickets for the racing we didn't see much of each other during the day but met up each evening at the campsite. Marc and Nadia, the other husband and wife team from Canada, also turned up for a chat. After eating we would sit around drinking *vino tinto,* regaling each other with biking stories from our travels and having a laugh.

Well that was all except for Clive, who only has a one-track mind (I'll leave it to your imagination) and shocked most of us, especially the women. But Sara, who is a gynaecologist, shocked everyone with a story about a jam jar going places it should not go – again, I'll leave it to your imagination. The one thing that everyone had experienced was the *Viento Fuerte* of Patagonia and all had been blown over numerous times. And finally I was trying to tell them about the tradition of naked drinking in the Commandos, but I didn't think they were quite getting it. So I decided a practical demonstration was called for but to retain some dignity as there were women present I kept my helmet on.

And so after a heavy weekend with *mucho vino tinto* drunk and great racing it was time to leave and go our separate ways. We took a lot of photos and bade farewell and I set off once more heading north for Alaska. As I left, Trevor the Aussie gave me a full-moon salute as I rode past – very appropriate. It was a fantastic weekend and I couldn't have asked for a better group of like-minded adventurers to spend it with.

I had to go back up past Salta again and so had booked into the Loki hostel to do some admin; laundry, rear brake pads and rest after my heavy weekend at the GP. Well, that was the plan, but on returning from town after getting some Adventure bike rider cards (business cards) with my name and blog etc. on them, I was surprised to find Clive there waiting on me. He had ridden up after getting new tyres and was going to spend the night at the Loki hostel with me. More red wine followed and more tales of his exploits as a formula 3 racing car driver in the 70s.

Stephanie and Marcel were still there and Stephanie wanted to talk to me again; why me? She confided in me that she thought she was pregnant to Marcel and didn't know what to do. I again gave her some fatherly advice. Marcel was now in plaster having broken his hand as a result of punching Stephanie, but they were still together. She had also arranged an appointment somewhere to have a proper pregnancy test. That night as we sat down to our evening meal with the rest of the guests, I introduced Stephanie and Marcel to Clive. Now, I had earlier confided in Clive the story of how I had met the two French youngsters and of their domestic situation. This would turn out to be a bad judgement on my part.

As the night wore on and Clive had more to drink he started questioning Marcel as to how he had broken his hand. None of the other guests knew why, but that was about to change. After making Marcel squirm with lots of probing questions about his hand, Clive let it be known that he knew exactly how it had happened. He also told him exactly what he thought of him, all in front of everyone present. As Stephanie looked at me in dismay, she knew I had betrayed her confidence and I felt embarrassed.

The next morning Clive had already left as I went to breakfast and I had to face Stephanie and apologise for my poor lack of judgement in telling Clive about their situation. She was very understanding and forgave me my indiscretion. She then told me that her pregnancy test results had proved positive and again she asked me for advice. This time, however, she was in tears, and again I asked myself, why me? I didn't have the answers, certainly not the ones she wanted to hear!

I would hear from her months later and she and Marcel were still together and had decided to keep the baby, much to my dismay.

The Loki hostel had a lot of other interesting guests; of note were two French guys riding unicycles around South America (gajociclo. com). There was also Jergen, from Norway; he was riding a Kawasaki KLR 650 and had a paraglider in a large bag (almost the size of a 50-gallon oil drum) packed on his bike, as well as all the other stuff, including a small helicopter packed in a Pelicase (plastic box) about the size of a suitcase. All this had previously been in a trailer that he had been towing behind the bike, but had got rid of, so it was now all packed on to the bike, unbelievable! He also had the largest tool roll I have ever seen, but he still had to borrow a socket from me to fit his rear-wheel spindle nut.

And finally I met Louis, another Canadian rider; looked like a hippie, baggy pants, long hair in a ponytail and long scraggly beard. He was riding a Chinese 250 thing and is as mad as a brush. Unbeknown to me he was also partial to getting naked as I found out weeks later when a photo of him naked on my Tiger appeared on Facebook. A great week with lots of interesting, kind and friendly people, more great roads, scary night-time riding and a very lucky escape, living the dream!

4.

Bolivia

Ruta 1 Bolivia, Potosi and Uyuni (Finally leaving Argentina)

After my 2,000km detour south from San Pedro De Atacama to Termas de Rio Hondo to see the Moto GP, I was finally leaving Argentina and heading for Bolivia. After two months in South America I had already ridden over 14,400km back and forth over the Andes.

After my rest and administration at the Loki hostel I was up early and away before most of the other guests were awake. I took *Ruta* 34 north towards the border crossing at Aguas Blanco; there was only one section of *ripio* and nearing the end of it I could hear something banging and rattling underneath the bike. I pulled over to investigate and found that the spring that keeps the centre stand up had gone AWOL (missing). I had a quick look around but it was nowhere to be found, it could have fallen off miles back. So I just had to bungee the centre stand up and continue on. My intention was to stop over for the night before crossing in to Bolivia in the morning; I had used all my Argentine pesos and hoped to use my debit/credit card to refuel before crossing in to Bolivia. No hope, none of the garages at San Ramon De La Nueva Oran would take any type of cards. So I had to look for a cash machine to get cash and then refuel. After getting money I filled up, including every spare can, and set off for the border.

Aguas Blancos was a lot smaller than I expected and looked like a little shanty town, and worse, there was no accommodation to be found anywhere. I now had a choice – to go back about 50km to the

92

last town I had come through or cross into Bolivia this evening. Into Bolivia it was. I took some time to get through the checkpoint and I was keeping an eye on my bike, which was parked right outside. Paperwork all done, I came out and immediately noticed that my 3ltr fuel can that I had just filled was missing. A bit annoyed but no great loss – it could have been worse. I set off and rode a few kilometres down the road to Bolivian immigration and whilst waiting for my visa it started raining heavily, a proper tropical downpour.

After getting my passport and other paperwork sorted out it was on with the waterproofs and off I went on *Ruta* 1 towards the city of Tarija, about 160km away. By my calculations it would mean maybe a half-hour riding in the dark. Well, it couldn't be much worse than riding in the torrential downpour that I was riding in at the moment. The road was twisty and surrounded on both sides by thick jungle-type forest. Thankfully after a short while the rain subsided and I reached the city without problems, except for the fact I had no Bolivianos (money). I found a hostel and then a bank and had an early night once again, exhausted after my 640km ride.

The next day I had my first experience of the strange petrol rules in Bolivia. As a foreign tourist some garages will not give you fuel and those that do, charge you more than the locals are charged, roughly double. The first three gas stations I went to wouldn't serve me fuel at all and only told me this on reaching the pump, after queuing for ages. I was getting rather pissed off with riding around town in the baking heat looking for garages. This was made more difficult by the fact that my satnav was not recognising Bolivia at all for some reason, so I could not use the 'find garage' app. Thankfully the fourth garage I found did give me fuel.

After re-fuelling I set off, still no satnav and by coincidence (bad admin) I did not have a detailed Bolivian map either, just the large-scale South America map. So I had to use the force (the sun) to get out of town as road signs were rather absent. Once onto *Ruta* 1 it was fairly easy; one road first heading west up and across two red sandstone mountain ranges, then another road heading north to Potosi. I have been going on about the roads here in South America and how good they are, but *Ruta* 1 has got to be the best tarmac/concrete road I have ridden in my life anywhere. For over 300km it twists its way through gorges and valleys with red sandstone mountains towering above on both sides, first westwards and then northwards in a constant series of switchback bends with perfect radius corners. The bike was only ever upright as I flicked from left to right and back again. It was now considerably hotter than it has been the whole trip and I had to ride with my jacket and all vents open too. I arrived in Potosi around 4pm exhilarated and full of the joys of motorcycling, rather than exhausted, which was a nice change.

I quickly found a cheap hotel at the bottom of a very steep road and then had a wander round. Potosi is a World Heritage site and is also the highest city in the world at 4,070 metres above sea level, so I decided to stay for two days to have a good look around. The big mountain that overlooks Potosi is in fact a massive silver mine, which has been in existence for over five hundred years. There are lots of lovely buildings and chapels in narrow congested streets that are mainly full of cake shops, *pollo* (chicken) fast food shops and *Peluqueria* (Barber) shops. I have honestly never seen so many barber shops in one place, hundreds! So I decided to have a haircut – at a good old-fashioned men's barber, with cut-throat razors, and a splash of aftershave, probably the best haircut I have ever had, and it cost me all of 80p, bargain.

An early getaway from Potosi on the Sunday morning was planned, as I still had no satnav and wanted to get out of town before it got busy. At breakfast I met Scott, a retired Canadian living in Nepal, and got chatting, a very interesting and well-travelled man, so that was the end of the early getaway. Trying to find the road for Uyuni proved to be difficult with no satnav. After several circuits of the narrow streets, not helped by the numerous confusing detours for roadworks, I was back where I started. The force was not working, but I eventually got out of town on to what I thought was the correct road. A few miles outside of town I came to a *peage* (toll booth) and asked if this was on the road to Uyuni. I was then informed that it was not, so I had to turn around and head back into town and around the now familiar streets asking everyone and anyone, '*Donde esta el carretera ruta Uyuni, por favor?*'

I was given lots of directions, most of which I didn't understand, but I nodded politely before riding off in the general direction. Whilst riding around I could see traffic on a road about 300 metres away across the top of some buildings, which looked as if it might be the one I was after, but how do I get to it? The beauty of having an off-road bike is it can go most places, so I took a direct route; across a building site, through some roadworks, then across a football pitch to the astonishment of those playing football and down a couple of small back alleys behind some houses and I was on the road. And thankfully it turned out to be the right road, as I saw my first sign for Uyuni.

Ruta 5 to Uyuni was similar to *Ruta* 1, not quite as twisty but series after series of perfect bends on perfect tarmac through similar terrain of red sandstone mountains. After a while the road opens out and the terrain is more a dirty mustard colour with small gorse type bushes, cactus trees and fields full of llamas and sheep. Whilst cruising along I had another heart-pumping moment when two llamas ran across the road in front of me. Mummy llama flashed across in front of me very quickly and was away even quicker. As I swerved, baby llama ran right in to my path, and I thought I was going to hit it with the inevitable crash. But I'll tell you this, I have never seen anything move so fast in all my life as it had a quick burst of speed and I just missed its back end. Disaster averted again, I came over the top of the last mountain range and got my first view of the city of Uyuni and the Salar de Uyuni (Salt lake) – what a beautiful sight.

I had planned to stay in Uyuni for a couple of days to look around. I was also going to ride across the salt flats towards the town of Llica. Llica lies some 160km away across the absolute nothingness of the dried salt lake. After sorting out accommodation for my stay I took a walk to the Train Cemetery, only a few miles outside town following the narrow-gauge tracks. It was a nice walk but I could feel the altitude affecting my breathing. The train cemetery is exactly that; lots of old rusting steam engines and carriages lying around. They all have graffiti and slogans painted on them and it is very popular with the tourists who clamber all over having their pictures taken. It is just like a large scrapyard, all just left here (but interesting all the same) in the desert, don't know why.

Back at the hostel I met a couple from Bristol, Joe and Lizzie, who had been cycling for over a year; they were dismantling a bicycle. Joe asked if I had a spanner that would fit the rear axle nut. I did and we got chatting and I gave him a hand disassembling the bike. I was shocked and saddened to hear that they were dismantling it for their friend, whose wife had been killed the week before cycling here in Bolivia. He (the friend) had flown back to the UK with his wife's body, all very sad and I could see that they were clearly upset. What a horrendous situation for a young couple to be in. I know from personal experience (having lost friends and soldiers in Afghanistan), that it's never easy when you lose someone and have to continue on.

So I arranged to meet up with Joe and Lizzie that evening for a pizza and to buy them a few drinks. They introduced me to Johan and Kevin, both 21-year-old German Adv motorcyclists in the last few weeks of a six-month trip. We ate pizza, drank *Potosini* (beer from the highest brewery in the world) and then some wine and had a good laugh and swapped stories of our adventures. Lizzie had had a narrow escape in Tierra del Fuego, when she was blown over the crash barriers on a high mountain pass with her bike. Fortunately she escaped with only a few grazes. Johan and Kevin also had stories of their adventure and coincidently had also met Clive, the 63-year-old Canadian biker (small world) some months earlier. We swapped stories of drinking with Clive, all very funny, and it was another great night with fellow travellers even though the circumstances of our meeting were rather sad.

Salar de Uyuni and the sandy track north to Oruro

I set off on the Tuesday morning with the intention of riding across the Salar de Uyuni to the town of Llica, where I hoped to overnight. I followed the track that runs north out of Uyuni to the town of Colchani, where I could get on to the Salar at the main entrance point. You can only get on and off the Salar at fixed access points, which are slightly raised, as a lot of the edges of the dried salt lake are swampy and watery. Once on there are a few main tracks that cross the Salar. The main tourist track runs from Colchani for about 60km to the island of Incahuasi which sits at 3,660 metres above sea level. This track was easy to follow as the normally pristine white salt was black from the amount of tourist traffic that uses it on a daily basis.

Arriving at the island I was not surprised to find dozens of SUV 4x4s and tourists all picnicking. I had lunch at the little restaurant there before setting off for Llica, another 100 or so kilometres northwest. So I took a compass bearing and off I went. The track to Llica was not that easy to see as none of the tourist companies go over that way, so the Salar was like virgin snow. On the first half of my ride across I was surrounded by SUVs; now, however, on this leg I was all

Crossing the Salar Uyuni.

ABOVE LEFT *Dakar Bolivia statue on the Salar Uyuni.*
TOP RIGHT *Sandy track north of Uyuni.* BOTTOM RIGHT *The Tiger resting after a particularly deep bit of sand.*

alone. Riding along keeping an eye on my compass, occasionally I saw some vehicle tracks heading in roughly the direction I was headed. Eventually I arrived at the far end of the Salar and found the track that would lead me off to Llica.

This track turned out to be a bone-shaker, all washboard-type ruts very close together, and I got a right shaking for the next 16km. On the outskirts of the village of Llica there was an Army checkpoint. The soldier on duty asked for my name and also asked why I was there. I duly told him my name and that I was just passing through. With that he lifted the barrier and waved me through and I rode into Llica. I rode down what looked like the main street, very narrow with single-storey clay-brick buildings on either side. It was also very rough, more of a rocky track than a road all the way to the opposite end of the village. I was now finding out why no one came here. There's weren't a lot of people about and it was very quiet. I rode around for a bit looking for somewhere to stay but to no avail. It was very much like the little Mexican villages you see on westerns. I did, however, find a nice little church in a small cobbled square so took a few photos before making a decision on what to do next.

It was now 4pm but I knew I could make it back across the Salar to Uyuni before dark if I got a move on. So off I rode back out through the Army checkpoint and onto the bone-shaker track to the Salar. Once on the Salar I put a bearing on my compass of due east, which would take me the direct route across, missing out the island with the café and hopefully straight to Uyuni.

The sun was on my back as I rode at 160kph across the virgin white salts of the Salar just following my compass. I kept the sun behind me as an extra bit of confirmation that I was going in the right direction (due east) to Uyuni. Saying that, it was very disorienting riding on the Salar, all the little islands and the surrounding mountains start to look the same and you start doubting yourself. But like all navigation you have to trust the compass as it's usually right. Arriving at the other end I now had to find an exit track, easier said than done.

It was now dusk and there were no other tourists 4x4s around to follow, so I had to ride around looking for the exit track. I almost got caught out in some soft mushy salt and had a brief moment of panic but powered out and back on to harder stuff, relieved I hadn't got stuck. I was starting to get a bit worried as dark was closing in and the thought of a night on the Salar was not appealing as it was bloody freezing. So I got out my binos, stood on the seat and had a look around the horizon. I saw what looked like a 4x4 in the distance and it seemed to be heading in the general direction of Uyuni, so I made the decision to ride in that direction and found a track that would get me off the Salar. And what a bit of track it turned out to be; twisty, not too rough, gently undulating and little berms following a narrow single-gauge railway line; it was like a little motocross track and very enjoyable.

I made it back to Uyuni just as it was getting dark and returned to the hostel I had been in the night before. Unfortunately it was now fully booked so I had to go to the hotel next door. Outside the hotel I was surprised to see another motorcycle, a BMW 800GS with a UK registration plate. As I was unpacking I met the owner, Charlie, who was an American and was on a world trip. Charlie had arranged for secure parking for his bike so after unpacking I went along with him. It was only across the road, a few hundred metres away in the yard of a local resident, and we secured our bikes for the night for only a few Bolivianos. That night we went out for pizza and a few drinks and swapped biking stories and he explained why he had a UK registration plate. Unfortunately we could not ride together as I was heading north the next day and he was waiting on friends. In the morning I had breakfast with Charlie and then I set off around 10am.

My destination for the day was the city of Oruro 320km to the north. There is a tarmac road which goes to Oruro but it would mean going all the way back to Potosi on the road I had come in on and then turning north, making the journey nearer to 480km. So I decided to take a *ripio* and sand track that runs due north for about 160km, before joining *Ruta* 1 and tarmac. It seemed like a good idea at the time; however, after a few sandy sections, it now seemed like a bad idea. Most of the track was fairly enjoyable and good riding but the sandy sections were very testing and physically demanding in the baking heat and the inevitable happened on a couple of occasions!

The first was on a small detour from the main track and it was really deep sand; the Tiger started weaving from side to side quite violently and it was hard to control. I veered towards the left side of the track and clipped the edge of the high sandy berm which was running alongside. That was when the front decided to dig right in to the sand and threw me off into the top of the bank. It was fairly fast and was a proper nose dive, and plumes of dust and sand enveloped me and the bike. I got up and dusted myself down and tried to lift the Tiger, which was buried deep into the sandy berm. As I looked across towards the roadworks there were a few workers running over to assist me. I was slightly embarrassed as they helped me lift the Tiger out of the deep sand and pointed towards a firmer section of track. After a quick check for damage and making sure everything was OK I thanked them and rode off.

I had now decided to go a bit slower as I was getting tired and all hot and bothered, keeping an eye out for the deep sandy parts which were hard to see and seemed to just appear out of nowhere. On spotting them I slowed my pace and gently rode through at about 15, 20kph with the Tiger weaving from side to side and me fighting to keep her in a straight line. As mentioned previously as a solo rider you have to compromise speed for safety. Going faster might make riding in the sand easier but the risk of injury is greater so you have to ride more slowly, which makes it very difficult but there is less chance of injury when you fall. And as expected the inevitable happened again and I hit a really deep patch and down I went for the second time; again very deep sand and a soft landing with no damage to either me or the Tiger. The difficult bit was lifting it back up in the deep sand – very tiring.

I finally reached tarmac just past the town of Sevaruyo and heaved a sigh of relief as I was physically exhausted and agitated with riding in the sand. , The sandy track – approximately 160km – had taken me four hours to cover, but the run in to Oruro was fairly straight and I could relax. The big Tiger definitely does not like deep sand and neither do I, a bit scary and the chance of injury ever present in your mind.

Oruro to La Paz

I had only planned on spending one night in Oruro so I found a little hotel in the centre before going out for a bite to eat. I had the usual *pollo* and potatoes in a little local café before retiring for the night. The following morning I had breakfast in the hotel restaurant, which had stunning views across the rooftops to the hills surrounding the city, before setting off. I thought I was going to have problems getting out of the city as I still had no satnav, but thankfully I managed to get out of Oruro fairly easily. Once onto *Ruta* 1 La Paz is just over 200km of straight boring road so it should be a relatively easy day's riding. Only the numerous *Desvios* broke the monotony and even these were boring, hard-packed gravel, easy to ride on.

Highlight of the day was when entering the outskirts of the city I spotted a small tyre garage on the way in, with a power washer. So I pulled over and in my best Spanish asked if I could use it. They agreed and I set about washing the salt and dirt off the Tiger from the previous few days' riding and all for the princely sum of around

£1. Tiger all cleaned I arrived in La Paz about 1pm and spent the next two hours riding around the gridlocked, chaotic city looking for somewhere to stay and getting all hot and bothered. Eventually I ended up back at one of the first hotels that I had seen on the main street when I had first arrived. It was nice, and fairly cheap, so I booked in for two nights as I had some maintenance to do on the bike and wanted to have a good look around the capital. In the evening after wandering around and having a meal I watched some entertainment and a military-style band performing in a square just down the road from my hotel.

I got up early the following morning and did a couple of hours' work on the bike; changed the air filter, adjusted the chain and gave it a general check-over for loose bolts. Job done I then went for a wander round town, which was a little disappointing with not really much to see. The roads in the city are congested; all the vehicles are constantly pumping their horns for no apparent reason so there is a continuous cacophony of horns which after a while drives you mad. The taxis (people carriers) and the old dodge buses, which are all brightly coloured, are a law unto themselves, with people jumping on and off everywhere and anywhere. If Potosi was full of barbers, La Paz is full of opticians – hundreds of them everywhere, which was handy as I had lost a screw out of my reading glasses so I went in to one and got them repaired for 50p – winner. Not a lot to do, found a Burger King and had a classic which was nice after a few days of eating local food, *pollo;* soup, grilled, fried and all with weird veg and horrible black potatoes.

I then went on the hunt for a coffee shop; you'd think there would be loads as it's a city, but no. I eventually found one and had a couple of nice coffees. Whilst in the coffee shop I met an 18-year-old English man from Cheltenham who looked remarkably like my son, uncanny. I walked around the overcrowded city some more, taking photographs of buildings and the busy streets. I also watched hundreds of Christian marchers or protesters go by and I was certain I had passed them the day before miles outside the city limits on the road into La Paz. I stood and watched them all go by with their banners, singing and chanting, all very entertaining. That night after something to eat I went to an Irish hostel called the Wild Rover to meet the young bloke I had met in the coffee shop and his friends for a few beers and a chat.

On the way back to my hotel just after midnight I stumbled across a rather nice plaza surrounded by government buildings that had a military parade ongoing. There were a few hundred soldiers and a band marching around the square. This immediately got my attention (being an ex-soldier) and so I decided to stay and watch. There were very few other people around as it was late but I was totally engrossed watching the soldiers drill. As they say in the Army, drill is like a pill, it should be taken thrice daily! It became obvious that this was a rehearsal for something as they marched around the square over and over again with the officer in charge shouting out orders and commands. The soldiers were all wearing berets, dressed in normal fatigues but with white cross belts carrying black leather packs with a red tube attached to the top. They had white slings on their old-fashioned-looking rifles, which also had bayonets fitted. After an hour or so sat on the steps in the plaza enthralled by the standard of drill or the lack of it, I decided to call it a night and head back to my hotel.

I had another early start in the morning so I could get out before the chaos; my destination for the day was the infamous Ruta de la Muerte (Death Road).

Gnarly track to Coroico and Death Road (Ruta de la Muerte)

Two and a half months into my ride through the Americas and I had already ridden some famous motorcycling routes; *Ruta* 40 Argentina, Carretera Austral Chile, both of which are mostly gravel and hard-packed dirt with some tarmac sections. I had also ridden across the Atacama desert in Chile and the Salar de Uyuni in Bolivia and other less well-known tracks, all of which were fantastic off-road biking routes. Some were rougher than others but all had tested mine and the Tiger's off-road credentials to varying degrees. But now I was going to ride the infamous Ruta de la Muerte (Death Road) in Bolivia and the Tiger would be tested to the limit, but not on the Death Road.

After two days in the busy overcrowded city of La Paz sightseeing and relaxing I set off to ride the Death Road. My satnav had not been working at all in Bolivia (no mapping whatsoever – thanks Garmin) and I had had to use a map and compass for navigation. I knew it was going to be difficult getting out of the city as I didn't have a city map and there were few road signs. And so it proved to be; two hours riding around asking directions, getting all hot and bothered and frustrated. Up and down streets I rode in vain, twice coming back to where I had started from. Some had smooth concrete surfaces with little traction and were so steep you felt as if you were going to fall off the back of the bike. Eventually and with great relief I got on to *Ruta* 3, which would take me towards the Death Road.

Once on *Ruta* 3 it was a long steady climb up over the mountains on a perfectly tarmacked road. As I neared the top of the pass it got really cold and then the fog came down (or I rode up into it) and it started raining too. With visibility reduced to a few metres I had to ride at about 15 or 20mph as I strained to see through the fog and rain. Steadily, I rode on and on and over the top of the mountain on the main road and down the other side. Due to the fog, having no satnav, poor maps and not really knowing where exactly the Death Road began, I somehow missed it. I had ended up on the far northern side of the town of Coroico at the bottom of a valley on *Ruta* 3. As I rode along I passed a small sign saying Coroico, pointing up what looked like a footpath; it looked too narrow to be a road so I rode on.

After a few kilometres I came to some roadworks where I asked the woman on the stop/go sign; '*Dónde está la Coroico por favor?*' (Where is Coroico?). She pointed back up into the thickly forested mountains to a red-brick town perched high above. So I rode back to where I had passed the small Coroico sign.

It was not marked on my map but the sign definitely said Coroico and was pointing up a very steep small track about four or five feet wide. It was overgrown on either side with pampas grass and trees, which hung down into the track. The track was made of a combination of grass and sort of jagged stones which were laid in the centre and slightly raised. There were rough ruts either side of the rocky middle section which could have been made by a 4x4 vehicle. So I got off the bike and wandered up and around the first couple of steep, tight switchback bends and had a good look at it. It was extremely steep as it started to climb up from the valley floor and got a lot rougher as well. It was maybe just wide enough to drive a 4x4 up, and the sign did say Coroico. I thought it must be the track up to the town and convinced myself it was and that I was going to ride it!

Decision made to take the gnarly track, I reduced my tyre pressures to 30psi rear and 24psi front and then set off. Once committed there was no turning back as it was too steep and narrow to turn the Tiger around. After I rounded the first few tight hairpin bends the drops at the side got steeper and higher, and I was already questioning my decision. The track was getting gnarlier and harder to ride on. On one side there was now a ditch and on the other a steep or vertical drop into the forest below. I also had to contend with tall pampas-type grass and branches overhanging the track on both sides that I had to duck under as I rode through, not easy whilst trying to concentrate on the track ahead.

The track was now getting rougher and rougher with long rutted rocky sections and scary drops down into the heavily forested valley below. Absolutely no margin for error; a fall would not be good, so I tried to relax. But I was tense, anxious and nervous as I muscled the Tiger up the narrow track and around the tight bends. All the while I was thinking if I make it up I'm never going to make it back down! Relax, relax, I told myself as I squeezed the tank with my knees and held the bars with a vice-like grip. Upwards and onwards I rode, fighting the Tiger's weight and trying to keep the momentum going as I bumped and banged across rocks. I was stood up on the pegs the whole way with the sump guard and the centre stand taking a hammering on the rougher sections. I spent most of the climb in second gear, sometimes first around the tight bends and having to feather the clutch. At one point I came across a Y junction in the track – which way? I came to a halt to decide but no sooner had I stopped when the Tiger started sliding backwards on the steep slope. I quickly dumped the clutch and gave her some revs, and thankfully the rear gripped and I was off and moving upwards. I took the left-hand track and hoped it was the correct one.

After God knows how long (forgot to check start time) I reached the outskirts of the town; I had covered only 11km but they were the most exhausting 11km I had ever ridden. I was drenched in sweat with the effort of riding up the track, which seemed to take for ever. Every muscle ached with the sheer physical effort of riding up the track and hanging on for dear life. The track was now wider as I entered the town, with walls and houses on either side. I rode on through the alleyways and eventually emerged in the town square. To my amazement and relief I saw medium-sized trucks, cars and vans of all sizes. So I knew there must be another road into town as they had certainly not come up the gnarly track that I had just ridden. I had never felt so happy and relieved to have arrived somewhere, and most of all I was happy I wasn't going to have to ride back down what I had just ridden up.

I found a hostel and asked the waiter in the restaurant about the roads in and out. And yes, there is a main road and he said I had come up some sort of hiking trail. As I sat in the pool overlooking the valley I had come up from I felt as if I had achieved something. Relaxing with a beer or two it now didn't seem that bad; in a warped sort of way I was glad I had done it. The Tiger had also proved to be very capable even if a bit on the heavy side for this sort of riding. She required a lot of effort and physical input but she had got me up. It was definitely the hardest, most anxious bit of riding I had done on this trip, maybe even in my life.

I also found out the directions to take me to the Death Road, which was just down the hill from Coroico on a wide track (the one I should have come in on) at the village of Yolisa. I was going to ride up the Death Road and it turned out to be rather disappointing after my previous day's ride on the gnarly track. It was three times longer at around 37km; three or four times wider (four or five metres in areas); and nothing very difficult or technical. On the way up I bumped into groups of mountain bikers coming down, all followed by minibuses. I stopped for a chat with some of them and all in all it was quite a pleasant ride to the top. There was only one section, a ride under a waterfall, more like a really heavy downpour on a narrow rough corner for around 50 metres, which was exciting, and that was it. The views when I could see through the mist were spectacular and the drops over the edge extremely steep but nowhere near as scary or as hard as the gnarly track!

On leaving the Death Road it was easy to see how I had missed it, as there are no signs or anything on the main road. I now had about 60km to ride back to La Paz and then hopefully find the road to Copacabana. Just outside La Paz I stopped for a pee and when I got back on the bike every time I selected first gear the engine cut out.

So I freewheeled down to a garage forecourt that I could see a few hundred metres away so as to get off the main road and investigate

Information sign on the Ruta de la Muerte, Bolivia.

Ruta de la Muerte.

the problem. I already thought it might be the side-stand switch, so that was the first thing I looked at and sure enough it was stuck; a quick spray with WD40 and a few pulls in and out with pliers and it was working again. I also blew my tyres back up to road pressures before setting off into the city.

As I rode off I thought I heard someone shouting and looked round to see one of the forecourt attendants waving at me. I wondered what he wanted so I turned around and rode back up. He preceded to hand me my glasses, which I had not packed away and which had then fallen off the bike as I rode off. I thanked him, packed them away this time and was off. Once in the city, I thankfully found the road for Copacabana quite quickly, and once clear of the suburbs had a relaxing ride across some great roads with fantastic scenery.

As I rode through the village of Huatajata I saw some sort of celebration (possibly Mother's Day) going on in the town square, so stopped for a look. There were around sixty or seventy people including a brass band with drums, and women in national dress, all wearing brightly coloured ankle-length dresses, billowing out from the waist like the ones worn in the Victorian era. Their heads were adorned with the traditional small bowler hats, which looked too small and were perched right on the top. All the men were wearing ill-fitting grey suits and Stetson-type cowboy hats. They were in a column four abreast like a squad of soldiers, with the women leading, followed by the men and then the band. They danced around the main square in a sort of two steps forward, one step back movement; it looked like it was some sort of line dance. Most of them, women and men, were carrying large bottles of beer, which they swigged from every now and then. The brass band and drums that accompanied them only seemed to know one tune. It was, however, a very catchy tune with a good beat and everyone looked like they were thoroughly enjoying themselves. I sat there for quite a while watching and soaking up the atmosphere and I felt like joining in as they looked like they were having great fun, but reluctantly I had to move on.

In the town of San Pablo there is a ferry service that takes you across Lake Titicaca. The ferries are not boats but flat wooden barges big enough to take a bus or a truck, or two or three cars. And they do take everything; trucks, buses, cars, motorbikes and foot passengers. They don't look very stable, especially the ones with buses and trucks on board, which were all listing heavily to one side. No health and safety here either as the passengers don't even get out of the buses. After the short ferry ride from San Pablo to Tiquina, during which I had to hold on to the Tiger to keep her stable as there were no tie downs, I then had a nice ride across a twisty mountain road and I arrived in Copacabana around 6pm.

Whilst looking for a hotel I was approached by some English people who introduced themselves. They were guides with Globebusters UK, who were here with some paying clients on a guided tour. After a brief chat they left as they were in another hotel and would be leaving early the next day. I managed to get a good deal on a hotel with superb views overlooking the lake for a few days to rest after quite a hard week's riding. There was a little English-owned bar on the main street so that was where I ended up after supper. During the course of the evening there was a massive thunderstorm and the whole town lost electricity, so I sat in the bar with a couple of blokes from London and other tourists drinking by candlelight as we listened to the thunderstorm crash overhead and the rain run down the main street, which now resembled a river. Living the dream!

There wasn't much to do in Copacabana apart from wandering around and relaxing. There are some nice restaurants and plenty of shops to while away the hours. There is also a very nice Church at the top end of the town which I spent some time looking around. That night after tea I was back in the English bar for a few beers and a chat with the owner before calling it a night. The following morning I had a lovely breakfast before setting off for Peru and the historic City of Cusco.

5.

Peru

Cusco (Historic city and muggers' alley)

I arrived in Cusco after nine hours of riding and covering 500 plus kilometres. I also passed the 16,000km (10,000 miles) mark on my trip and I was only in Peru. Yet again the satnav was not working so I had to ride around Cusco in the dark looking for somewhere to stay. Once in the historic old part of the city I eventually got a nice hotel and booked in for three nights. Cusco's historical centre is lovely, lots of cathedrals and churches, narrow streets and alleys (more of which later), and nice old buildings with balconies overlooking the streets and plazas.

The following morning I took a bus tour to see more of the city, some Inca ruins and the statue of the Jesus Blanco that stands atop a mountain and overlooks Cusco. It was a great couple of hours riding round the city relaxing and seeing lots of great architecture. The numerous churches are a reminder of the Spanish colonisation of the past. Whilst on the tour I received a message from Dan and Sara, the Canadian husband and wife team that I had met last month at the Moto GP. They were coming to Cusco (small world) so I decided to stay a couple more nights and also to move from my hotel to the same hostel as them to catch up.

When I met them I told them about my lack of Bolivian mapping on my Garmin satnav SD card and the problems I was having as a result of it. Dan had other map data on his laptop that he kindly offered to give me, and we went shopping for another SD card so I could load the new mapping on to it and keep the Garmin one separate. Dan downloaded all the maps for South America onto my new card, which will hopefully make life a lot easier. We also had with us a young German rider called Marius, who had bought a bike here in South America and was now riding around on his own. He had only just passed his test before leaving Germany and had never ridden anywhere before. He also didn't know much about bikes and complained that his clutch or gears weren't working properly. Dan and I had a look at it and after a quick adjustment of the clutch cable (which was far too tight) the problem was solved.

We spent the day wandering around the alleys and hills in the city and again we bumped into some of the riders on a tour with Globebusters UK that by coincidence Dan and Sara had also met previously. We chatted for a while and swapped biking stories before going our separate ways. On the way back to the hostel we decided to drop into Paddy's bar, which lays claim to being the highest Irish bar in the world, for some drinks. In the bar we met another German, called Karlson, an engineer working out here for Siemens, whom I had met the day before. One drink turned into two and then three and then we decided to just stay there and drink the night away. A great night was had and it's fair to say we drank quite a few beers. Around midnight Dan was first to succumb and decided to leave and go back to the hostel. He was followed about an hour later by his wife, Sara, and Marius, whilst Karlson and I stayed for a while longer and one more drink. I had eventually had enough also so bade farewell to Karlson and left to make my way back to the hostel, which was only a few hundred metres and a couple of streets away.

Whilst I was walking back down the street, minding my own business in my pink polo shirt and shorts and looking every bit the vulnerable tourist and obviously slightly the worse for wear, three guys appeared from one of the little alleyways. I didn't think anything of it as they started to walk towards and past me. One went to my left, another to my right, when suddenly they grabbed me. It was fight or flight time and I instinctively (I had no choice) went into automatic fight mode. A furious scuffle then ensued as they tried to push and bundle me into the alley that they had just appeared from. Not an ideal situation to be in; I sensed real danger and fear!

I've been in a few fights over the years and boxed earlier in my Army career. But this was not the boxing ring and it was not a Saturday night scuffle – these were dangerous men and they probably did this all the time. Part of parachute training was an event called milling, or fighting with controlled aggression. Milling is basically two guys in a ring and you have to fight (not box, fight) for a whole minute, during which you are assessed for; courage, strength, stamina, willpower and the tenacity to keep going, whether winning or losing. Well this was milling now, not pretty but effective. I fought with all the fury and might I could summon and threw lefts and rights like a whirling dervish.

They seemed shocked that I had seized the initiative. All three of them were pulling and pushing me in an attempt to get me on the ground but I had other ideas and continued to fight and try to break their grip. They clearly weren't expecting my violent frenzied onslaught of wild flying punches and refusal to give in. As first one, then a second got beaten off, the third assailant took a little more effort, holding on tightly to my shirt collar and neck. But eventually I managed to throw him off and break free, ripping off my shirt collar in the process. It was all over rather quickly – 30 seconds to a minute maybe – but it seemed like a lifetime.

I ran across to the other side of the street and thankfully my assailants didn't pursue me. As I reached the other side of the road a passing car pulled up beside me whose driver had obviously seen the violent scuffle. He asked if I was OK, which I was, but I was now very angry and a bit pissed off to say the least, mainly for having let myself get into that situation and the fact that my pink polo shirt was now ruined. My three potential muggers were still in the alley watching and I shouted a few obscenities at them before walking down to my hostel less than a hundred metres away.

I don't know whether they had weapons or not. If they did they thankfully didn't use them, otherwise the outcome could have been so very, very different. I also wondered why I had fought back, (maybe it's because I'm Scottish) as I didn't have any of my bank cards with me and had no money left after my long day's drinking, just an empty wallet. The front door of the hostel was locked and I had to knock for a few minutes to get in, all the while keeping a watchful eye over my shoulder. Tucked up safely in my bed I reflected on what had just happened and knew I had been lucky. Still, no harm done and lesson learnt, but the outcome could have been a lot worse.

Cusco to Machu Picchu (Another crash)

After my eventful few days in Cusco with Dan and Sara, I set off on the Sunday morning for Machu Picchu with the new maps loaded into my satnav. They worked fine and got me out of Cusco and on to the road for Urubamba. Unfortunately after Urubamba the satnav stopped working again and wasn't showing any roads, so I had revert back to the map and ask locals for directions to Aguas Calientes, the small tourist town at the foot of Machu Picchu. After passing through the town of Ollantaytambo the road starts to climb up towards the Paso Abra Malaga. Occasionally you catch a glimpse of other traffic higher up the mountain, which gives an unbelievable perspective of how far you have still to climb. It is a fantastic road, switchback bend after switchback bend as it climbs higher and higher up the twisty mountain pass unlike any I had seen before, to a height of around 4,500 metres before dropping down the other side again on twisty hairpin bends into the valley below. It then straightens out and becomes more flowing as you ride on to the small town of Santa Maria.

It took about four and a half hours to cover the 208km to the town of Santa Maria, mainly due to the slow average speed with the number of hairpin bends on the fabulous pass. Santa Maria is where the tarmac ends and you turn off on to a gravel track which takes you up towards Aguas Calientes and Machu Picchu. So I decided to stop and have lunch and a rest before tackling the ripio! Lunch was in a little roadside shack, not much choice so had the standard *pollo* soup, which is the safe option, you can't really go wrong with soup. Fed and watered I was ready for the first leg on the ripio, which would be for around 32km to the town of Santa Teresa. Now, what I didn't know was that you cannot ride or drive any vehicles to Aguas Calientes. The only way to get there is by narrow-gauge trains. One leaves from Cusco and goes direct to Aguas Calientes, a journey of around 128km (the one my friends Dan and Sara had taken) and is the main transport for the majority of tourists visiting Machu Picchu. The other leaves from the Hydroelectric, which is 16km further up the track from Santa Teresa on the other side of the mountain. From there it is a 13km train ride up the mountain and there are only a couple trains each day. The other thing I didn't know was that I would have to leave my bike at the Hydroelectric station whilst I went on to Aguas Calientes and Machu Picchu.

A few miles after leaving Santa Maria the track starts to climb following the contours of the mountain gorge. The gravel track was in quite good condition and well used by cars and minibuses transporting tourists up to the Hydroelectric train station. It was carved into the rock face and there were sheer drops down into the riverbed below on my left. And as always the views and scenery were fantastic. Riding along at a fair pace, stood on the pegs to soak up the bumps and enjoying the ride, I suddenly and unexpectedly lost the front end. It happened really quickly, as it does, and before I knew it I was crashing hard into the ground. Thankfully I was on a left-hand corner so slid towards the rock face and not the drop into the valley. I hit the ground harder than I can ever remember (except for the time I broke my back and pelvis moto crossing) and felt for sure a trip to hospital was on the cards. I landed on the left-hand side of my back and a searing pain shot through me, my left elbow also took a knock and I had the wind knocked right out of me. My head took a bang and my left foot got crushed slightly under the bike as I hit the ground.

I took a few minutes to gather myself as I was briefly disoriented and couldn't breathe. I pulled my left foot from under the bike and sat there trying to take stock of the situation and figure out how badly I was hurt. I struggled for breath and tried to stand up; I only managed to get on one knee as I gasped for breath, and the pain was almost overwhelming me! I'm not a doctor, but I knew my ribs were broken for sure, nothing hurts like broken bones and ribs are particularly painful as I know from having broken them in the past. I also know that there isn't a lot you can do so you just have to suck it up and cope with it.

As I knelt in the gravel unable to get up, with the Tiger still on its side, a thousand thoughts coursed through my mind; what am I going to do? How badly am I injured? Will I need to go to hospital? Where is the nearest hospital? Thank fuck I've got insurance! Is the bike OK? When will someone come and help me? Is this the end of my trip? All the while struggling for breath and wincing with the pain. I hadn't been sitting there long before a small car appeared, coming round the corner ahead of me. It came to a halt a few metres from where I was sitting in the middle of the track and stopped, but no one got out to come and help me. I could see two men in the front but they just sat there looking at me. Now, it was obvious I needed help as the Tiger was still on its side and I was sat in the middle of the track covered in dust a few feet away. I had to gesture for them with my right arm and hand to come and assist me. Eventually the two occupants got out and walked across to where I was sitting and helped me up onto my feet.

They then lifted the Tiger up and manoeuvred it to the side of the track. They also picked up my left pannier, which had come off, and put it beside me and the bike. As I sat down on the pannier still struggling for breath they walked back to their car. Then without saying a word they got in and drove off, leaving me sitting there at the side of the track wondering what the fuck, and in agony. And unbelievably over the next few minutes whilst I was sat there three tourist minibuses passed by and not one of them stopped to ask if I was OK! Maybe they thought I was just resting?

Now that I had calmed down and assessed my injuries I knew I was going to have to pick myself up and ride out of there. A sense of déjà vu came over me. As I said I'm no stranger to crashing and being injured and I had had a similar incident at the start of the Iraq war in 2003. Whilst on a mission to brief another unit near the Kuwait–Iraq border I crashed my Harley Davidson MT 350 crossing an anti-tank defensive berm. As I cartwheeled down the other side of the berm my left foot got caught up in the frame, dislocating and breaking every single metatarsal in the process. Again I was alone with my left foot twisted almost right around in my issue desert boots. After assessing my options I picked myself up, picked up the bike, dusted myself down, administered a syrette of morphine and rode for another five kilometres across the desert to get medical help, all the while with my foot dangling at the side and in a fair bit of pain. And to cut a long story short from there it was a one-way ticket on the casualty evacuation chain to Selly Oak Hospital in Birmingham.

Now here I was again, injured and alone, so I delved into my pannier, got my first aid kit out and took a handful of painkillers and anti-inflammatories (unfortunately no morphine). Then I had to make a decision; do I go back or do I go on? Might as well go on, I thought, as it's only broken ribs and I've already got a ticket for Machu Picchu; also I'm meeting Dan and Sara, who's a doctor, well OK she's a gynaecologist but she's still a doctor, I reasoned. So onwards it was.

No stranger to self-help, I sat for a while to give the drugs a chance to work and tried desperately to take deep breaths. This proved to be very, very difficult but I had to summon the willpower to get up and check the bike over. Clutching my chest and doubled over I got on with checking out the Tiger. All seemed to be OK apart from the left wing mirror, which was smashed, and my left pannier, which had come off yet again in the impact, only this time it had taken a right bashing and wouldn't fit back on the frame. I got out my tool kit and my stumpy hammer and set about trying to bash and bend the pannier back into shape – not easy at the best of times, but I could only do little baby swings with the hammer and I was almost passing out with the effort. I had to stop after every hammer blow to try and breathe and cope with the pain. Eventually I managed to get it to fit onto the frame and prepared myself for the ride up to Santa Teresa, still some 16km further up the track.

Immediately on setting off I realised the bars were twisted, not much but enough to be very off-putting, which made for an interesting ride. The adjustable clutch lever was also broken, the small spring was missing and a little bit was broken off the adjusting mechanism where it meets the mounting point, but working. So I decided just to ride it as it was and fix it later when I got somewhere and was feeling better. Sat on the bike and with my arms on the bars, I was still hurting badly and still struggling to breathe but it was bearable and I was able to ride, so I pottered along very gingerly in second gear, taking it easy.

After only a few hundred metres my heart sank as I came round a corner and I was confronted by a river crossing about 10 metres wide and maybe around a foot or more deep. At this point I thought again about turning back, but as I said I had a ticket for Machu Picchu (which had cost quite a bit) for the following day. So I took as deep a breath as I could and went for it, steady on the throttle and gassed it through the river and thankfully got over with no dramas.

Arriving in Santa Teresa and onto concrete I got off the bike outside a café and sat on a kerb again to assess the situation and try and recover a bit from the ride up. As I sat there, Nick, a German tourist, came over and started talking to me and asking me questions. I could barely speak and again thought I was going to pass out as I tried to speak with him. All he got was a few grunts and groans and I tried to ask him if he knew where the track to Aguas Calientes was. He wasn't sure and had to go as his minibus was leaving.

Still thinking I could ride to Machu Picchu I asked some locals directions for Aguas Calientes, and for the first time was told you can't ride there, by several people. I was also told I could ride there and given directions by several others. I was confused but again I set off in pain towards where I had been directed. After a few kilometres down a steep dirt track I came across a couple of small buildings and some *aguas calientes* (hot pools) but clearly not the town I was looking for. There was a small campsite there too and again I felt like stopping as at this point I was beginning to feel really low and totally demoralised. But I decided to ride back to Santa Teresa to look for somewhere to stay with a bed so I could lie down and give in to the pain. But once back in Santa Teresa I decided to ask once more for directions and this time a guy told me to follow a white minibus that was going to the Hydroelectric train station. I duly followed, about another 19km further up on a dirt track, but I got there without any more dramas.

Arriving at a little shack at the end of the track, I now found out for sure that you can't ride to Aguas Calientes. I had to leave my bike and all my gear here and get the train, and the last train was leaving in thirty minutes from the station four hundred metres further on. Not a problem when you're fit and well, but I was in agony, I couldn't breathe, couldn't bend over and now I had to get changed out of my riding gear, unpack, repack, park my bike, and store all my gear in a little room. Then I had to cover the four hundred metres on foot to the train platform in time to get a ticket and get on the train. Talk about testing yourself! I was then guided by Wilfredo from the shack to a small compound where I had to leave the Tiger and all my gear. Trying to change, I again thought I was going to pass out as I struggled for breath; I tried to explain to him in my best sign language that I was in fucking agony!

Quick change parades used to be a regular occurrence in my early days in the Army, designed to put you under pressure. But this was self-inflicted pressure and I wondered why I was doing it. Still, all that training was now paying off; in less than fifteen agonising minutes I changed into my walking clothes, packed a daysack with washing kit, repacked my panniers, stored all my bike gear in a little bedroom in the compound, and locked the bike. I made sure I had everything: wallet, camera etc., and we were off en route to the station. Wilfredo must have understood and seen I was in pain and very kindly carried my daysack for me from the compound to the train station. I struggled behind him and couldn't walk upright, having to walk like a half-shut knife to ease the pain emanating from my ribs.

Once at the station I was dismayed to see a large queue but Wilfredo ushered me right to the front. I bought a ticket and got on the train, where I sank into my seat and looked forward to relaxing for a while. The train would take roughly an hour to get to Aguas Calientes as it slowly wound its way in a zigzag motion up the steep mountain track. When I arrived at Aguas Calientes I quickly found a hotel, disregarding the cost (there's nothing cheap here anyway), and went on the internet to get in touch with Dan and Sara and tell them of my predicament. I also took the time to call home to my wife.

My injuries soon paled into insignificance as I was shocked and stunned when she informed me that my 20-year-old son had been rushed into hospital at 4am seriously ill with glandular fever and an extremely high temperature. The infection had spread to his internal organs; he was in intensive care and in a very bad way, but stable. She told me that the doctors said he would be fine once the antibiotics started doing their job and his temperature came down. I told her I was going to come home but she said he would be fine by the time I got back so I might as well stay on my trip. I felt helpless, powerless and lonely; there I was on the other side of the world and I could do nothing. I questioned why I was doing this and why I wasn't with my family. Melancholy descended over me, so I needed to find my two friends, as a problem shared is a problem halved, so the saying goes.

Thankfully Aguas Calientes is not a big place – only two small main streets – and I met up with Dan and Sara a little later on the bridge in the centre of town. I told them of my son's illness and Sara (the gynaecologist doctor) reaffirmed what my wife had told me regarding my son's prognosis. She reassured me that all would be fine, so I felt a little bit better. She also gave me a quick check over (thankfully I wasn't pregnant) and more importantly gave me some special painkillers, the kind that only doctors get! She also gave me enough to last for a couple of weeks and I must say they did the job.

The town of Aguas Calientes is the jumping-off point for Machu Picchu and was built specifically for tourists. There are two ways to get up to Machu Picchu from town, the first and hardest option by walking, which takes around two hours, all uphill and also means a 3am start. The second is by the numerous little buses (the only vehicles here in town, brought in by train) that ferry tourists to the main entrance, thus saving you walking. The first option wasn't appealing to me as I didn't think I could make it with my broken ribs, but Dan and Sara, who had arrived earlier in the day, had already got me a ticket for the bus that would take us to Machu Picchu in the morning. How relieved was I, and they hadn't known that I was injured until I'd arrived and told them, so I was very grateful.

That night I had a sleepless night as I couldn't lie on either side, nor my back or front as everything hurt; that and the fact I was in a hotel room directly over a raging, roaring white frothing river that runs through the centre of town. Still, I managed to get up at 4.30am in the morning (well I was awake anyway) and had breakfast of an egg roll, a can of Red Bull and a handful of painkillers and anti-inflammatories. I was supposed to meet Dan and Sara but there were hundreds of tourists waiting to get on the buses and I couldn't see them anywhere, so just I joined the queue and got on the next available bus up to Machu Picchu.

Getting off at the entrance to Machu Picchu along with the hundreds of other tourists I still couldn't find Dan and Sara, so I set off for the Sun Gate, which is the second highest point on Machu Picchu and about a kilometre up a steep footpath. Hard enough to walk up to when in the best of health but I'd got broken ribs and I was about 2,500 metres above sea level, where breathing was difficult, to say the least. I had to stop occasionally to try and suck in air as my chest felt like I had a python around it crushing me. The only other people who were struggling were the old and the fat and I could see other tourists looking at me as I struggled to draw in breath; they must have thought I was really unfit, which was a bit embarrassing. However, once the drugs had kicked in and I was warmed up I felt OK. I managed to get to the top and also get around the rest of the ruins at Machu Picchu. On the way down from the Sun Gate my

The track to Aguas Calientes (Machu Picchu).

Me with Dan and Sara at Machu Picchu.

arthritic right knee started hurting even though I had taken lots of tablets. Still, it took my mind of all my other aches and pains, so that was a bonus.

As I sat at the top of the ruins talking to four Australians I was surprised to see Dan and Sara appear from out of the clouds coming down another footpath. Reunited, we spent the next few hours wandering around taking photos of ourselves and the ruins. And I must say it was well worth the effort and pain, what an amazing unbelievable place, totally awe-inspiring – it needs to be seen to be appreciated, absolutely incredible! Back in Aguas Calientes after lunch we went to the hot springs (from which the town gets its name) for the afternoon. Very, very relaxing and we sat in there for quite some time drinking cocktails and generally doing nothing. On the way back to my hotel I managed to buy a small shaving mirror, which I intended to fit into my wing mirror as a temporary repair.

Machu Picchu, Ollantaytambo to Lima (Out of Los Andes)

The next day I bade farewell to Dan and Sara and I got the train back down to the Hydroelectric, where I would be reunited with the Tiger. Now that I was feeling a bit better and had some time I spent an hour or so doing some repairs; hammering the pannier back into shape, straightening the bars, taping in my little mirror to the left wing mirror etc. and trying to fix what I could, all the while helped by Wilfredo, the ticket guy. I couldn't take too long over it though, as I had booked a hostel in the town of Ollantaytambo some 160km away and needed to get there before dark. So I did what I could and set off down the gravel track that I had come up on and had my crash on. I took it very easy and was not looking forward to the river crossing but managed to get across OK. I also stopped at the crash site and tried to see where I had gone wrong. There was a deep rut that followed the corner all the way round, with a prominent ridge in the middle of the track, around 8 to 10 inches high, covered with a fine layer of talcum powder like dust – difficult to see in the sunlight as it looked flat. I think I must have been on the ridge going into the corner and as I'd tipped the Tiger in, it had just slid off the top and down it went, dumping me in the process.

I had to stop and readjust the bars as I'd moved them too far in the other direction, which was annoying. All this time wasted trying to fix things meant I was yet again looking at another ride in the dark for maybe an hour so. The problem this time was that I was heading back up the mountain to the Paso Abra Malaga and into thick cloud. So for the last 60km up and over the pass and down to Ollantaytambo I rode in the cold darkness. Visibility was reduced even more by fog and rain. There were countless hairpin bends and the odd truck coming the other way with its blinding lights. Occasionally I had to swerve around big rocks that had fallen on to the road, as they loomed into view through my headlights. And not forgetting the pack of dogs that chased me around one particularly long slow bend. I couldn't accelerate away because of the corner so I had them snapping and barking at me all the way round; a bit scary as I was leant over and they were right beside me. All very tiring, eyes on stalks, I arrived yet again at my destination relieved and exhausted – adventure bike riding, you gotta love it!

After some food I had an early night and the following morning decided to stay for two days to rest and check the bike over properly. There was a lot more damage than I had originally thought; panniers and frames bent, bars still twisted, clutch lever broken, left fog lamp mounting point broken, left wing mirror smashed, left indicator smashed and engine crash bars pushed right into the engine casing, so a few jobs to be getting on with. I spent the next five hours replacing the clutch lever, taping the small shaving mirror into the wing mirror, straightening handlebars, pannier frames and crash bars, gluing the indicator and the fog-lamp mounting point and generally checking the Tiger out all over. I also did some routine maintenance; chain adjustment, coolant and oils. After it was all done it was now as good as new, but not me, as I was still hurting badly. Ollantaytambo is a lovely little town with some ancient Inca ruins not quite on the same level as Machu Picchu but interesting to look at just the same. There are also some nice restaurants and a small plaza to sit and relax in whilst watching the world go by. Whilst wandering around the little alleys and tight streets I found a pharmacist and stocked up on more anti-inflammatories and painkillers; you can get just about anything here without a prescription.

After two days and nights in Ollantaytambo fixing the bike and resting, I awoke to driving rain and considered staying for another night as I was still hurting and struggling to breathe from my crash. But time was against me, so it was on with the waterproofs and I set off for Abancay, 132km east of Cusco. Passing through Urubamba I had a ride around the town looking for a tool shop or something similar to try and get a new 6mm Allen key as I had rounded off the one I had. It was now hammering it down and I was piss-wet through. I eventually found some little car accessory shops and pulled in. No luck in getting a new one, but one little garage shop had a grinder, so I got the guy to grind the damaged bit off the Allen key and square it all off; it was now as good as new, and it only cost 25p.

It was now raining even harder as I set off up over the pass back toward Cusco. With the satnav now working again it should have been straightforward to get to Abancay but the satnav was trying to take me down a wet and muddy gravel and dirt track that said Abancay 74km. The thought of doing 74km in the driving rain on a muddy slippery dirt track didn't appeal to me and the thought of falling off again was even less appealing. So I had a quick look at the map and decided to take a longer route that would take me back towards Cusco. I turned around, rejoined the main road for Cusco and let the satnav recalculate. Passing near Cusco I was sorely tempted to stop and call it a day, and go and meet up with Dan and Sara again, as I was piss-wet through, cold and hurting, but decided to press on for Abancay.

I continued on and the route took me across two *abras* (passes) on route 3S; the first was Abra Huillque at a height of 3,715m above sea level and then over Abra Sorllaca at 4,000m above sea level. It was cold and it rained all day and I'd only put on my Hein Gericke nylon waterproofs and not the ones that go inside my riding suit, so I was soaked right through and freezing. Still, even with the rain the road was superb as it rose up and down with hairpin after hairpin. My Full Bore tyres were proving that they were more than competent in the wet as I could lean the Tiger over confidently on the rain-lashed tarmac.

Abancay was not much to look at, rather grubby-looking, so I found a hotel and then had another look at my handlebars that were still not quite right. After another few adjustments I thought I'd got them aligned correctly, then the mechanism in my ratchet tool broke in the process of tightening up the pinch bolts. After a bite to eat I remembered that I hadn't oiled the chain so decided to give it quick oil. Now if you remember I tore a muscle in my right calf back in March trying to lift the Tiger fully loaded on to the centre stand. Well, just for good measure I was about to tear the left one trying to do the same, all for the sake of the few minutes it would have taken to unload the panniers and kit. As I tried to lift the Tiger I felt that awful familiar snap in the back of my calf followed by searing pain and instantaneous inability to bear weight or walk. How fucking stupid was that? I thought.

I hobbled back to my room and had a thousand thoughts running through my mind; what was I thinking? How could I do the same thing twice? What am I doing here? Why am I crashing? Why won't the rain stop? Why am I in so much pain? Who is doing this to me? Why am I not with my family? My son is in hospital severely ill and I'm here, why? I'm missing my wife, I've had enough, solo adventure biking is lonely; I'm getting the next plane home! Melancholy descended over me like I'd never experienced before. There I was sitting hurting in a dingy hotel in an even more dingy town and the TV in my room didn't even have an English channel to watch, living the dream!

I called my wife who mercifully had good news; my son was on the mend so at least I could stop worrying about him. I took more painkillers and anti-inflammatories and went to sleep; maybe I'd feel better in the morning. I awoke the next morning after a restless night, my left calf had swollen like a balloon, it was still raining and I still felt melancholy. However, I couldn't stay here, it was shit. Digging deep I packed and set the satnav for Huancayo, which sits about 500km further north up in the Andes, and rode off into the rain. The satnav didn't take me where I wanted to go, it took me towards the coast (west) on route 26A and the long way round. On the bright side the rain had now stopped and it was getting hotter and I was able to ride the bike OK without much pain, so things were looking up.

I checked the map to see exactly where the satnav was taking me before riding on. This route would take me about 480km west towards the coast. It's an absolutely fantastic twisty mountain route carved into the rock face. First it follows the river Huanca for about 130km, following every curve of the valley floor as it winds its way west. It then rises over the Abra Huashuccasa to a height of 4,300m and across a *plato* and then drops down an unbelievable series of bends to the town of Poquio. It then rises again to the Abra Condorcenca which sits at 4,390m, before descending down towards Nazca. Once again there were more hairpin bends than I ever dreamed of and passes with climbs and descents that blow your mind away, brilliant bike riding roads, a must for any rider.

At one point I was passed on the opposite side of the road by about 20 BMW riders. Riding along, I came across one who had stopped so pulled over to chat; he was an American and was with the group who had just passed me. They were all on an organised trip with Moto Adventura, a tour company. Not my thing, I prefer the loneliness of the long distance solo adventure rider, or do I?

When I realised I was headed for the Pan American (Pan Am) highway I made the decision to continue. I hadn't intended on riding the Pan Am but a couple of factors were foremost in my mind; firstly I was injured and secondly I needed to be in Alaska by August so as to beat the arrival of winter, and I'm still in South America. So I decided to head for Nazca and ride the Pan Am. It would give me a chance to rest as it's a tarmac road and cruising territory and I can make full speed ahead north. You could spend a year riding in the Peruvian Andes, but unlike my fellow adventure riders that I had met on this trip, I didn't have a year or two, so northwards it is.

I spent the night in Nazca and as luck would have it right opposite my hotel was a small hardware shop and I was able to buy a new ratchet at a cost of 15 soles, just over £3. My leg was already feeling a bit better but still swollen, my ribs were still hurting but the sun was out. For breakfast I'd just eaten four rolls of egg and bacon with the now usual handful of drugs before setting off for the Nazca Lines. These are drawings that were carved into the desert floor thousands of years ago. Now you can go up in a plane to see these but it's expensive so I decided to ride there and see them from a viewing tower at a cost of two soles (50p). The guy at the bottom was a bit light on his loafers, if you get my drift, and sold me two Peruvian string bracelets. Well, what can I say, the Nazca lines are the most underwhelming thing I've seen so far. To be honest I've seen better crop circles. Maybe they look better from the air or if you're an alien looking from outer space, but I doubt it!

After the disappointment of the Nazca Lines I set off for Lima and arrived around 6pm after 500km of relaxing riding on the Pan Am. That was except for dodging the trucks, buses and maniac car and 4x4 drivers. I also got my first puncture of the trip as I was riding through the town of Ica. At first I thought the road surface was rutted or the tarmac was melting as the front end started acting all weird, but then as the tyre totally deflated I lost control and the bike veered across the other side of the road and into the path of an oncoming bus. I regained control and narrowly avoided a collision before pulling into the side of the road. I got out my tools and set about changing the inner tube. Putting the new tube in and getting the tyre back over the rim was very difficult but I got there in the end. Only problem was it would not inflate, so off it came again as I thought I'd probably pinched the tube putting it on. On taking the tube out the problem was very apparent; I hadn't pinched it but taken a big tyre-lever bite-sized chunk out of it, a brand-new tubing ruined. So I had to repair the one I took out and thankfully I got it back in and on with no problems and once more I was off.

I had the usual scary *Death Race 2,000* riding experience in South American big cities on arrival in Lima, so I booked into the first hotel I came to as it had been a long hot day. It was nice but a bit expensive and breakfast was rubbish so I moved across town to another hotel. I had a problem finding it, but a friendly policeman called Arturo, who was standing guard outside a police HQ, gave me directions and was very helpful. I spent the day wandering (hobbling) around Lima doing a little bit of sightseeing. I saw some sort of clown parade and came across some more dancing with a brass band and drums providing the music. This was similar to the celebration I had seen a few weeks earlier in Bolivia; one tune, similar moves (dad dancing, two steps) but outside a church and no beer drinking, only Inca Cola. But wonderful just the same and it lifted my spirits (I need to get the album), very basic with a catchy rhythm. Everyone looked like they were enjoying themselves immensely; I sat there for half an hour enjoying the atmosphere and watching the dancers. Lima, like all the other big cities, was far too busy, so I planned to leave in the morning and beat the chaotic traffic, hopefully.

The past few weeks had been eventful, but my son was now out of hospital and getting better, I was still hurting but no longer melancholy and life was once more great. And despite all the ups and downs (attempted muggings, crashes and injuries) I was still riding and still enjoying it, heading north, 'North to Alaska' as the song says!

Lima to Huaraz, back into Los Andes (Highway robbery)

After my two days in Lima I had decided to head for the town of Huaraz some 500km northeast and back into the Andes, as I wanted to ride the famous Canyon del Pato. It's a high mountain pass and is carved into and through the mountains with lots of tunnels and sheer drops, so I planned a route that would take me back into the Andes and through the canyon. I had heard rumours that the Canyon was due to be tarmacked over and even some that it had already been done, so I set off hoping that it would still be gravel as this might be the last opportunity to ride it in its present state.

But first I was going to go to a Triumph garage in Lima that I had found on the internet, so I set off on Monday morning in search of it to see if I could get a wing mirror, a centre-stand spring and a front tube. According to the satnav it was only 6km away across the city. After an hour and a half in the chaotic traffic during which time my panniers were bumped into twice, once by a bus and the other by a little Nissan people-carrier, I couldn't find it. So I gave up and headed for the Pan Am highway, which runs right through the centre of Lima. It was very busy and just as chaotic as the main streets so it was a relief when I cleared the suburbs and the road got quieter.

There wasn't a lot to look at travelling north out of Lima on the Pan Am although it does go through some very large sand dunes for a bit, but is mainly straight and boring. I was constantly having to overtake the numerous trucks and buses that use the highway. Somewhere near the town of Huaura I overtook (crossing double yellow lines in the process) a slow-moving truck going up a hill. Unfortunately for me there was a *Policia Carretera* (Highway Police) patrol vehicle sitting at the top of the hill and I was waved into the side of the road. I switched off the engine and took off my helmet and waited on the patrolman to come and speak to me. He informed me in Spanish that I had committed a traffic violation and proceeded to demonstrate this by putting his fag packet on my bike seat and drawing two lines beside it before describing my manoeuvre with his fingers.

The conversation then went something like this, the policeman speaking in Spanish with one or two words in broken English i.e. ticket and solution:

POLICEMAN (PM) Papers *por favor*, I need ticket you.

ME OK [handing over my passport and V5 document].

PM You will have to go to police station in Lima and pay ticket. [Don't know if I would have had to? And it was 200km back down the road.]

ME OK ticket. [I'm just going to ride off with it and not pay and he knows this.]

PM *Solucion trescientos soles* [solution 300 soles – about £60.]

ME *No entiendo* [I don't understand]. Give me a ticket.

PM Solucion trescientos *soles*.

ME *No entiendo,* give me ticket.

134

PM *Solucion* trescientos *soles.*

ME Give me ticket.

And so it went on!

We were in a Mexican stand-off, I couldn't just ride off and he stood there with his right hand on his pistol grip trying to look menacing and repeating his mantra of *Solucion, Solucion*. But I just found it funny as he clearly wasn't going to give me a ticket. He just wanted to take money from me and he kept repeating, *Solucion, Solucion trescientos soles*. After ten minutes or so he started to reduce the solution fee, *Solucion doscientos soles*. It was obvious I wasn't getting a ticket and he eventually came down to *Solucion ciento soles* (about £20). I could have maybe kept shrugging and saying, '*No entiendo*' for a while longer but we had now been stood bartering for about fifteen minutes.

Maybe I could have got him lower but I wanted to get away, so I said in agreement *Solucion ciento soles*. Getting my wallet out I duly handed it over like you do in the movies, all shifty and with a shake of the hand. I was then waved off. Corrupt fucker, anyway I don't know what the going official rate is for crossing double yellows, whether I'd have got the ticket or even if I would have had to pay it, but £20 was worth it for the experience. I must say though, every policeman I had met or been stopped by in South America had been helpful and very friendly, and I'd met loads. Even this one was friendly and wished me well on my journey as I set off.

Now, there are a few reasons I decided to go back into the Andes; one, to ride the Canyon del Pato; two, the roads are quieter; three, they are more interesting, twistier and have better scenery; and now four, after today's experience with the corrupt policeman, another reason to head for the hills, as there are no police sitting on mountain tops waiting to fleece you. I left the Pan Am highway a few kilometres further on from my policeman and rode northeast back into the Andes.

I took *Ruta* 16, which follows the Rio Fortaleza from Paramonga and then climbs up to the town of Conococha around 4,100m above sea level; another fantastic twisty climb on perfect tarmac with glorious weather. On reaching the top it started to cool down just a bit but not enough to need warm clothing. Then the road flattened out before gently descending in a super-fast series of high-speed curves following the valley floor beside the Rio Santa. Huge snow-capped peaks over 5,000m above sea level jut out from the landscape ahead and loom over the town of Huaraz.

Huaraz to Chiclayo (Canyon del Pato)

I arrived in Huaraz after a particularly long day's riding and I took a little time to find the hotel I had booked. I was having satnav issues again, but I eventually found it. Once into my hotel I met a German and his wife who were fined 300 soles for not having lights on their car at the same place a day earlier, probably by the same police. So another different but interesting day as an adventure bike rider, living the dream! I had some *pollo* for supper again before having an early night.

Awoke the next morning and my ribs and left lower leg were absolute agony so I had breakfast followed by numerous painkillers and anti-inflammatories before setting off for Canyon del Pato. On way out of town I saw a small bike shop so I stopped to try and get a new front inner tube to replace the spare one I'd damaged earlier. They didn't have one but I got guided by a bloke on a scooter to another shop and got a spare tube and a new spring for my centre stand. Then it was back onto *Ruta* 3N, which follows the Rio Santa with brilliant views of Mounts Huascaran (6,768m), Huandoy (6,395m) and Alpamayo (5,947m), all bathed in brilliant sunlight looming over the valley on the right-hand side as I headed north.

After about 100km on fast sweeping A-type roads the tarmac ended and I entered the Canyon del Pato, and despite all the rumours was glad to see it was still gravel, but not the usual type; this was small, like peas. The track through the canyon is a narrow single track but wide enough, just, to drive trucks and buses along it. The gravel was a few inches deep, not that great to ride on, so I had to try and ride in the tyre-width clear bits made by the four-wheeled traffic. The canyon runs for approximately 10km and is carved into and through the mountainside with numerous tunnels varying in length bored into the rock. The Rio Santa runs through the bottom of the canyon and the rock face rises almost vertically on either side of the canyon. Some of the drops at the side of the track are sheer and there are no barriers so a fall would almost certainly be bad news.

There was the occasional traffic, cars and trucks coming the other way, thankfully not too many. I always came to a halt and let them past as I was on the right side of the track with sheer drops at my side. Sounding the horn was mandatory when entering the tunnels to warn other traffic of your presence. In some of the tunnels you can see the exit and others you can't as they're longer and pitch dark and some are slightly curved. I was maybe 50 meters in to one long tunnel when I was confronted with a large truck coming the other way. I squeezed right into the side but there was no room for him to pass. He obviously couldn't reverse so I had to dismount and manhandle the Tiger round in the deep gravel as it was too narrow to do a U-turn, not easy with sore ribs and a painful left calf. After doing a bit of to-ing and fro-ing, I got it around and rode back out only to have to repeat the process again to go back in.

Riding through the canyon I couldn't help comparing it to the Ruta de la Muerte in Bolivia. The canyon I thought was better, not the same scenery and not as long but more interesting, and what an amazing feat of engineering. Leaving the canyon I then joined

Ruta 12 still following the Rio Santa, which would take me west back towards the coast and the Pan Am highway. *Ruta* 12 is similar and just as amazing as the Canyon del Pato with tunnels and vertical rock faces rising on either side, only wider and with hard-packed dirt and gravel, much better for riding on. Still unable to stand on the pegs for long due to my sore left calf, I motored along at a good pace slowly getting my confidence back after my recent visit into the gravel. I occasionally rode in the loose gravel in the centre of the road, again trying to rebuild my confidence, and thankfully there were no dramas.

After around 100km of great riding on the gravel I reached tarmac and also a police checkpoint where I was waved to the side of the road. I thought, oh no not again! But this time they just wanted to talk and asked me the usual questions; where are you from? Where have you been? Where are you going? Are you alone? Then I was waved through with a smile and no money changed hands. Arriving at Chimbote near the Pacific coast I refuelled at a service station and asked if there were any hotels nearby or on the way up towards Trujillo. The two petrol-pump attendants told me not to go to Trujillo as it was dangerous. I had previously been told this by an English teacher from Lima – that this was a particularly dangerous city and the chance of robbery and murder were high. The two attendants confirmed this by making pistol shapes with their hands and putting them to their heads and pulling the imaginary triggers and saying '*No, No Trujillo*'. It was clear that they were telling me not to go to Trujillo as I would get shot.

So I had a quick map check and decided to ride back to a little town named Santa a few miles down the Pan Am. I thanked the two petrol-pump attendants and rode off. Riding through the main street of Santa I saw a small hotel and thought, that will do nicely. It was nice and cheap but when I was shown to my room it looked a bit strange and weird! The mattress, which was a double, was on a concrete base like the kind you see in a prison cell. The headboard was made of red leather about a foot thick, four feet high and in the shape of a heart and there was a full-size mirror on the wall next to the bed. Maybe it was a Peruvian honeymoon suite or maybe I was in a brothel. It also had a nice view of the building next door's brickwork, which was only a few feet away through the window; still it only cost about £4 – bonus. For supper I again had *pollo* in a small family-run restaurant round the corner from my luxurious digs, followed by another early night.

I got up early the next morning and as I was leaving had a look in some of the other rooms that were open. They were all furnished the same as the one I'd been in, strange place. I made a nice early getaway straight onto the Pan Am, and on reaching Trujillo rode straight through. It was still nice and early so I managed to avoid the robbers and murderers. I rode for over 300km up the Pan Am at a fair pace, no police around so I did plenty of overtaking on double yellows, before deciding to stop in Chiclayo, Peru's fourth largest city. Ribs and leg seemed to be getting worse so I was going to find somewhere to lie up and rest for a few days. I stopped in one of the main plazas and walked (hobbled) around for a bit looking for a decent hotel to rest in. I found one just off the main plaza, which was a bit expensive but nice, so I booked in for three days. I spent the next couple of days and nights sitting in my room watching TV and drinking *vino tinto*. And when I wasn't sitting in the room I hobbled round to the plaza and sat in the sunshine watching the world go by. I also found the best ceviche restaurant in Peru, again just off the main square.

I was starting to get bored after my two nights and three days sat in the hotel resting my ribs and leg, watching crap Peruvian game shows (a bit like *Gladiator*) with scantily clad women and even more scantily clad men; I had had enough. I decided to set off for the Pacific coastal resort of Mancora in northern Peru. Thankfully, I was still able to ride my bike with minimal pain and the weather had got decidedly warmer. So I would be moving further up the coast for a few more days relaxing on the beach before moving on to Ecuador.

Chiclayo to Mancora (Sad news)

I had pre-booked into the Point hostel, which was located right on the beach, for three days for more rest and recovery, again to try and heal my ribs and leg. It would be an easy ride of around 450km on tarmac. I chose not to go on the Pan Am highway and to take the scenic route which runs due north through the desert. Well, it was marked as scenic on the map but it turned out to be very un-scenic as the road went through small town after small town and then on through desert scrubland. There were some hills and the last 30km near the end of the day's riding as I came down towards the coast were quite twisty, but all in all very boring and not a lot to look at.

Arriving in Mancora I paid one of the little Tut Tut taxis (three-wheeled trikes with little canopies) a few soles to guide me through the maze of streets to the hostel. The Point hostel, as I said, was right on the beach and I was looking forward to my few days' rest. First though I had to service the Tiger, so I spent a few hours going round town trying to find some sort of container to drain the engine oil into. I eventually got a plastic food container from a little market and set off back to begin the service. I changed the oil, oil filter, air filter and spark plugs, and checked the bike over thoroughly

Jobs all done I set about the hard task of relaxing and spent the next three days eating, drinking *vino tinto* and swimming in the warm clear Pacific waters. The hostel had a good mixture of guests, mostly from the Scandinavian countries. I spent a lot of time talking to a young Israeli guy who was ex-Navy and Air Force and had some really amusing stories of his short time in the Israeli defence force. And it

ABOVE LEFT *Coming to the end of the Canyon Del Pato, Peru.*
ABOVE RIGHT *One of the many tunnels on* Ruta *12, Peru.*

LEFT Ruta *12, Peru.*

Mancora, watching the sun set over the Pacific, not knowing that the sun was also setting on my brother's life and he would be dead by the morning.

confirmed my suspicions that forces personnel are the same the world over. Now this was the first hostel I had been in that didn't stock wine, only beer and spirits, and there were signs all over saying only alcohol purchased on the premises was to be drunk there. I had a chat with the manager who was very friendly and asked why they didn't stock wine. He explained that it didn't sell well with the younger clients. I asked if he minded if I drank my own and he said no, so off I went in a Tut Tut into town looking for a *botelier* (off licence) to get some *vino tinto*. Mission accomplished I arrived back at the hostel with two bottles of Casillero del Diablo and set about drinking them. As I sat there drinking red wine and watching the sun go down over the Pacific, unbeknown to me, the sun was also setting for the last time thousands of miles away on my brother's life.

The next morning I was woken early by my phone ringing, which was unusual, so I knew that something was wrong. My first thoughts were that my son who had been in hospital a few weeks earlier was ill again. I had lots of missed calls and text messages from my wife and daughter asking me to ring home. The good news was that my son was indeed OK, but the devastatingly sad news was that my younger brother (by a year) William had been found dead in his home. For the second time this trip I sat in a little room feeling alone and wondered what I was doing here. Thoughts of my family were again foremost in my mind and I wondered what I was going to do now; how am I going to get back? Where am I going to get back from? What am I going to do with the Tiger? Should I cancel the rest of my trip? Should I just continue regardless? You can't bring people back and these trips don't come around every day!

I had been in a similar situation back in 2001 whilst deployed overseas in the Oman and my mother had gone into a coma and was dying. Now when you're in the Army and things like this happen the system JCCC (Joint Casualty and Compassionate Cell) kicks in and they arrange everything for you; your movements, transport, flights, trains, taxis etc., and how and where you are going to get back from. You also have your friends and comrades around you for support, but I'm a civilian now and don't have any of that; I was alone and thousands of miles away from home. My younger sister was also alone in Scotland and trying to deal with the death of my brother (who had no family) so I would need to get back. So the first thing I did after speaking to my wife was to ring my sister and see how she was.

I also emailed all the other Adv riders that I had met on my travels who had come down through the Americas. I informed them of my predicament and my options; cancelling the remainder of trip, not flying back to Scotland, flying back to Scotland for the funeral then returning to continue the trip. I asked them for help and advice or if they knew anywhere or anyone who could look after the Tiger whilst I went back to the UK. I also rang James Cargo, the shipping company who had brought the Tiger out, to see where and if they could get it back. They could only fly the Tiger back from Buenos Aires, some 7,000km and at least a two-week ride away. The other option was from Bogota which would be difficult and very, very expensive, so bringing the Tiger back was not an option. My wife and sister also said I should continue with my trip, so decision made, I needed to leave it somewhere and return after the funeral.

Without exception all the other adventure riders got back to me immediately with offers of help, advice and suggestions of where to go. Dan and Sara, the Canadian adventure bikers that I had spent some time with, and Andi and Ellen, the two Kiwis I had met at the GP earlier, put me in touch with Salvador (Salvi), a biker from Bogota who had offered to help me. So after much deliberation I decided that I would ride to Bogota. This would still mean a five-day ride through two countries to get there. I would then leave my bike with Salvi whilst I went back to the UK. Then I would return after the funeral and continue my biking adventure to my final destination of Alaska.

My brother was a year younger than me and had had a bike before me as a teenager. He was also a lot better at doing wheelies than me and probably most other people. He could wheelie any bike either off the throttle or by using the clutch and then ride it almost vertical up through the gears for as far as he wanted.

William Roy Stewart 1963–2014

6.
Ecuador and Colombia

Dash to Bogota Airport, Colombia

With the decision made to continue my trip after returning to the UK for my brother's funeral, I needed to make haste to get to Bogota. This would mean a mad dash from Mancora (Peru) through Ecuador and Colombia to catch a flight back to Glasgow. I had already booked a flight from Bogota that left in six days. I had also arranged to leave my bike with Salvi so I needed to get there (2,200km away) as quickly as possible. So I packed up and I set off for the border with Ecuador about 160km further up the Pan Am highway. I spent the night in the border town of Huaqaillas which straddles the Peru–Ecuador border so that I could get through the border checkpoint and immigration early the next morning. You can actually enter Ecuador from the town as half of it is in Peru and half in Ecuador, as I found out when I was looking for a petrol station.

However, I needed to go through the actual checkpoint in order to get my visa and my import paperwork for the Tiger. So I had to turn around and ride back out of town and follow the signs on the Pan Am towards the main border crossing, which was thankfully well signposted and only a few miles away. I arrived at the border crossing and it didn't take long to get through the immigration even though the Peruvian and Ecuadorian offices were quite a distance apart. I had breakfast at a little café before riding the next few kilometres to the *aduana* office where I would get my Ecuadorian import paperwork for my bike. Again this was fairly quick and straightforward although for the first time at any of the borders I'd crossed they took photographs of the bike and the frame number.

Setting off from the border and moving slightly inland from the coast the change in the vegetation was very noticeable. It had now gone from desert scrubland to thick green vegetation with banana plantations for mile after mile before giving way to thick tree- and grass-covered mountains. The banana trees were full of bunches of bananas all of which were encased in some sort of plastic bag or wrapping of differing colours whilst still attached to the tree. The road itself is very twisty and winds its way up and down through the mountains, badly potholed in places but very little traffic and generally OK.

I initially followed route 25 north for a bit before turning onto route 80, which is a toll road, the first of many in Ecuador. Route 80 runs northeast through the banana plantations, not a bad road, quite twisty but not great scenery unless you like looking at banana trees. After about 100km the road then merges with route 35, the main Pan Am, and swings due north. This is where the banana plantations end and where dense forest and cultivated fields rise unbelievably right up into the mountains and are every shade of green. The tolls through Ecuador were numerous and very cheap but also really annoying as it meant taking off gloves and fumbling for change before trying to force sweaty hands back into sweaty wet gloves. It was a long hard day due to the heat, the rain and the twisty mountain roads and after just over 480km (which took all day due to the low average speed) I arrived at the town of Riobamba halfway through Ecuador. I went straight to bed after a meal as I had an early start the following day to cover as much ground as possible.

It was raining when I woke so the waterproofs were worn from the off and the rain was slowing me down as the road looked slick and slippery. The road heads due north as it snakes its way up and down through the tree-covered mountains, through village after village and toll after toll. On reaching the city of Quito the road changes into a three-lane highway, super twisty with perfect tarmac and just like all the other mountain roads only wider as it winds its way up and down through the mountains around Quito. There was quite a lot of traffic but the road is wide and I was able to weave in and out of the trucks and cars. I used every inch of space available as I went from the inside lane to the outside around the corners and back again. This part of the road runs right through the city and for a fair bit afterwards, and it was a joy to ride. But it doesn't last and the road changes back to a normal A-type road with traffic going both ways. However, on the plus side the rain had now stopped so I was able to get a bit of a move on.

Leaving the town of Ibara I got detoured onto route 187, which took me on a north-easterly loop for about 60km up a twisty mountain pass and back down again before rejoining the Pan Am. Another long day and again, just over 480km covered before reaching the town of Tulcan, a few miles from the Colombian border. I covered Ecuador in two days and I hadn't seen anything apart from what I had time to look at as I rode through. I was also starting to get tired both mentally and physically due to the constant braking and cornering for mile after mile on the mountain roads and I still had another three days' riding to go before I reach reached Bogota. That night I ate pizza and decided to have a quick trim at a barber's before going to bed. Bad idea, it wasn't the usual man's barbers but a woman's and my neckline was all ragged and squinty to say the least, still it only cost about £1 – bargain.

Crossing the Ecuador–Colombia border (More bribery)

I left Tulcan just after sunrise and I soon arrived at the Ecuador–Colombia border, which was very busy even at this early hour. Leaving Ecuador was easy, as was getting through Colombian immigration.

Whilst there, I met some Colombian English students who asked if they could speak with me to practise their English. I duly obliged and spent about half an hour chatting with them before going on to the *aduana* to get my bike paperwork sorted. I was told I needed photocopies of all my paperwork; passport, V5, driver's licence, immigration stamp etc., another first. So I had to trundle off to the little photocopy shop which is conveniently nearby and get copies of everything (at a small cost) before returning to the customs office. Paperwork all sorted and bike and frame number photographed again, I was informed that I had to stop a few miles up the road at a supermarket and purchase third party insurance so that I was covered in Colombia, 'the same as you did in Ecuador,' the official said. I didn't have insurance in Ecuador. So as I rode past the supermarket I didn't stop and I didn't get insurance as I thought, nobody has checked my insurance since I've been in South America so I'll take the chance of doing without.

Not as much distance covered today, only 400km, but still another long day before arriving quite late in the beautiful city of Popayan, which has a lovely Cathedral in the centre and lots of old-looking buildings all of which are painted in brilliant white. I had a short walk around before going for something to eat, very beautiful. I had supper in a really posh restaurant before retiring for another early night. Another early start as I set off from Popayan on the main route towards the town of Cali, which is a nice road with long sweeping bends as the terrain here is fairly flat. Just before Cali and all the way to the town of Tulua the road changes to a two-lane dual carriageway, super-smooth with very little traffic, and it gave me a chance to relax and was a nice change from the twisty mountain roads. No bends and no braking except for the occasional roundabout and it was great just cruising along. One thing that I noticed and was pleasantly surprised about in Colombia is that the roads have road signs everywhere so the towns and routes are well signposted, which was good as my satnav was not working properly again. The other things that became apparent were that small bikes were more numerous in Colombia than anywhere else I had been and they were everywhere. There were also police and Army checkpoints in every town and also all over the countryside, with small Army detachments on all the bridges, which have defensive Sangers at each end.

After Tulua, the road then heads east back into the Andes and climbs up over the Paso La Linea, which rises to about 4,500 metres above sea level before dropping down the other side towards the city of Ibague. It had now started raining torrentially and I was piss-wet through again. This pass was unlike any other I'd ridden; yes it's steep, high and as twisty with hairpin bends like all the others I'd ridden, but the difference on this pass was the volume of traffic, 18-wheel trucks were everywhere, as were cars and hundreds of small motorcycles. The bends are unbelievably steep on the inside and very, very wide; wide enough for three trucks to go round at the same time. The trucks seemed to take this as a licence to try and overtake each other going up the hill regardless of the fact that they were all moving at a similar speed. Then there were the trucks coming down towards you also trying to overtake and coming straight at you so you had to pull right into the side.

Basically there seemed to be no law and no road or lane discipline, everyone – cars, bikes, trucks – were overtaking anywhere and everywhere; blind corners, over double yellow lines, anywhere that they thought they could get by. The trucks were only doing about 10kph on the steep road, two or sometimes three abreast. This added a new dimension to riding when trying to overtake them as you had to weave in and out as you rode up and around the corners. There were also a lot of roadworks at various points along the road with manned stop signals. All the bikes came to the front and lined up en masse, and as soon as the signal was turned around to GO, it was like being in a mad motocross free-for-all start. Engines revving like mad, wheels spinning furiously as they sped off, weaving, bumping and jostling to be first into the next corner, total madness!

As I was coming down the other side of La Linea, I overtook a slow-moving truck in the driving rain on double yellow lines as I approached a right-hand bend. As I passed the front of the truck, I saw too late a police checkpoint and a frantically gesticulating policeman waving me into the side of the road. I briefly considered riding on as I was already past the checkpoint but decided it would be better to pull in, so I came to a halt some 100 metres past him; maybe they will just wave me on, I thought. But no, he came down and directed me to go back up to the checkpoint, so I had to turn around and ride back up. Bike parked I took off my helmet and hoped for the best, but it didn't look good. He proceeded to explain to me with the aid of sign language that I had broken the law by crossing the double yellow lines. Next he got out his ticket book and asked for all my documents. I immediately thought fuck, I don't have any insurance. I handed over my passport, V5, driver's licence and import document. As he checked them over he seemed happy and didn't ask for insurance. However, he then explained to me that I would receive a ticket and that the bike would be impounded. I would need to get a bus to town, pay the ticket and then return with the receipt before I could get the bike back.

Not what I wanted to hear as I had a flight to catch in Bogota so I could get to my brother's funeral. So I got out my Spanish phrasebook for the first time on the trip and in my best Spanish and sign language told him that my, '*hermano la muerte, el avión mañana par Inglaterra*' (my brother is dead and I need to get a plane tomorrow to England). As he closed his ticket book, I thought he had understood and was going to show me some leniency and compassion, but no, he then looked at me, held out his hand and simply said 'MONEY'! I thought, oh no here we go again, but he then gestured for me to follow him and led me away from all the other policemen and through a door. I thought I was being led to an office but as he opened the door I realised that it was a toilet and he ushered me in. Once inside he held out his hand and again said 'MONEY'! How much do you give a policeman in Colombia I wondered? Not knowing the going rate and not wanting him to see how much I had, I turned around, got out my wallet and extract 50,000 pesos (about £15) and handed it over to him, hoping that this was enough. Thankfully it was as he took it before ushering me back out and gestured for me to be on my way. I quickly grabbed all my paperwork off the desk, put on my helmet and sopping wet gloves and rode off quickly just in case he changed his mind.

It rained continuously for the rest of the day and I was glad to reach my destination for the night, the town of Ibague. I found a hotel fairly quickly and by chance there were two bars right next door. I decided that I needed a beer or two so after eating I went into one of the bars, which was quite busy. There were a quite few couples and a few men sitting around watching a big screen with salsa music videos playing and I thought, this looks all right. I went to the bar and sat between four blokes and ordered a beer. I had only just started drinking it when the two guys on my left engaged in a full-on kissing and cuddling session; I could hardly believe my eyes. So I looked round at the two on my right and they too were holding hands and cuddling. I then had a quick scan around the bar and even though there were quite a few women, I realised that everyone else in the bar were gay couples and most of them were snogging. I hadn't noticed this on my way in, honest; I quickly finished my beer and left.

Outside it was still raining torrentially and the water running down the hill was four or five inches deep. The doorman had an umbrella and I asked him to cover me as I ran across the road to the other bar and he duly obliged. As I entered the other bar I made sure I had a good look around first before buying a drink and all was fine, much better. It also had salsa-type music playing but it was full of couples (men and women) dancing. I had a few beers and watched the dancers; some were very good and others not so good, but entertaining just the same. Outside it was still hammering it down and I stood on a balcony watching the rain pound down onto the street, which now resembled a raging river. I watched a guy in the doorway opposite wearing only a pair of baggy shorts, completely soaked through. Every now and then he was approached by someone or a car pulled up and someone got out and they huddled together under the doorway. He was obviously dealing drugs as I could clearly see them exchange money and small packages. I watched for a bit, intrigued, before going back inside and watching the dancing for a while longer. The rain eventually subsided so I headed back to my hotel for another early night. I had to meet Salvi and three of his friends at 10am the next day. I had arranged to meet them at a town called Giradot about an hour and a half ride away from where they would then guide me into Bogota.

Rendezvous in Giradot and the ride to Bogota

After my interesting night in Ibague I had breakfast of sweet cakes and coffee in a small patisserie before setting off. I was again off early to make sure I made it to Giradot on time, the sun was already up and I rode off into brilliant sunshine. The road to Giradot was another piece of motorcycling delight; dry, smooth and fast sweeping corners. I arrived at Giradot at 9.30am and parked up at the garage where Salvi had arranged to meet me. It was now red-hot and the petrol-pump attendants came over and told me to sit in the shade as I had been waiting for over an hour. Another hour passed and I was beginning to wonder if I had got the right location, but eventually Salvi and his three friends turned up. After we introduced ourselves we went for a coffee and a chat.

Salvi told me he had planned to take me back to Bogota on a more interesting and scenic route. We set off and it became apparent immediately that the pace was going to be quick and I wouldn't get to see much scenery as I concentrated intently on the road. Salvi and two of his friends were riding KTM 990s and the other was on a 1000cc Suzuki V Strom, and they could ride them and ride them quick! Once out of Giradot we took a B road that followed the river Magdalena. It was fairly flat with long straights and sweeping bends, the road surface probably the worst I had ridden on anywhere in South America, potholes of every size were everywhere. It looked like it had been on the receiving end of an artillery bombardment. The pace was hot and the temperature was now even hotter and it was an effort to keep up on the fully laden Tiger.

Some parts of the road were rougher than others and I also hit a few potholes that were unavoidable. Going round one particularly rough corner I grounded the side and centre stands and had to sit the bike up as I thought I was coming off. On reaching a junction that would take us on to a proper smooth main road through the mountains, I noticed that my side-stand base plate was missing. It must have come off when it ground out on the corner, which wasn't that far back. One of Salvi's friends had run out of fuel so he required a tow and they set off for the nearest station a few kilometres away, and I set off back down the potholed road to look for my base plate as it wasn't that far. As I was riding back I hit a massive pothole, which sounded horrendous as the suspension bottomed out and shook me to the core. On reaching the rough corner I found the base plate straight away and then made my way back to join the others at the gas station.

After refuelling we set off up over a mountain pass with plenty of hairpin bends and smooth tarmac. Only problem now was it had started raining and it rained all the way back to Bogota. Just short of Bogota the rain became torrential and for the fifth time in the five days it had taken me to get to Bogota I was piss-wet through. At one point the rain was so heavy it was lying three or four inches deep on the road. As Salvi's KTM cut a swathe through, there was a five-foot plume of water coming off the rear wheel that absolutely drenched me as I rode behind. The others peeled off as we entered the suburbs to make their own way home and I continued along with Salvi. The pace hadn't slowed that much and I now had the added scary excitement of the city traffic.

Salvi had briefly mentioned the traffic to me and the fact that lane-splitting was allowed. So as we headed deeper into the city and the traffic got busier I had difficulty keeping up, as Salvi weaved in and out of the traffic like a man possessed. All the other bikers in the city rode similarly, every one madder than the other; London despatch riders would struggle to keep up here! I struggled to keep up too as the width of my panniers was limiting my ability to squeeze through the traffic. Eventually we reached the Hotel Continental where I would be living for the next two nights before my flight, and boy was I glad. The hotel is a combination of rooms and private apartments of which Salvi had one. The views from the apartment across the city to mount Monserrate, which dominates Bogota, are spectacular. Once in the apartment I met his wife, Paola, who is a journalist. They have only been married six months and I am the third adventure biker that they have given accommodation to. They had also looked after the two Moto Kiwis – the husband and wife adventure bikers from New Zealand – a few months earlier. Not many wives would put up with that, certainly not in the first year of marriage, and now they were going to look after me.

I've now ridden in quite a few of South America's cities since I've been here; all of them are chaotic and mad but Bogota is by far the maddest yet. The rules are, there are no rules and there certainly didn't appear to be any speed limit. I mentioned earlier that there were also a lot more bikers and scooterists here than anywhere else and they were all mad. If arriving was an experience, the following day I was going to get it all over again with added spice. Salvi had arranged new tyres for me, which I was going to collect the following morning. After a good night's sleep Salvi and I set off to get my new tyres, which were at the other end of town. I should have taken off my panniers but didn't, so I struggled again to keep up with Salvi as he dashed across town like a drug-crazed despatch rider. Some of the speeds we reached as we scythed our way through the early-morning traffic were ridiculous, and if done in the UK would certainly result in a lost licence and possibly a spell in jail. But we were not in the UK and anything goes here in Bogota. I had opted for Heidenau tyres, which were recommended by other adventure riders. The owner of the shop is also a rider and a friend of Salvi so we sat for a while and had a coffee and a chat. I couldn't get the tyres fitted there as they only sell them, so after strapping them to the rear of the Tiger I had another ride across town to the tyre fitters, yee ha!

Whilst waiting to get the tyres fitted I noticed that the on the left side of the front wheel there was a big dent and a flat spot in the rim. Not too bad and obviously not affecting the bike but I borrowed a large hammer from the mechanics and set about trying to hammer it back into shape before the new tyres were fitted. After some serious hammering it was almost as good as new. I also took the opportunity when the wheels were off to clean the brake callipers and fit new front brake pads. Tyres fitted and balanced I then had to make my way back across town on my own as Salvi had gone to work. My satnav was again not working properly so it took me a while and several circuits of downtown Bogota to get back to the apartment. I still had a few little jobs to do on the Tiger; I refitted the side-stand base plate, filled and adjusted the flow rate on the Scottoiler and tried once more to realign my handlebars, which were still not quite right from my crash at Machu Picchu. Neither for that matter were my ribs, which were still hurting.

Jobs all done and handlebars at last perfect I was looking over the bike when I noticed a hairline fracture on the main frame just below the weld where the rear sub frame joins the main frame. I first thought it was caused by my crash as it was on the left-hand side. But on checking the right side there was an identical fracture; not good. I called Triumph UK and told them of my problem. They told me they had not had any other reports of this nature and asked if I could bring the bike in. I explained I was in Colombia, so no I couldn't. I would need to get some sort of temporary repair done. Salvi had come back from work and I told him of my problem. He was on the phone right away to a friend who had a metal fabrication shop, and once again we were off on a mad dash across the city to get the Tiger some cosmetic surgery. I figured a couple of little spot welds would do the job and the welders agreed; all I had to do was remove the rear brake reservoir, and it took less than half an hour. Hopefully this would do and stop the fractures becoming any worse.

The Tiger was in severe need of a wash so we went to a little power-wash shop around the corner and sat and drank Coke whilst both bikes got washed. Salvi's bike was finished in no time, but after an hour watching the wash guy, who was now on his sixth soap, scrub and rinse sequence on the Tiger, I had to tell him enough was enough, it wasn't going to get any cleaner. The Tiger was now looking brand new and ready for the next leg of my trip. I then had the prospect riding back across the mad city again and it was now dark. The ride back didn't disappoint; very fast and very scary.

Now I also had to get the bike to Salvi's friend Juan's house (who would be storing the Tiger for me), which was another 40 minutes' ride away up a mountain outside the city. Thankfully Salvi was taking the car as his wife Paola was also coming and we would pick her up from her office after dropping his bike back at the hotel, so the ride up was quite sedate. Juan's house was very impressive, set in a secure compound surrounded with barbed wire fences and a manned security gate at the entrance. Juan had cooked a meal and insisted that we all eat, so we ate and drank a few beers except for Salvi who was the designated driver. I found out that Colombia has a zero drink and drive policy. Thank God for that I thought, as all the drivers and bikers were mad enough without adding drink! Juan and his wife were excellent hosts and had great stories to tell, and if I wasn't catching a flight in the morning we could have stayed drinking and chatting all night. So around midnight we had to bid our hosts farewell, a great and thoroughly enjoyable evening under the circumstances.

I had to leave the apartment at 5am to get to the airport for my flight at 9am, and Salvi had booked a cab for me from a safe company. Apparently the cabs (not all of them) can be dodgy here in Bogota and work with organised criminals to rob fares. The MO that the robbers use is; whilst the cab is stopped at traffic lights, two men will jump into either side of the back of cab and rob the occupant of their money and bank cards, sometimes even taking you with them to an ATM to empty your account! This had happened to one of their friends, who coincidently happened to be a US Drug Enforcement Agent working here in Bogota. He had been stabbed and died during an attempted robbery whilst sat in the back of a cab. That story didn't fill me full of confidence but Salvi assured me I would be OK. Back at the apartment I packed some clothes for my trip back to Airdrie and managed to get four hours' sleep before getting the taxi to Bogota airport for my flight home. Every set of traffic lights we stopped at made me nervous, as the story of the DEA agent was fresh in my mind, but we got there safely enough.

Since being told of my brother's death, it had been an emotional, eventful and tiring five days of virtually non-stop riding through two countries on demanding mountain roads. I had managed to sort out all my flights to Scotland for the funeral and return flights back, including my flight and the Tiger's cargo flight to Panama. I'd also found time to get lots of jobs done on the Tiger in readiness for my onward trip north to Alaska, none of which I could have done without the help of Salvi.

The funeral and Loch Lomond, Scotland

After two flights that took me from Colombia to Newark in the USA and then on to Glasgow, I arrived back in Scotland on Tuesday 10 June exhausted. It had taken me eight days after first hearing the awful news of my brother's death to get here. My brother-in-law was at the airport to meet me and drive me back to Airdrie. Arriving at my mother-in-law's I had a quick shower and then went to see my sister to discuss the final arrangements for our brother's funeral. It was an emotional meeting as we hadn't seen each other for some time and now we were meeting under the saddest of circumstances.

We had to take a drive to the funeral directors to finalise the details of the funeral. It was scheduled for the coming Friday and my wife had taken time off work and was driving up from Plymouth on the Thursday evening. The funeral went as well as could be expected, with lots of relatives and friends coming to pay their last respects, some of whom I hadn't seen for twenty, thirty years or more. And embarrassingly, I didn't recognise some old friends and even some relatives were unrecognisable. The service was conducted by Kay, the local minister who had grown up and been to school with us, so it had a real personal touch as she had known my brother very well.

My wife was staying for the whole weekend and as we hadn't seen each other for over three months, we went away for the weekend to Drymen near Loch Lomond after the funeral. We were booked into the Buchanan Arms Hotel in Drymen a few miles from the loch. It is a three-star hotel but after some of the hovels I have been in in South America it seemed like a ten-star. For a start the showers were hot, there was coffee in the room, it had a restaurant, a swimming pool, a Spa and of course a bar with real beer, living the dream! In the evening we ate *nouvelle cuisine* in the hotel's restaurant which was superb, and drank fine wine. The next day we took a ferry from Balmaha across the loch to the small picturesque village of Luss. The weather was not that great, warm but overcast. On coming back to Balmaha we then took a leisurely drive to Aberfoyle and Callander. Memories of my youth flashed through my mind as these were the roads that my brother and I used to ride around as teenagers. We also went to Stirling and visited the memorial to the Battle of Bannockburn, which began on 24 June 700 years ago, and is where Robert the Bruce, King of Scots defeated the English Army of King Edward II. Scotland has scenery to rival anything that I had seen in South America – the mountains might be smaller but they are just as beautiful.

I had ordered a new wing mirror, and an indicator, which had been smashed in my crash at Machu Picchu, and two top yoke bolts that had been missing since early in the trip. These would be delivered to my mother-in-law's house so I could take them back with me to Colombia. A very sad and emotional week, but as funerals tend to do they bring family and friends together who haven't seen each other for some time, so it was great to catch up and reminisce about my brother and everything else. All too soon the weekend was over and my wife had to return to Plymouth, and I had a flight back to Colombia to continue my motorcycle trip with the Tiger. Losing my brother had made me determined to achieve my goal of getting to Prudhoe Bay. Life is sometimes too short and this past week had given me lots of time for reflection, and these opportunities don't present themselves every day. My wife and I had also decided that she should come out and meet me somewhere during my trip. So we had booked a holiday in Mexico for the last two weeks in July, only just over a month away. The following day my wife dropped me off at Glasgow airport early on Tuesday morning before returning to Plymouth. After 19 hours and two flights, I arrived back in Bogota, still sad but ready to continue, north to Alaska.

Bogota (again) to Chicamocha National Park

I got a taxi back into town, still wary when it stopped at lights and junctions but again I arrived back at Salvi's apartment without issue. Salvi had offered to give me a bed again before I set off to continue my trip. Time was now definitely against me reaching Alaska before the first snows of winter. I intended to leave Colombia and head straight to Panama, but Salvi had insisted that I spend some time here and see some of the country. He had even gone to the trouble of planning a route for me that would take me in an anticlockwise direction around the country. He had marked some of the cities and touristy areas that I must visit before coming back to Bogota for mine and the Tiger's flight to Panama.

The following morning after a good night's sleep I went for a wander around Bogota and also tried to get a decent road map of Colombia. Not much luck with the map so I had to buy a little map book from which I cut and Sellotaped some pages together to make one for my planned route around central Colombia. In the afternoon I collected the Tiger from Juan's house up in the mountains, and as Paola, Salvi's wife, had their car, I now had the scary prospect of riding pillion with Salvi (or as he put it, be my bitch). Now I have only ever ridden pillion a couple of times in my life, the last being over twenty years ago. I didn't like it then and I wasn't going to like it now either, having seen Salvi ride!

I was hanging on for dear life as we cut through the city traffic and then up over the mountain pass to Juan's. The KTM is a tall bike and sat on the back it seemed even taller and I felt as if we were leaning over at extreme angles, but probably weren't. I think he was taking it easy but now and then he would accelerate hard past slow-moving traffic on the twisty mountain road and then brake hard and I held on with a vice-like grip to the pillion grab rails. Arriving at Juan's I was relieved to be back in control of my own destiny! I had taken my new indicator and wing mirror so whilst I fitted them Salvi and Juan fitted mini indicators to Salvi's KTM. I didn't take long with my two little jobs and then gave a hand with the KTM as fitting the rear indicators meant stripping the whole rear end of the bike. Jobs eventually done I bade farewell to Juan and headed off back to Bogota.

Whilst waiting for the lift in the apartment building in the morning before going to collect the Tiger, I had met Michael, an investigative journalist from Ireland who was here looking into the drug murders that are still prevalent in the country. We got chatting and went for a coffee across the street and arranged to meet later for a beer. However, on returning from Juan's that night the travelling had caught up with me and by 8.30pm I was in bed sleeping. The following morning I packed up, said goodbye to Salvi and headed for the coffee shop to have breakfast before leaving. As luck would have it (small world) I bumped into Michael again so we had a good talk about his job. He had been a journalist for over eighteen years and had travelled all over world. He was there to interview murderers and drug dealers and was heading off to the coastal city of Buenaventura, which by all accounts is a really bad place. Murder is an everyday occurrence and body parts are routinely left in the streets as a warning to others; a bit like medieval times when heads, arms and legs were displayed in cities. Whilst I was chatting to Michael he received an abusive phone call warning him not to come to Buenaventura. He told me that he had had hundreds of these calls since he'd been here, what a job!

It had been raining all morning and I was in no rush to leave but I needed to get going, so I wished Michael luck and I set off with full waterproofs on. I took the road east out of the city and over the pass towards the town of Calera. This would take me on a more scenic route as it swung north hugging the east shore of Lago Guatavita. After around 80km it then rejoined the main route (*Ruta* 55) towards Tunja. I rode all day hoping to reach the picturesque mountain village of Barichara, but it was getting late so I decided to stop in the town of San Gil, 16km short. I found a nice cheap hostel right by the town plaza and after a shower I went for a walk. Colombia had just played and won their second match in the World Cup so the plaza was full of people with their football shirts and flags drinking, dancing and celebrating. I had a few beers and watched the revellers for a while before retiring for the night.

The sun was up when I woke the next morning and it was already red-hot. I set off for Barichara and the road up was an absolute cracker, twisty and smooth and totally devoid of traffic. Barichara is set on a high plateau overlooking a vast valley that stretches as far as the eye can see. The houses are all painted white and are set in neat rows all running parallel to each other. In the town centre there is a lovely church, which dominates the main plaza. I had a wander around taking photos and then went for a coffee and some cake before heading off again down the same route I had come up. I then continued on *Ruta* 55 north towards Bucaramanga. About 60km short of Bucaramanga is the Canyon Del Chicamocha, the second largest canyon in the world, which is in the Chicamocha National Park. There is a tourist park with a cable-car ride called a *teleférico*, which runs down into the canyon and across the Rio Chicamocha and on up the mountain on the other side before coming back again.

So I decided to stop and spend a few hours looking around and take the *teleférico* across. It had now started raining heavily and the cable car had stopped for lunch, so I also had lunch and spent an hour or so wandering around looking at the different attractions. The main feature at the top of the mountain is an impressive monument depicting an uprising of the peasants that took place in 1780. It is a massive multi-figured sculpture called Monument to the Santandereanidad, built on top of the hill. It sits on a giant metal frame in the shape of a tobacco leaf (the main product of the region at the time) and points towards the nearby town of Socorro, where the uprising took place. The Spanish had been taxing the people to fund the war in Europe against the English, which they obviously weren't happy about (who ever is?). The statues on the monument are of some of the main players in the revolution; the woman who started it, Manuela Bertran, and the traitorous Archbishop Antonio Caballero who betrayed the commoners, among others.

I then took the *teleférico* ride down into the canyon and over to the other side of the valley. It was still raining so the views were obscured by the rain and low cloud but still very impressive and a nice relaxing ride. By the time I got back to the start (the whole cable-car ride took about an hour) the rain had stopped and I was looking forward to riding down into the canyon, as I had seen the twisty serpent-like road that descends down into the canyon from the *teleférico* and it looked amazing.

It was now 5pm and the rain had subsided as I left Chicamocha National Park so I decided I would ride to Bucaramanga about 60km away and find somewhere to stay for the night. Riding through the city it didn't look that nice and I had trouble finding a hotel, but eventually I found a good one and at a reasonable price. Later that evening, I sat at a bar with an open front on a crossroads across the street from my hotel and watched the traffic and the mad bikers as they tore away from the lights, very entertaining.

The next morning I was off and heading for Guatapé, a large rock formation that juts out from the earth. I took *Ruta* 66 out of Bucaramanga, which winds its way west through fantastic scenery, and then I took a small B road to the town of Barrancabermeja. The road was littered with potholes but it was only about 22km before I joined *Ruta* 45, the main route southwest. There were some nice straights with long sweeping bends which was a nice change from the continuously twisty mountain roads. However, due to the twisty nature of the road and slow average speed I was not going to get to Guatapé on time to do any touristy stuff, so decided to head straight for Medellin and go back to Guatapé in a few days.

Medellin

Ruta 62 was superb and I arrived in Medellin just as it was getting dark, but yet again I was having trouble with the satnav not recognising the postcodes.

After over an hour riding around I eventually found the street I was looking for. There is a bar there frequented by adventure motorcyclists called Patrick's bar, the only real fake-Irish bar in Medellin. It is in Parque Lleras, a touristy area with lot of nice bars and restaurants. By sheer luck there was also a nice fairly cheap boutique hostel across the road so I booked in for two nights. After the usual booking-in routine I was shown to my dorm and on entering I met the other only other occupant. I got the fright of my life; my roommate for the next two days was Beth, not her real name to protect her identity just in case some of what she would later tell me had any truth in it. She looked about 100 years old, and in the middle of the room there was a dismantled bicycle with bits and pieces spread all over the floor.

Beth was one of the strangest people I had met on this trip so far, half British, half American, half eccentric, half bonkers and totally mad! As I said she was very old, probably around 65or 70 but looks older. Her hair was long, grey, wiry and unkempt, long grey hairs sprouted from her wrinkly chin, she had no front upper teeth and the bottom teeth were a dark brown-yellow colour. She was never without a cigarette in her nicotine-stained fingers and her hands were all gnarly like a bricklayer's. She was wearing dirty ripped blue jeans and a check shirt, neither of which looked like they had seen a washer for some time. She told me she had been travelling all her life and this trip has been going on for 12 years. And to be honest she looked like she'd been living rough for all of it; I have seen healthier-looking, better-dressed and better-smelling vagrants.

Beth talked in riddles and never completed a story, or told you just enough and was always cagey, leaving you wondering what the hell she was on about. She asked if I liked the Beatles and then proceeded to tell me a story about how she met them back in the sixties. She told me bits of a story about being in the back of a limousine with all four of the Beatles. From what I can gather, reading between the lines as she never gave too much detail and spoke in riddles, she had had some sort of sexual encounter, experience or something; maybe she was better-looking then? She also said she had contacted them (the Beatles) over the years to talk about what happened. She knew John Lennon was dead, but asked me if Ringo Starr was still alive. She also said she had spoken to Paul McCartney and Yoko Ono on several occasions regarding what happened to her and was trying to get closure. All very bizarre, strange or sad depending on whether or not what she says is true.

She asked if I had any tools and if she could borrow them as she was trying to fit head bearings to her bicycle. I offer to help but Beth has her own way of doing things, so I let her get on with it. Anyway I was tired so I draped my towel down over my bunk as I didn't want to see anything scary during the night, put my earplugs in and went to sleep. The next day as I was having breakfast I was joined by yes, you've guessed it, Beth. She was having nicotine and caffeine and has slept in the clothes that she was wearing when I arrived. Can't remember what we spoke about as I had now just started nodding in agreement as the subjects were weird and she seemed a little unhinged as she jumped from one subject to the next. She asked for more tools (it's a big job) so I just gave her my whole tool kit and told her to help herself, made my excuses and went for a walk around Parque Lleras.

After lunch I decided to go to Patrick's bar and when I arrived it was full of Americans waiting on the USA–Portugal World Cup football match to kick off. So I joined some of them; Jamie, Richard, Sam and a few others, the atmosphere was great and we watched a great game. The USA should have won, in my humble opinion, not being that much of a fan or expert. After the game we continued to drink and chat and even though the Yanks were a bit disappointed with the result it didn't dampen their spirits and we had a great evening. Jamie told me that the owner, who was called Albert, was also a fellow Scot and a biker. He then got the bar manager to send him a message telling him that I was there.

The next morning as I was sitting at the front of the hostel having breakfast, Albert turned up looking for me. He introduced himself and asked if I'd like to join him for a coffee. Albert was indeed a Scot, originally from Crawford, and had been in South America for many years; initially in Ecuador before moving to Colombia. He now owned Patrick's bar, but his main occupation was as a gold-prospecting consultant and advisor. We talked for a while reminiscing about Scotland, and arranged to meet for a drink that evening at the bar. That meant I would have to change my plan and stay another night. That afternoon I also met up with Sam from the previous night and had a few beers. I asked him if he would like to join me and Albert later. Returning to the hostel I met Beth again, who had returned from a shopping trip with a bag of groceries and asked if I would like to join her for supper. I politely declined and told her I was meeting friends.

Sam was first to arrive and he told me a bit about himself. He was an anaesthetist and was there on holiday from Texas, and was also a veteran, ex-US Army, so we had something in common. Sam had a large gun collection (unusual for a Texan), which included a .50 rifle, and invited me to Texas to go shooting. Albert turned up next riding a mint KTM 990 super moto with the loudest exhaust ever. Quite a few others turned up during the evening including Gordy, an ex-Royal Anglian (British Army) soldier who ran his own little security firm there in Colombia. He'd been here for seven years and knew a few of my friends from 29 Commando (small world). We all had a laugh, spun dits and generally swung the lantern, and drank lots of beer. As it got later and we sat there drinking, the streets were getting busy, but not with people, rats! Hundreds of them, the most I had ever seen anywhere, had come out and were scurrying around eating from the garbage bags just feet from where we were sitting! Another great night spent laughing and drinking with interesting, like-minded, great blokes. I eventually had to bid farewell and head off for bed as I had been there a day longer than planned and I wanted to get on the road early.

One of the other guests at my hostel whom I shall mention is a Colombian guy called Elke, who was very nice, very articulate and also spoke good English. He was living in the hostel with his mother and two kids. Elke comes from the Darien Gap region, one of the most dangerous places in Colombia and the bit I have to fly over to get to Panama. And he confirmed its notoriety by telling me he has had to *vamos* from town after his brother was shot twice in the head for going out with a girl that he shouldn't have. I spoke with him for some time during my stay, very interesting guy and an interesting but scary lifestyle living up in the Darien Gap.

The Tiger had been parked on the pavement for the duration of my stay due to there being no secure parking at the hostel. Each morning when I woke, I wondered and hoped it would still be there, so it was a relief that I was leaving and it hadn't been stolen. I'd had a fabulous few days in Medellin, which was once one of the most dangerous cities in Colombia. It used to be run and controlled with extreme violence by the infamous Pablo Escobar; he was the boss of bosses and headed probably the biggest drug cartel in the world at the time. And on the recommendation of Albert, I was going to go and visit his (Pablo Escobar's) former home, the Hacienda Nápoles. It is located near the town of Doradal and is now a macabre memorial/museum and safari park. First though, I had to go back and visit Guatapé.

Guatapé and Hacienda Nápoles

It was a bright sunny day as I set off for *Ruta* 60 out of Medellin and as luck would have it, it was a straight road that led me out of the city before it started to climb up a twisty mountain pass. *Ruta* 60 then runs southeast through some fantastic rolling mountains and as with most of the roads I have ridden in Colombia the road surface was perfect and the surrounding countryside every shade of green. I then took a B road towards the small town of El Penol and Guatapé; it was only around twenty miles but it was a never-ending series of twists and turns.

The only fake Irish bar in Medellin, Columbia, with Sam (the Texan anaesthetist), Oz and Albert, the owner and fellow Scot.

ABOVE *At the Hacienda Nápoles. The picture behind has Pablo Escobar dressed as a Mexican bandit and lying dead on the rooftop after he was shot by the police.* LEFT *Piedra del Peñol at Guatapé, Columbia. The 740 stairs can be seen on the face of the rock.*

Arriving at Guatapé I parked the Tiger and had a wander around the shops and restaurants at the base of the rock before having something to eat. The 'Peñol Rock' (La piedra del Peñol) is a rock formation, that formed along the Antioquia Rock Base (batolito de antioquia) 70 million years ago and is estimated to weigh 10 million tons. With two thirds of its mass below ground, the exposed vertical face juts up over 200 metres from the surrounding plain and is visible from miles around. The rock is almost entirely smooth except for one long crack running top to bottom on one of the faces.

I had now been on the road for four months and the longest period I think I have ever gone without doing any physical training of any sort. With my torn calf muscles now healed and my broken ribs still hurting but not quite as painful, I decided to test myself ascending the staircase (740 steps) that is built into the rock face as quickly as I could. The temperature was around 25 degrees celsius and wearing motorcycle boots and trousers I set off to try and get to the top without stopping. I have to admit that I did stop briefly on a couple of occasions but only to admire the view (honest). On reaching the top I took my pulse and it was roughly 165 bpm which is only four below my theoretical maximum.

I spent a fair bit of time admiring the views (and recovering from the climb) and I have to say they were spectacular. I then had the prospect of going back down and as I had now come to realise going down was more painful for my arthritic knee. And so it turned out; it seemed to take for ever and my right knee was killing me. On reaching the bottom I had a severe case of disco legs as my thigh muscles quivered uncontrollably. I definitely had some work to do regaining my fitness levels after this trip was over.

Back on the bike I had a relaxing ride to the town of Doradal and the infamous drug cartel boss Pablo Escobar's hacienda. This is where he lived during his reign and it is located a few kilometres outside the town. The whole estate has been turned into a safari park and his house, Hacienda Nápoles, is now a macabre memorial, not just to him but to the hundreds of people killed during his time as the biggest drug boss in Colombia, if not the world. All that's left of the actual hacienda is a shell with a canvas roof erected over the top to keep out the elements. Inside the walls and windows are covered with large photos and information panels depicting the man himself, his family and the people that met a violent demise on his say-so. These included three presidential candidates and hundreds of soldiers and policemen, as well as thousands of civilians who were caught up in the drug wars. He was also responsible for some massive car bombs in most of the major cities in Colombia.

His reign at the top came to an end in 1993 when a manhunt that had gone on for months came to a conclusion on a rooftop near Medellin, and he was machine-gunned to death by a special police squad that had been hunting him. All very interesting and not for the faint-hearted as there are lots of pictures of dead people. My only criticism is that all the narratives that accompanied the pictures were in Spanish, so I had some difficulty understanding some of it. But definitely worth a visit and very easy to find as his light aircraft is mounted over the gate at the entrance. The park entrance is on the main road, *Ruta* 45, just past Doradal between Medellin and La Dorada.

I then set off for La Dorada to spend the night, and 32km out the skies became so dark it looked like the end of the world. It then started thundering and massive bolts of lightning flashed across the dark brooding horizon. Then the rains came and for the umpteenth time I was soaked to the skin, as when it rains here it rains heavily. I pushed on as I only had a short way to go and it was now almost pitch black. The road now looked like a black oil slick as the rain lay two or three inches deep on the surface. As I entered La Dorada there was fortunately a hotel right on the outskirts so I stopped and booked in. After getting out of my soaking wet riding gear, I went into the town centre to find a bank and whilst there saw hundreds of motorcyclists riding round and round the town square for ages. They were all waving Colombian flags and wearing Colombian football shirts, pumping their horns and blowing trumpets as they celebrated another win for Colombia in the World Cup.

Bogota (yet again), Lyncargo air freight and Panama City

The following day I rode the short distance of 237km to Bogota where I had pre-booked a B&B near the airport for ease of getting to and from the cargo depot and for my flight to Panama. But as I arrived back in Bogota on the Wednesday evening I yet again had trouble with the satnav finding postcodes. After riding round for an hour I reluctantly paid for a taxi to guide me to the guest house; he also had trouble finding it but we got there eventually. He then tried to charge me double the agreed price of 10,000 pesos (£3), so I gave him 12,000 and told him to fuck off!

I had to be at the Lyncargo offices at eight the next morning so I put in the co-ordinates that they had given me and thankfully I got there with no problems. It then took just over four hours to sort out the paperwork for shipping the bike to Panama. This was due in some part to the fact that the woman dealing with me didn't speak English and I don't speak that much Spanish. So we were relying on Google translator to communicate with each other. I was sat on one computer and her on another beside me as we messaged each other back and forth, thank God for modern technology. I was then guided by one of their employees to the freight warehouse in Bogota airport. Once at the airport there was more paperwork to do at the customs office and then I rode the bike into a warehouse where it was weighed.

The Tiger weighed in at 291kg with all the luggage but no fuel in the tank or spare fuel so I reckon it is around 320kg when fully fuelled, and probably more when carrying water and rations for camping! After the weigh-in, I was left at a café inside the secure freight compound for three and a half hours whilst I waited on the police coming to do drug searches and security checks on the Tiger and my gear. There were a lot of menacing-looking bikers hanging around the café all dressed similarly with dark riding suits, radios on their chests and earpieces in their ears. It was quite funny as they were on all sorts of little 125 or 200cc motorcycles, mostly Chinese or South American brands. Most if not all of them I had never heard of, though there were also a few Japanese bikes. I got chatting to them and discovered their job was to escort all the trucks that leave the secure compound to their destination just in case they are hijacked. They are not armed, they just report over the radio if anything goes wrong. They were a great bunch of blokes.

At around 5.30pm the police turned up with a sniffer dog and I had to empty out the panniers, my bags and open everything up including the fuel tank. The dog went about its business of sniffing for drugs; they must be able to smell them over the smell of petrol as it had its snout right in the opening of the filler cap and my spare fuel cans. Obviously there were no drugs in the bike, so I was given the all-clear to pack up and the bike was then labelled and ready for shipping. There was no need to take off screens, wing mirrors or disconnect the battery or any of the other stuff that was normally done elsewhere, the bike was just put on a pallet strapped down and was good to go. I was due to fly the following morning (Friday) with the Tiger flying the day after.

That night I ate the best pizza I think I have ever eaten anywhere in the world in a little pizza shop in a suburbs a few kilometres from the airport. It was owned and run by Beano, an Italian pizza chef, who cooked in a wood-fired oven, brilliant! Arriving at the airport I tried to check in and the girl there said I needed a flight out of Panama or proof of onward travel. I tried to explain I was on a motorbike and showed her all my documents. The girl went away and came back still insisting that I needed a flight out of Panama. I tried to remain calm as I explained again that I was on a motorbike and gave her my export paperwork for the Tiger. Again she went off to speak to someone, probably a superior, and after about thirty minutes she came back and I was given my ticket to board.

7.

Central America and Mexico

Panama, and the Tiger is delayed again

No sooner had I arrived in Panama than I received an email from Lyncargo informing me that the Tiger would not be there until Thursday (five days later than agreed) due to the aircraft needing maintenance. I was not happy since this meant I would be stuck there for a week with no bike. I sent Lyncargo an email asking for an explanation and compensation but there was no reply and as it was now the weekend there was nothing I could do until Monday. The first night in my hotel I met Bob, a retired pharmacist who lives locally and uses the hotel bar. Originally from Ghana, he was educated and worked in the USA for most of his life. I drank with him on a few occasions over the weekend; Bob was well known in the area and took me to some interesting bars where I met some of his friends. A great character, slightly mad, very talkative and very amusing.

I also met Richard (from Leeds, England) and his girlfriend Katrina (coincidently also from Ghana) who were in Panama looking for a new yacht. Here's their story: Katrina, who couldn't swim, got a job as a chef and crew member on a two-man yacht that was going to cross the Atlantic. She wanted to escape her life in Ghana and was prepared to do anything to get away. During the crossing they were chased by Venezuelan pirates, almost shipwrecked and because of bad weather and storms took longer to cross than expected. They also ran out of food so hadn't eaten for the last few days when they arrived in the Canaries at 3am on a dark winter's night. Cold, hungry and desperate for food she went looking around but everywhere was closed. Walking around the deserted town she met Richard, who was the only person sitting at a little café. She was immediately attracted to him and she invited him to her boat for lunch the following day. Richard was a bit sceptical as he said 'the only people arriving in the Canaries from the Atlantic in the off season are drug smugglers or refugees,' but he went along anyway. Katrina asked him to come along the next day as well but before he got there the boat's skipper put to sea, much to Katrina's disappointment. Arriving in another port further up the coast Katrina jumped ship and made her way back to where she had come from in search of Richard. They had now been together for one year and Richard had taught her how to swim, all very romantic, almost brought a tear to my eye!

They were now back on this side of the Atlantic trying to buy a boat to go sailing together.

The heat was stifling; humidity levels were high, very cloudy so not a lot of sunshine and it had rained every afternoon since I arrived. When it rained it rained heavily so I bought myself an umbrella for walking around with. I spent the weekend doing the tourist thing, visiting the old city of Viaje and Casco Antiguo and also spent a day walking round and shopping in the more modern new city. Panama City has a fabulously impressive skyline with towering skyscrapers. It also has massive modern shopping malls, fine restaurants and even finer bars. I also watched more football that week than I have watched in the past thirty years. And to be honest it was quite enjoyable. They are passionate about it here regardless of who is playing, but obviously the best atmosphere is when the Latin American countries are playing. There is a large Colombian population here and I watched the Colombian game in Hooters bar. The bar was full of super-excited Colombian supporters all dressed in their national team shirts; dancing, shaking their booties, blowing horns and whistles, total madness!

I eventually got a reply from Lyncargo, no offer of compensation but confirming that the Tiger would arrive on Thursday at eleven o'clock. But it had not all been bad, it had been a great week and again I had met some mad and interesting people. I had moved hotels to a cheaper place as I had to stay longer than I'd expected, and by sheer coincidence (small world) met Richard and Katrina again a few days later when they moved into the same hotel. I also met Chris, a schoolteacher from London, and we all had a good time chatting and laughing at Katrina's stories of her escape from Ghana and her subsequent adventures in modern countries, she was Ghana's version of Crocodile Dundee – not used to modern conveniences! That night Chris and I went to one of the many casinos here and played a bit of Blackjack; not really my thing but as long as you were playing the beer was free, bonus! It was not a bad evening and we were only playing for a few pounds. Needless to say we didn't win anything.

The Tiger arrives in Panama, *Vamos* Costa Rica and Nicaragua

Thursday morning arrived and I set off for the airport to collect the Tiger. I got a taxi from the hotel and had some difficulty getting the taxi driver to understand that I wanted to go to the *Aeropuerto Internacional*. The journey should have taken 15 minutes but took over an hour as he went through the back streets of the city trying to avoid the toll road to the airport. The taxi had no air conditioning, no door handles, no seat belts, it didn't sound too healthy and he was quite an erratic driver. At one point I almost got out as I was getting really frustrated, but just decided to shout at him in English, 'WHERE THE FUCK ARE YOU GOING?' It fell on deaf ears as he just kept going on regardless.

Eventually we arrived and I got out all hot and bothered only to find out that the cargo area was at the other side of the airport. So another taxi ride followed, but thankfully this one knew where he was going, had air conditioning and spoke a little English. Girag, the warehouse where I had to collect the Tiger, was easy to find. However, when I got there they informed me that the flight would not be in until one o'clock, so I had lunch at a small takeaway shack whilst I waited for the Tiger to arrive. The flight came in at 12.30pm and in less than two hours I had the paperwork done and was ready to leave. When I put the key in the ignition the Tiger wouldn't start; I tried several times and it still wouldn't start. What was the problem, I wondered? I checked the fuel and the battery and both were OK. So I tried again; still no joy, but eventually after several minutes she kicked into life with a mighty roar and I breathed a sigh of relief. I don't know why it took so long to start; maybe it was due to being left idle for week. Or maybe it was after riding at altitude (Bogota is about 2,640 metres) and then flying to sea level, the ECU just needed time to readjust itself, I don't know, but fortunately it had started and I was once more an Adv rider and not a frustrated taxi passenger.

After a week in Panama City waiting on the arrival of the Tiger I was looking forward to getting back on the road. However, because I had now lost a week's riding time I was going to have to do another mad dash through several countries. I now only had fourteen days to get to Playa del Carmen on the Yucatan Peninsula, Mexico, where I was meeting my wife. That only gave me a couple of days in each country and it meant riding almost every day for the next two weeks. Oh well, I thought, that's why this is called riding the Americas!

The following day I said goodbye to my companions and I was off. My satnav was working and I wanted a look at the Panama Canal before heading out of town on the Pan Am highway, northwards. Not long after leaving the city I was stopped by a highway patrolman for speeding; he spoke quite good English and informed me that I was doing 100kph on an 80kph road. I just shrugged my shoulders and said, 'Was I?' He then asked for my documents and told me it would be $20 ticket and I thought, oh no, here we go again! On looking at my passport he then asked where I was from and I told him Scotland. He looked at me and smiled before handing all my documents back, then told me to carry on. I asked, 'No ticket?' And he just gestured me away and said, 'Slow down, mister.' So Panamanian police are not corrupt, just good eggs.

The Pan Am is not very interesting but I needed to make some time up after my delay so rode at the speed limit (honest, officer) to the industrial town of Santiago. What a dump, and all the hotels are very expensive as they are on the Pan Am. I found a cheap and nasty little hotel called the Cion Hotel. It was also on the main road and it was the filthiest place I had ever stayed in in my entire life. The bed was absolutely filthy and underneath there was all sorts of foul detritus; the shower's walls and floor were covered in slime, and I considered leaving. I have honestly never seen anywhere quite like it except for on those TV programmes where they go in to clean out filthy houses – truly disgusting! But it was really cheap and it was late so I spread my basher over the bed and slept in my sleeping bag. The next day I was off early and rode to the town of David, again along the Pan Am. This stretch of the road was in a very bad state of repair, full of potholes and really bumpy in places. I had pre-booked a little hostel called Bambu and it was quite nice. It had a swimming pool so I had a nice relaxing swim and met some of the guests, who were not a bad bunch.

The following morning I had planned another early start as I had a border crossing at Costa Rica to get through before heading for the little surfing town of Domical. The border crossing was a slow process, not helped by the unfriendly *aduana* office who were just rude and lazy. It was, however, fairly quick (only two hours) once I had got photocopies of all my documents and paid $22 for ten months' insurance even though I'm only going to be in the country for a few days – all a bit of a rip-off! I had had enough of the Pan Am so took the Pacific coast road *Ruta* 34, which was a lot quieter and a lot more interesting with great views and sweeping roads. On arriving in Domical and after getting somewhere to stay I went for a swim in the Pacific, which was nice but the rip current and the big waves made for an interesting time.

Sitting in a bar near the beach I saw two people on a motorcycle with Spanish plates ride by and wondered where they were from and where they were going. Returning to my hostel I was pleasantly surprised to see their bike parked next to the Tiger (small world). I introduced myself and after a chat we went for supper; their names were Juan and Amanda, (boyfriend/girlfriend) and they had been on the road for just over four months, doing roughly the same route as me. Juan was originally from Argentina and Amanda was from Mallorca, Spain. We had been to many of the same places at roughly the same time but this was the first time our paths had crossed. We decided to ride together the following day and head for the Park National Volcan Arenal and the small town of La Fortuna. We followed *Ruta* 34 for a few more hundred kilometres before turning east onto route 142 which is a narrow B-type road that follows the edge of the Laguna Arenal all the way to La Fortuna. On the way we stopped at a river, where we watched dozens of wild caiman lying around on the muddy banks soaking up the sun.

Unfortunately the Arenal volcano was shrouded in clouds as we arrived in La Fortuna, so no chance of a photo. That night we dined in a fine restaurant owned by a friend of a friend of Amanda's, called Ronnie. He sat and chatted with us all evening and was constantly getting the waiters to top up our glasses with wine. We all had pizza and I have to say they rivalled the one I had in Bogota – very good. At the end of the night when Amanda asked for the bill Ronnie said it was on the house. So on that note I have to say that the pizzas were better than Beano's in Bogota, as they were free and were washed down by copious amounts of *vino tinto*.

Ronnie had recommended that we go to the waterfall just outside town where you can swim in the pools at the bottom. So the next morning we rode the four kilometres to the National Park, paid $10 and swam in the cool clear waters at the base of the falls. I then had lunch with Juan and Amanda before setting off for the border with Nicaragua. I took a different route out to the one I had come in on and as I was riding along I got smashed in the helmet by a bird. Thankfully it wasn't too big and I escaped without incident, but the bird didn't come off quite as well as I had to wipe blood and feathers from my visor! I followed *Ruta* 4, which runs from La Fortuna back west towards the Nicaraguan border. It is a small B-type road with no road markings but twisty and smooth and enclosed on both sides by thick vegetation. There was also a small stretch of around 30km of gravel, which is the first I'd been on for some time and it felt good. I had intended to find somewhere to stay and cross the border the following morning, but yet again I couldn't find anywhere to stay so decided to cross the Nicaraguan border that evening instead.

Whilst filling up at the petrol station I met Remi, a Brazilian biker who had just ridden down from Alaska on a Yamaha XT 660. He said he had ridden 6,000km in the last six days – that's 1,000km (600 miles) a day, hard core! Due to my setbacks and delays I thought that I might have to do some similar mileages if I wanted to get to Alaska before September; not exactly what I wanted to be doing but at least I knew I could get there quickly if I needed to push a bit, as after my holiday with my wife I would have a month to get to Alaska before temperatures started to drop below zero.

The Nicaraguan border was chaotic; the officials don't have uniforms so you don't know who is an immigration officer and who are just helpers/fixers or whatever. I was being accosted by a middle-aged man called Charlie who was shouting at me, telling me where to go and saying he was the only one that spoke English. I ignored him at first as I didn't like his tone but I was confused. There were no signs, and no office buildings to speak of, so I reluctantly obeyed Charlie's commands, following him and going where he told me.

Officials wearing light blue polo shirts wandered around and Charlie was continually telling me what papers to show them, and occasionally tried to take them from my folder. All very annoying and I was on the verge of knocking him out as he was irritating the hell out of me. However, I didn't think I would get round the confusing bureaucratic system and the dispersed offices without him, so I bit my tongue and duly continued to go where and produce what he told me to. I spent two and a half hours with Charlie running around lots of different offices in the sweltering heat and humidity. I was sweating like a racehorse and very agitated to say the least. I paid for immigration tax, import bike tax, environmental disinfectant spray for bike wheels, local council tax and all at a cost of $26, and I was done. Or so I thought, but then Charlie wanted paying. I was in two minds whether just to tell him to fuck off but to be honest it would have taken a lot longer without him. So I offered him $2 and by the look on his face I knew it wasn't enough so I upped it to $3 and he was happy and so was I.

It was now around 6.30pm and it would be dark soon so I set off full steam ahead for the Nicaraguan coastal resort of San Juan del Sur, only around 80km away, first up the Pan Am (*Ruta* 1) for 30km and then left onto *Ruta* 16 towards the coast. Not a lot of time in Costa Rica but what I saw was beautiful and I would only be spending a few days here in Nicaragua as I still had over 1,600km and another four border crossings to go to get to Cancun, where I was meeting my wife.

San Juan del Sur, Nicaragua to Puerto Cortes, Honduras

I arrived just after dark and booked into the first cheap hostel I came across. I then went for a quick wander around the small coastal resort before going for something to eat. I found a nice little restaurant with an Indian-sounding name, and the menu was all Asian-type food, curries and stuff. I had a curry that was almost as good as a proper (English) Indian curry, not quite, but a nice change from the standard South American fare. After my curry I went across the road to a little bar where there was a pub quiz taking place. I could hear that the questions were in English, so I went in and ordered a beer. I listened to the quiz and then got chatting to some expats (Brits, Aussies and Yanks) who were all living or working out there. I was introduced to Jameo, an ex-Royal Welch Fusilier who was working as head of security for the US reality show *Survivor*. They were there filming a new series in a part of the jungle and a beach just up the coast from San Juan del Sur. I had a good chat and a few more beers, which led to shorts with Jameo, before calling it a night and going back to the hostel.

The next day I did some maintenance on the bike; chain adjustment, tyre pressures and a general check of all nuts and bolts etc. In the afternoon I went to watch the World Cup semi-final football match between Holland and Argentina, in a German bar that was full of Dutch supporters all dressed in orange. The bar opposite was full of Argentinian supporters also all dressed in their national football team colours. At first when I entered the bar I couldn't get a seat as it was very busy, so I sat on a little tiny stool beside an eccentric-looking old lady also dressed in orange who had braided hair, full of glass beads. What I didn't know was that the stool belonged to her pet spider monkey, which I hadn't seen. The next thing I knew I had a monkey on my head with its arms and legs wrapped around my face. It gave me a little bit of a start, as I wasn't expecting it. I jumped up out of my seat wondering what the fuck was going on as I managed to prise it off. Embarrassed, I moved around to the other side of the table out of the way of the little critter. I'd watched a fair few matches over the past few weeks, all with a great atmosphere, but this one surpassed them all as the crazy Dutch danced and sang to all sorts of weird Dutch pop music.

In the evening I went for something to eat at Big Wave Dave's bar where there was a live jazz band playing. Great music and great food, and in the interval they played Johnny Cash; life doesn't get much better. Later I moved around the corner to the little expats' bar I had been in the night before and as luck would have it Jameo was sitting at the bar. Jameo as I said was ex-Royal Welch (14 years) and had also spent 12 years with 21 SAS Reserves. He was on the security circuit for much of that time as well, before landing this job with the *Survivor* reality show, which was then filming its thirtieth series. I also met William, who is in charge of the diver rescuers who are responsible for the contestants' safety when they are doing water-based challenges. We drank quite a few beers (again) and had a good laugh chatting and spinning dits about our time in the Army and subsequent lives.

I got up early the next morning and went for a swim in the warm, clear waters of the crescent-shaped bay to erase my little bit of a hangover. I then packed up and had breakfast in a little café opposite my hostel. I was sitting eating breakfast when an elderly gentleman said hello and we got chatting; he was German and was a doctor or surgeon of some sort. He then started to tell me that he was at the forefront of stem cell therapy and had a clinic here in the town. He also told me he was practising here as he was banned from working in Europe and the USA – I wondered why. He told me about everything that stem cell therapy could cure and I was obviously very sceptical. He asked if I had any ailments. Now, I've got lots, and just to be polite I told him about my arthritic knee. His eyes lit up as he excused himself and ran off to his car before reappearing with a folder. He then proceeded to show me documents and photos of himself, his staff and his clinic. The folder was a cheap Nirex-type and some of the photos in it were clearly very old. I made a joke of it as he was much younger-looking with dark hair, whereas now he was old and bald. Then he made his pitch and offered me a course of stem cell therapy for my knee and told me I would be pain-free and able to run at the end of it. It was all very convincing, if you were stupid and gullible. I asked him how much it cost and how long the treatment took. 'Normally it is $20,000', he said, but he would do it for me for only $10,000, with the course of injections taking four weeks – bargain. I thought he's clearly some sort of dodgy quack, you don't get banned from practising for nothing and I was not convinced, and neither was I that gullible! So I told him it had been nice chatting to him, thanked him for the offer, made my excuses and left. As breakfast chats go it was one of the strangest, most interesting and weirdest on the trip so far.

I took the same road out as I'd come in on, since there is only one road, and it was then back on to the Pan Am, which follows Lake Nicaragua's western shoreline. After the town of Nandaime, I took *Ruta* 4 to avoid going into Managua, the capital. I had to take a few other back roads – namely *Rutas* 18, 11B and 11 – and then go through the small town of Masaya, where I stopped for a coffee. *Ruta* 11 then rejoins the Pan Am at Tipitapa and runs north towards the Honduras border. I stopped for the night 16km from the border in the town of Ocotal, and booked into the Frontera Hotel, which had an armed guard on the front gate. He had a pump-action shotgun, so the Tiger and I would be safe. There wasn't really that much to see or do so I just had a wander round town for an hour or so. I then went back to the hotel for a good night's sleep, before the now dreaded border crossing nightmare in the morning. Maybe it would be smooth and easy?

I awoke early in the morning and after breakfast went to refuel the Tiger with what I had left of Nicaraguan cordobas; $140 or about £3, and got four litres for that. The guy at the filling station told me to be careful in Honduras and to be cautious as it's a dangerous country. With that advice, I set off for the border crossing of Los Manos just up the road where the usual Central American scene of chaos greeted me. As I rode in there were trucks, cars, coaches and people all over the place. Most bizarrely, there were also horses running around, in and out between the lines of static traffic and pedestrians.

Now, I had learnt from the last crossing that the Nicaraguan officials wore light blue polo shirts with BDA printed on them and there were signs above the wooden office buildings saying Migration and *Aduana*. So all the little fixers who were trying to offer their services to me (the guide-gullible tourist, not) got a fuck-off tablet! First, I went into the Nicaraguan migration office to get an exit stamp, which cost me $2. I didn't have change, so I had to change a US $20 bill into cordobas with one of the *cambio* (money exchange) guys who hang around the borders. I then changed the cordobas to Honduran lempiras, each time losing a few dollars in the exchange. It had also now started raining again and as usual it was torrential. Still, at least I was not riding in it. Bike exit paperwork done and finished with Nicaragua, I then moved along to the Honduran immigration office.

After standing in a queue for ages I was handed a form to fill in. I then had to stand in the same queue again to get my tourist visa with the filled out form, and this time it cost $3. Now, at the start of this process I had $41 US; I now had $21 US and a few Honduran lempiras. I then moved onto the *aduana* to start the import process for the bike. First, I had to go and get three copies of all my documents again at a small cost. Then it was back to the *aduana*, where I was told the import fee was $36! Now I didn't have that left; I had $21 so I was $15 short! I asked if I could pay by credit card and they said no. My last chance was the small bank the size of a cupboard that is in the middle of the border crossing. I asked at the bank if they had an ATM or if I could withdraw cash with my cards, but the answer to both questions was NO!

I was now stuck between countries and didn't have any means of getting money or paying the import fee. I went back to the *aduana* office and pleaded my case to the woman behind the counter. At first I was getting nowhere but then she took all that I had; $21 and a handful of lempiras, and started counting, but I was still quite a few dollars short. She then spoke to another guy at the back of the office before coming back and informing me I couldn't get my import licence as l didn't have enough money. I didn't know what I was going to do; I was stuck in no man's land. So I stood there repeatedly trying to explain my lack of money and the fact that I couldn't get any from anywhere. After about an hour of me standing around pleading and shrugging my shoulders she took all my money and papers and disappeared off into a back office. When she re-appeared my paperwork was all stamped up and I was eventually given my import licence for what cash I had, happy days. And I'd done it without the help of the annoying fixers. After two and a half frustrating hours at the border the rain had stopped, I had a full tank of fuel, not a single penny left, but I was on the road and off into Honduras.

I planned to ride right through the country from the south to the north-eastern sea port of Puerto Cortes around 480km away. After leaving the border I followed *Ruta* 6, which was in quite a bad state of repair with potholes everywhere, so I was constantly swerving to avoid them. The scenery was not too bad, a change from the jungle-type forests to rolling hills covered with some sort of pine or fir trees. After the city of Tegucigalpa I took *Ruta* 5, which is a superb piece of dual carriageway; perfectly smooth, super-fast bends as it twists and winds its way up over and through a couple of small (2,000 metres or so) mountain passes. On reaching Lago de Yojoa I decided to get off the main road and I took a little back road that followed the lake for around 30km before rejoining the main route. It seemed like a good idea at first, great lakeside scenery, not a bad single-track road with plenty of twists and turns, but then it turned into a pothole nightmare. I couldn't ride in a straight line and my speed was reduced to running pace as I weaved around the crater-sized holes in the road. Occasionally one would catch me out, bottoming out the suspension, and the shock waves travelled up my arms and back. I was soon back on the main *Ruta* 5 from where it was only an hour to Puerto Cortes.

As I arrived in Puerto Cortes I followed signs for Playa del Rio Mar beach and had a look round for somewhere cheap to stay. All the hotels had armed guards. That was one thing I noticed here in Honduras – the number of guns that are around; they're everywhere. Now I don't know if it's a good gauge of how dangerous a country is or not, but in every country I had been in there were guns. Usually they were carried by the police or the guards at banks; however, here in Honduras there were guards everywhere and they were all armed; at petrol stations, shopping malls, car parks, and even the hotels. Most were armed with pump-action shotguns and here at my hotel the two guards had pump-action shotguns and six-shooter pistols strapped to their hips. They were also wearing Stetson-like cowboy hats. Does it make me feel safe or is it really dangerous here?

Anyway, I would be here for two days relaxing before heading to yet another border crossing, this time for Guatemala. Playa del Rio Mar is just a few miles outside the city along the coast from a Honduran Naval base. It is a beach-front holiday resort with a few decent hotels and bars. All of the other tourists seemed to be locals, as I was the only *gringo* in town; there were no westerners or Europeans anywhere. Puerto Cortes is apparently one of the most violent and dangerous cities in the whole of Central America. Except for the couple of hours riding around town trying to find a bank that would dispense cash, I spent the next two days swimming in the Caribbean Sea, drinking in the local bars and generally relaxing at my hotel.

Honduras to Guatemala

After my relaxing couple of days it was another early start. The thought of crossing the border was not appealing to me, as I thought it was going to be similar to the one I had crossed on the way in. Arriving at the border after about a twenty-minute ride I was surprised to find it virtually deserted and no annoying helpers/guides to be seen. I went straight to immigration and my passport was stamped, then across to *aduana* and the paperwork was sorted. In less than 15 minutes I was good to go and no money had changed hands – great! Whilst waiting at one of the offices I was approached by a local guy, who introduced himself as José. José owns a chain of motorcycle shops here in Guatemala. He offered me free servicing or any assistance that I needed whilst there. It was very good of him, but unfortunately I didn't need anything done and I was riding straight through. He also introduced me to his wife and son who all spoke perfect English; we had a brief chat before I had to get on my way.

I then had about 16km to ride to the Guatemalan immigration office. As I was riding along, one of my gloves, which I had tucked in behind the windscreen, suddenly flew up past my head. As I turned my head to see where it had gone an ominous-looking black 4x4 sped past me. I immediately braked and pulled over to the side, then turned around and rode back looking for my glove, but it was nowhere to be seen. So I got off the bike and started walking back down the road looking in the grass verge for my glove, when the dark 4x4 appeared behind me. I felt a little bit nervous as it pulled alongside me; I wondered who they were and what they wanted. As they rolled down the window I was surprised to see it was full of policemen. I was even more surprised to find that they had my glove. The reason I couldn't find my glove in the road or on the verge became apparent. It was the police truck that had been behind me when the glove blew off, and it had landed on their windscreen and got stuck on the wipers, so they had come back to give me it – bizarre.

Glove returned I set off for immigration and it was another quick and easy process: one man in a little office, all smiles, welcomed me to Guatemala and again no money was asked for. Passport stamped, I then had another five kilometres to go to the *aduana* and when I get there, it was another small office with one young guy inside. He took my paperwork, looked at it and then said there was a problem. He then explained to me that as it was a Sunday and the bank that you pay the import tax to was closed and wouldn't be open again until tomorrow. I thought I was going to have to spend the night there, so I asked if there was any way this could be sorted today. He then rang his supervisor and when he came off the phone told me there was a solution. Thankfully, it was not the 'give him money' solution.

He told me I could to ride to Puerto Barris some 24km away, go to the customs office and then to a bank in town that was open on a Sunday and pay the import tax. I asked for an address but the import guy told me it was easy to find (really?) or just to ask when I got there as everyone knew where the customs office was, (sure they do!). I was about to get the run around and a mystery hunt looking for different offices and a bank somewhere in the city. He then gave me the paperwork I needed to get signed and stamped, as well as the tax sticker that I had to stick on my windscreen. Take them with you as they don't have them in town, he said. I considered just riding off and not bothering with looking for the customs, as I'd got the tax sticker, but I thought maybe I would have problems leaving the country, so I decided to go look for the customs office and the bank.

Arriving in town I followed trucks to the port thinking the office would be there, but no, it was not. I asked a few truckers if they knew where the customs office was; blank faces and shrugs were all I got. I then rode around using the force and by sheer luck stumbled across it, tucked away at the end of a road in a compound. Once inside I hung around for a while as they looked at my paperwork and then they told me I had to ride to the bank, which is in a shopping mall another eight kilometres away, and pay the tax. I was given directions to the shopping mall, but finding the mall turned into an epic. Nobody seemed to know where it was or they didn't understand me. I rode around for a while before eventually finding it. Once inside I was confronted with a large queue outside the bank and the door was locked. I duly queued with everyone else for about half an hour; the doors eventually opened and a lot of people were let out and some more were let in. After about another half an hour I was let inside and I then joined another queue. When I eventually reached the teller, I handed over the paperwork and

I was fleeced for more money (about £12) before getting my import tax receipt. Still, at least I was getting somewhere.

I was now hot and bothered again with all the messing around and as I was getting on my bike in the car park I got stopped by a security guard. He was rambling on about a ticket or something; I was not amused, I had now been running around for a few hours, I was tired, frustrated and started shouting at him, but he insisted that I come with him to the office. I uttered a few choice words and thought about just telling him to fuck off, but he was armed with a six-shooter, so I decided it was probably best if I went with him; I wouldn't have wanted to get shot over a ticket. Arriving in the office, I started ranting at the two female clerks sitting behind a desk, asking what the fuck the ticket was for. They then handed me a card and I realised it was the ticket I got given when I entered the Mall car park; I had left it on the bike and it had been handed into their office. They only wanted to give it back to me as I needed it to exit the car park. So no fine, I felt a little bit embarrassed but not too much as I was still hot and bothered and pissed off with the delay! Ticket in hand I headed off for the customs office.

Eventually I got back to the customs office and handed over my receipt from the bank. Now you would think they would have had all my paperwork ready for me returning, but no. I had to wait around for another half-hour and at last I got the import document. Five hours after I arrived I was at last on the road north. I took *Ruta* 13 west out of Puerto Barris towards Guatemala City and then *Ruta* 9 north. I was headed for the town of Rio Dulce, which sits at the narrowest point of Lago Izabel, where it meets El Golfete. Crossing a bridge I stopped to take some photos and I saw a hostel below, on the banks of the lake, so decided to stop there for the night.

What a good decision, it was a lovely little place right on the shores of the lake; I managed to get a private room and it was very cheap. I ate in the hostel restaurant, which was perched on a wooden floor that stretched out across the lake. Whilst eating I met Jackie, a fellow Scot who was here on holiday with her husband (who was Guatemalan) and two kids. We had a chat for a while about my trip and they told me some things about Guatemala. The next morning I went to the restaurant for breakfast and ordered the equivalent of a full English breakfast. After about an hour I still hadn't been served and asked several waitresses what was keeping my breakfast. They all shrugged and said something in Spanish before running off. I asked again but no one seemed to be paying any attention to me. I was hungry and frustrated and for the second time in two days (I must have been getting tired) I let rip with a rant in English! As I got up to leave I was shouting across the room at the waitresses telling them to forget my fucking breakfast. Which I think they already had anyway. So I packed and set off, starving and very agitated.

I rode across the bridge and around to the old Spanish fortress of Castillo De San Felipe which was built on the Northern edge of the lake at the narrowest point to protect Lago Izabel from pirate raids. Before I went for a walk around I broke into my emergency rations (a tin of tuna) as I was starving. The fortress was built on the advice of the Governor at the time who had informed King Felipe II of the numerous pirate attacks in the lake. The construction of a protected tower which was manned by twelve soldiers and twelve pieces of artillery was begun in 1595. From what I could gather (all the info is in Spanish) it was attacked and or destroyed a few times over the centuries but rebuilt afterwards and most recently in 1955. I spent the morning in the castle wandering around taking photos and wondering what it must have been like to have been stationed here. They must have been small in those days as the passageways are narrow and so are the stairs that lead to the battlements.

After I had a good look around I set off for Flores, a few hundred kilometres north, with the intention of overnighting there. I took *Ruta* CA13, which is a fast but uninspiring road and it was overcast and occasionally rained. I stopped just before Flores to refuel and tried to use my travel card to pay as I only had 41 quetzals (£3) left. The machine wouldn't accept it so I had to use another card and thankfully the payment went through; I then had something to eat but now none of my cards would work, including the one I'd just paid for the fuel with. The woman at the counter pointed to a cash machine in the corner so I went over and gave it a try. Thankfully it accepted my card and I got 100 quetzals (£7.50) out to pay for my lunch.

Now with a full tank and a full belly I set off feeling a lot better. I was riding along contented, daydreaming and not paying attention properly, when I was suddenly going into a bend far too fast. I had to brake hard to scrub off some speed, but was still on the brakes as I went deep into the corner. The Tiger went into a massive wobbling session and bucked and weaved left then right, then the back tyre started slipping and sliding as it lost and then regained grip. I thought I was off, as I struggled to regain control and tried not to look at the barrier on my right. After a few arse-twitching seconds the Tiger settled and I got round the bend and away. My heart was pounding and it was my first real scare for quite some time.

The next scare came sooner than expected, too; there are lots of sleeping policemen in Guatemala and they are big and unmarked. I was again travelling at a fair speed, around 110kph, when suddenly the Tiger was airborne and I felt the rear end kick up behind me. The Tiger then nose-dived into the road with the back end bouncing around like a pogo stick. It's not a moto crosser, sprung to mind again, but it settled quickly. There wasn't any real danger, I just wasn't expecting it, and still it was exciting, though. I then arrived in Flores and it was a dump so I decided to ride through and head for the border town of Melchor de Mencos, which sits right on the border with Belize only 80km further on. I should have realised at the time that all this bouncing and unsettling behaviour was due to the fact that my rear shock was on the way out, more of which later.

Thirty kilometres out from Melchor de Mencos the road ended and it was now a muddy slippery track. I thought this was now going to take forever, as I was reduced to 15–20kph. Thankfully it ended after only a few kilometres and I had tarmac all the way to the border. I was looking forward to getting to Belize as their first language is English and I intended staying for a few days. A few miles after the border on the Western Highway I planned to stop and pay my respects at a roadside memorial. It was erected in 1985 in memory of some soldiers from 29 Commando Regiment, who were tragically killed in a road traffic accident whilst serving here.

Belize and the search for the 29 Commando Memorial Stone

At the Belize border I used my last 41 quetzals (qtzs) for a few litres of fuel and changed a $20 bill into Belizean dollars with a *cambio* guy. I then went down to the bridge that would take me over to Belize; there was a toll booth where they wanted 20qtzs to cross and I'd just got rid of them. So back I went to the fuel station where I changed another $20 to get 20qtzs so I could pay the bridge fee; quetzals in hand I duly paid the toll and then rode the short distance to Guatemalan immigration and *aduana*. They then took my tax sticker back, signed and stamped my papers and I was done, all in a matter of minutes. Then it was off to Belize immigration, only a few hundred metres away too, and it was also done in a few minutes. And at last I was speaking in English, of sorts.

I then had to go to the Belizean customs, which was in the same building and clearly signed in English. Again it was all very quick; no photocopies required and even better, no money to pay; in less than 20 minutes I was back on the bike and ready to ride through the barrier into Belize. I got stopped at the barrier and asked if I had anything to declare, and if I could open my panniers. I declared two warm bottles of beer that were in my top box and the customs official said that they were not allowed, but let me keep them anyway. As I was about to ride off into Belize he then told me I had to stop at a red-roofed building 400 metres away and buy insurance. So off I rode and when I got to the insurance building, I duly stopped and bought insurance, honest!

Belize City was only about 100km or so away but as I mentioned, first I was going to visit the 29 Commando memorial. I had a military map with the memorial location marked on it, on the road leading to Holdfast camp (there is only one road) near the town of Esperanza, so it should be easy to find. I rode up and down three times and couldn't find it, so I stopped and asked a guy who was wearing a Belize Defence Force uniform. He didn't know anything about the memorial and called over an elderly local guy. He asked him about the memorial and he immediately pointed to the area of the road that I had marked on my map. He said he remembered when they were killed and that there was a memorial stone and a sign there, but unfortunately it disappeared a few years ago, he didn't know why.

With that, I set off for Belize City and I hammered it all the way there. The road was quite narrow and for the most part very straight so nothing too demanding. I arrived just as it was getting dark and found that Belize was more expensive than I thought it would be. The first two hotels I went to wanted the equivalent of £50/£60, far too expensive. So I rode around for a bit and eventually found one for £17, bargain. There was no TV but I only wanted to sleep; I'd covered nearly 500km today and the past few days had been long and tiring. I had some supper from a little fast food stand up the road, where I was pestered by some local prostitutes. Back at the hotel I decided to update my blog and whilst typing away with my headphones on listening to some music there was a knock on my door. I wondered who it could be. When I opened the door a woman stood there in her night clothes. I was puzzled; what could she want? She then said to me, 'Can you please stop whistling? I'm in the room next door and you're keeping me awake.' I hadn't realised I was whistling but apologised anyway and agreed to stop – strange!

The next morning I wondered if the 29 memorial had been relocated when the British Army withdrew from Belize. There was now only a small training detachment here; British Army Training Support Unit Belize (BATSUB). They worked out of what was formerly Airport Camp, now Price Barracks and occupied by the Belize Defence Force. I thought maybe the memorial was now in there. I sent a message to my friend Gib, 29 Commando's Quartermaster (QM) and asked if he knew anything. He got back to me confirming my suspicions, it had indeed been moved. Now, anyone who knows me knows that I am not one for misplaced sentiment; I also don't like buying flowers as I think they're a waste of money. However, I thought it was only right and proper that I visited the memorial and laid a wreath to my fallen comrades. So off I went in search of flowers, but trying to find some in Belize City proved to be impossible. I was going to give up when I saw some in a shop window as I rode by; unfortunately they were plastic, but they were nice, so they would have to do. They would also last longer; value for money.

Flowers secured to bike, my next stop was Price Barracks. I used my old Army ID card and got in OK. I was then directed to BATSUB, where I met the Regimental Administration Officer WO1 Graham Stewart (no relation) and also a fellow Scot. I told him why I was there and he was more than happy to assist. The 29 Commando memorial is now situated beside three other memorials; the larger of the four stones has a marble plaque engraved with the names of

Costa Rica with Amanda and Juan.

LEFT *The staff at BATSUB Belize, RAO (Graham) and the OC (Suan).*
RIGHT *Laying flowers at the 29 Commando Memorial Price Barracks, Belize.*

all the soldiers who have been killed here in Belize. I was shocked at the number of fatalities here over the years; 60 soldiers have died whilst serving here, quite a high number for a training environment. I laid my little bunch of flowers, paid my respects and then took some photographs for posting on the Commando veterans' website.

I asked Graham if it would be possible to stay for a night or two before heading up to Mexico and was glad when he said, yes not a problem. He then sorted me out with the best room I've had for ages; I was billeted in the Warrant Officers' and Sergeants' mess, which was formerly the British Commanders house, very plush. Later on I met some of the other staff stationed here; there were only six in total. I also met Steve the QM (for a unit that I can't mention, sshhh) who was out here with an advance party of fourteen men. The main body, some 100 men, were due to arrive at the weekend. Steve invited me out to dinner with some of the others on the advance party. It was great to be in the company of soldiers again spinning dits, drinking and eating good food. It wasn't a late night as they were all jet-lagged and had to get up early the following morning.

The next day I wandered into Ladyville, looking for breakfast and a coffee, and didn't have any joy with either. I did, however, find a chicken barbecue stand selling BBQ chicken at nine in the morning, so I had some for breakfast and it was delicious. Back at camp I pottered around doing some admin and in the afternoon went for a swim in the camp swimming pool. That evening I had been invited to go for a meal and drinks with the BATSUB team at the recently opened swimming pool bar and restaurant. Again it was great to be in the company of soldiers, spinning dits, drinking *Belikin* beer and having a laugh – what a great bunch.

For the first time since retiring I missed the Army, if only just a little bit. I had had a fantastic few days in Belize. I had paid my respects to fallen comrades and had been superbly hosted. I had also met some great guys, all of whom until a couple of days before had been complete strangers. But we were all comrades with something in common, something that you can't buy or manufacture. And they made a nice change from backpackers and tourist-types.

Belize to Mexico and meeting my wife

It was time to head north to Mexico and meet my wife Mags for a two-week relaxing holiday. Mags had organised everything as this was her holiday and we were booked into a five-star hotel just a few miles up the coast from Playa Del Carmen. I dropped by the BATSUB offices to say goodbye to the team and thank them for their hospitality and then I was off. It was only around 160km to the Mexican border and as with the other road I came in on from Guatemala, it was long and straight, no road markings, little traffic but fairly smooth. So it didn't take me too long to reach the border.

In the Belize exit hall I had my passport stamped and was told I had to pay $18 exit tax, around £10, and there was me thinking I hadn't anything to pay as you normally paid on the way in, bummer. Next up was the motorcycle paperwork, very easy and I had nothing to pay. I then went on to the Mexican checkpoint, which was a little bit confusing as there was some roadworks going on and I went a little bit the wrong way. You could actually ride into a small border town without going through customs, which is where I'd ended up. However, as I was sat on my bike obviously looking confused, and started shouting at me. As usual I ignored him as I thought he was one of the annoying helper/fixers. But he came over and spoke to me in English and told me the checkpoint was back up the road I'd come down and round to the left, and he pointed in the general direction.

I thanked him before riding off and five minutes later I arrived at the border crossing. I was directed to an office complex and was surprised at how efficient and quick it all was. First I got my visa, then I was directed over to another window, which was a bank where I paid my taxes and got my motorcycle temporary import paperwork. I was charged $25 exit charge (and I'd only just arrived?), $100 import fee for the bike and I also had to leave a $400 deposit refundable when I left the country with the bike. It was all done on my bank card, very efficient, and in a matter of minutes I was back on the bike and into Mexico.

I took the main highway (307) north towards Tulum and Playa Del Carmen, my destination. The road was wide, straight, well surfaced, well signed, and well boring! The temperature was now in the high 40s and for the first time on the trip I was feeling really tired; not tired in a physical way as it had been a short day's riding, but I was actually sleepy and beginning to fall asleep on the bike, not ideal. I can't ever remember feeling like this ever on a motorcycle so I could only put it down to the extreme temperature. However, I pressed on but then I actually dozed off for a split second. I got the fright of my life as I swerved across the road before waking and regaining control of the bike, so I decided to stop there and then, only 50km short of my destination, as it was the safest thing to do.

I was in Tulum, and I rode down towards the seafront looking for a hostel or a hotel of which there were plenty, but they were all expensive. I headed back into town and found a hostel right on the crossroads of the main road. After a good night's sleep, I set off to complete the last 50km to my hotel for the next two weeks. As I was riding through Playa Del Carmen, I was surprised to see a Triumph shop, as it hadn't come up when I had done some research before my trip. I pulled over and popped in to say hello. It was right on the main road that runs through Playa Del Carmen and was owned by Javier. He told me it had only been open three months, hence why I didn't know about it. We had a chat over a coffee, took a few photos and he asked if I need any servicing or work done. I did; full service, new chain and sprockets, etc., but I had all the parts and intended doing it myself.

I explained this to him and that I was meeting my wife Mags who was bringing with her an air filter, an oil filter and other bits and pieces. Now this was an issue with my wife as her suitcase was filled with spares for me, taking up her valuable space and weight. If only I had known the shop was there I could have saved her the trouble and me the earache! I told Javier I would pop back during the week if I needed anything, and set off for the hotel.

At the hotel I checked in and enquired about taxis to the airport where I had to pick up Mags. They told me it was $60 for a taxi, so I decided to ride there, meet my wife, and get her a taxi back which I intended to follow, bad idea! After an hour or so at the airport I realised that I'd been waiting at the wrong terminal; the one I should have been at was a few miles away. So I set off for the correct terminal and hoped my wife wouldn't be too upset that I wasn't there to meet her. Arriving at the right terminal I was lucky and glad to see that my wife's flight had been delayed, so I'd got away with my mistake. My wife eventually arrived and I could tell straight away by the expression on her face that she was not happy with something and that something was the fact I was on the bike, faux pas!

She immediately told me she was not impressed that I was going to put her in a taxi on her own. I didn't think it would have been a problem, but was now finding out too late that I had clearly upset her. Too late now, so I got a taxi and paid the top rate of $90 for a direct trip to the hotel. Shared minivans are cheaper at $60 but as Mags was clearly upset I stumped up for a direct trip with no stops back to our hotel. So when the taxi controller told her to get in a van that had pulled up I questioned what was going on. He told me it was only her that was getting in and it would be going direct to the hotel. With that, I walked across the road to where the Tiger was parked and as I was getting on the bike, I saw four or five other passengers getting into the van. I ran back across and started arguing with the taxi controller but he was still insisting it was direct trip. I told him I had paid for my wife to be in her own taxi and as it was now shared it should be cheaper.

Too late; as I was arguing with the controller the van drove off with my wife and the others in the back. I cut my losses and ran back to my bike, donned my helmet and gloves and set off after it. Now, it was a busy airport with white minivans everywhere and they all looked the same and I couldn't see the one with Mags, anywhere! It must have already got to the main road, so I hammered down the road like a maniac looking in all the vans that I passed. She was nowhere to be seen. And when I say hammer it, I mean I was doing over 100mph trying to catch up with this van. Now, I don't know what speed he was doing but I eventually caught up with it about 30km up the road. My wife's face was a picture of incredulity as I gave her a reassuring wave before slotting in behind them. I was then surprised to be waved in front by the driver and he gestured that he would follow me. I was confused, but Mags shouted out the window, 'He bloody doesn't know where he's going.' I ended up having to guide the taxi to the hotel; well, at least he went straight there like I'd asked for, even though I had to guide him.

Once back at the hotel I got Mags settled in before we had a couple of much-needed relaxing cocktails. After calming down Mags forgave me for my error in judgement.

Mexico (Servicing and Tulum ruins)

After a couple of days relaxing on the beach with my wife it was time to carry out some jobs on the Tiger. Mags had brought me out new air and oil filters but first I needed some sort of receptacle to drop the oil into. We also needed a helmet for her so we could get around on the Tiger; in the morning we went shopping for one so that we could go exploring the Yucatan peninsula together. We managed to get a helmet from Wal-Mart which was nice (pink) and cheap (£22), DOT stamped so not legal in the UK but good enough for using around here for days out. Whilst wandering around I found a wash-down so took the Tiger back later for a wash before doing the servicing. Now, I can't be sure but I think they might have dropped it whilst moving it around the wash-down as my wing mirror was all loose and twisted and when riding back to the hotel the steering was slightly off again, no visible damage though.

My first job on returning to the hotel was to change the oil, oil filter and air filter. Yet again the air filter was full of dirt and sand and I hadn't even been doing much off-road stuff since breaking my ribs on the way to Machu Picchu. Which, by the way, were still hurting over two months later. They should have healed by now but thankfully they'd not been affecting my riding. Once I'd done the basic service it was time to change the chain and sprockets as the chain was right on the limit of the adjustment on the swing arm. Over the past two weeks or so, I had had to adjust the chain after every day's ride and it was now right at the end of the swing arm, but I had decided to leave it until I reached Mexico. On breaking the chain and removing the front sprocket I discovered that it had virtually no teeth left on it. In hindsight, I should have realised that my rear shock was also to blame as there was very little damping and it was virtually useless, but because it was happening gradually I hadn't noticed. It would completely give out a week or two later and I would need to have it repaired. I then loosened all the front end: top yoke, bottom yoke, front spindle and mud guard, and realigned everything. All done ready for our trip down to Tulum ruins the following day.

Tulum is only an hour's ride down the coast and as Mags doesn't have proper riding gear we rode down in shorts and T-shirts, and not forgetting her snazzy £22 pink helmet. Even riding in shorts the heat was relentless as there was no cooling breeze; it was like riding in a hairdryer on hot! The heat emanating from the engine was almost unbearable on my bare legs. Once in Tulum we had to buy some cowboy-style straw hats to keep the sun from our heads as we wandered around the ruins. We had a great day at Tulum but as I said the heat was unbelievable and as it was now late afternoon the ride back was even hotter than the ride down. We went back and forth to town on the Tiger a few times in shorts and flip-flops but decided against doing any more long trips as it was just too bloody hot.

I wasn't looking forward to resuming my trip proper next week when I would have to don my adventure suit again. Meanwhile our holiday continued, we met some great people and had a relaxing time eating, drinking and generally doing nothing.

Chichen Itza, Mexico

Playa Del Carmen was only a few miles up the coast so we took a trip on the bike to do some shopping and have a look around. Very touristy, a bit like Spain, with all the shops selling the same tat and people pestering you to buy stuff. We had planned to visit the Mayan ruins of Chichen Itza three hours' ride away. But as I said, due to the excessive heat we chose not to ride there, but instead booked onto a day trip provided by one of the many tour operators.

We were picked up at 7am in a little Toyota minivan and then went into town to pick up other day trippers. At the first hotel the driver couldn't find the two passengers who were booked on the trip, so off we went to the next hotel a few miles further on. Again the day trippers were not around and the driver had to go looking for them. They eventually turned up, four young French girls, and off we went to the next pickup. Thankfully they were waiting, a young Mexican couple, and then we set off for Chichen Itza, or so I thought. We were actually going back into town to the tour office where we waited yet again whilst the driver went inside. He eventually came back after about ten minutes and again I thought at last we're off to the ruins. But no, we then drove back to the first hotel we had been at to pick up the two girls, both Hispanic, who had not been there the first time around. It was all getting a bit annoying now and I was all hot and bothered and struggling to remain calm. We had now been in the minivan for nearly two hours and we still hadn't left Playa Del Carmen.

Eventually we got under way for Chichen Itza. The first stop was a fresh water sinkhole (cenote) that had been formed by the limestone rock above collapsing to reveal freshwater pools and caverns. Mexico has the largest network of these underwater cave systems in the world, with over 6,000 cenotes in the states of Quintana Roo and Yucatan! The driver gave us a brief and a time to be back in the van ready to move onto the next location. We changed into our swimming costumes and made our way down to the sinkhole. There was a steep set of steps carved into the rock, which led us down into the cenote. It was absolutely stunning, clear blue water illuminated by shafts of sunlight pouring in from a couple of large holes in the cavern roof. The water was cold and apparently bottomless with lots of small fish swimming around. We spent an hour there swimming and taking photos before moving back to the changing area and getting ready to move to the next location, where we would have lunch. But yet again the two girls who had been late in the morning were late and the driver had to go and look for them and hurry them up. A theme was now starting to develop and Mags and I tried to remain calm; they are Hispanic after all, so they don't rush and timings mean nothing!

Arriving at the lunch location we were greeted with a large restaurant building with a larger shop and hundreds of other tourists. Again we were briefed on the timings for lunch then we moved into the large dining area where the food was an 'all you can eat' buffet. The attached shop was selling the usual tat; sombreros, all kinds of other hats, ponchos, stones, knives made of stone etc. We sat at a table with our other companions for the day and watched a small slim French girl eat about twenty pieces of chicken and two plates of rice; she definitely got her money's worth! After lunch it was back on the minivan and would you believe it, the two Hispanic girls were late again. If it was *Coach Trip* (UK reality series), they would have been voted off on the first day!

We eventually arrived at Chichen Itza and were introduced to our guide Thomas. Thomas would guide us around and brief us on the history of the Mayan pyramid, temples, ballpark and everything else within the Chichen Itza site The whole park is one big tourist trap with stalls everywhere selling (or trying to sell) the now familiar usual touristy tat, set up so that you needed to walk through them as you went around with the guide. It was like running the gauntlet with everyone trying to sell you some sort of rubbish! Most annoying of all were the jaguar call pipes, which were driving us crazy. It was also now absolutely red-hot and everyone was suffering in the heat. They should learn from the Peruvians and how they run the Machu Picchu site, where there are no vendors at all, you can't even buy water! Anyway the tour took one hour and was very informative, especially the bit about the ball game where the winning Captain is sacrificed to the Gods. Brings a whole new meaning to the army saying, 'It pays to be a winner.' Not!

It was now 5pm and time to go, and would you believe it one of the Hispanic girls was late again. This time her friend went to look for her and we got under way heading back to Playa del Carmen. After a three-hour trip back, we dropped off all the others around the various hotels before going back to our hotel. We were so tired we never even went to supper and went straight to bed completely exhausted after our day out.

It was a great day despite the unpunctuality of our fellow day trippers and Chichen Itza was worth the visit, very impressive, but could have done without the touristy stalls which as I said were very annoying. In hindsight we should have gone on the Tiger.

Our two weeks at the luxurious five-star hotel had been great and very relaxing. Other than the couple of days sightseeing and shopping, we spent our days by the beach and the pool generally just lazing around sunbathing, swimming, eating and drinking cocktails. In the evenings we ate great food and drank fine wines whilst chatting to the other guests. The whole experience was of relaxed quiet refinement, no families, mostly couples of all ages. There was also a dress code in the evenings in the hotel restaurant where soft music was played whilst you dined, all very posh! Some of the guests we met were very interesting and had their own stories to tell.

Firstly there were Peter and Beatrice, both journalists for CNN. Peter was an investigative journalist and had some great stories to tell that kept us enthralled. He was originally from Peru but had fled to America to avoid conscription when he was 18. He had actually escaped (well he just took the opportunity and left) whilst attending the medical, and no one noticed until it was too late. The one story that stuck in my mind was about a man who had been chained to a wall in a basement by his elder sisters in Mexico for thirty years. Peter had uncovered this after hearing rumours which he eventually exposed, and saved the man. He was released from his captivity and the reason the sisters gave for their cruelty was; he had been drinking and womanising too much when he was a teenager and they had to put a stop to it. Sadly there wasn't a happy ending; after being released from his shackles the man died a few weeks later from shock whilst in hospital recovering from his ordeal.

Secondly there were Doug and Raschelle (who was also a journalist), both from Texas; more of them later as I would meet both of them some weeks later when I was passing through Texas.

And lastly there was Ian and Heather, both aging hippy types in their sixties who made the whole stay a lot more interesting and exciting than we expected. We first met them one evening in our first week whilst in the restaurant. They were on the table opposite with one of the hotel salesmen, a large Texan with grey hair and a long grey handlebar moustache; He looked like the Sergeant Major in the movie *We were Soldiers*, starring Mel Gibson. And it became apparent very quickly that they were all very drunk! The hotel had a sort of timeshare thing going on and there were numerous salespeople around trying to sell rooms to prospective clients. Normally we only saw them during the day, usually at breakfast with guests before giving them the three-hour sales pitch. Now it was clear that Ian, Heather and the large extremely loud Texan had done a deal and were celebrating it with a few drinks, all on the house.

So there we were sitting quietly minding our own business when Ian heard my Scottish accent and called over to me in a broad Glaswegian accent, 'Where are you from?' I replied 'Airdrie', and before I knew it he was moving his table and chairs along with his wife and the Texan over to join us. He then told me both he and Heather were Australian but he was originally born in Scotland. He was one of the last £10 Poms (assisted migration scheme that operated in Australia after World War II) who emigrated to Australia. It became even more apparent that all three of them were absolutely hammered. The Texan salesman couldn't even talk and just mumbled and slavered as he tried to drink more whisky. Ian, on the other hand, was very vociferous and kept shouting at the waiters to bring him more fucking whisky.

This went on for some time, causing me and Mags some embarrassment as we cringed every time Ian abused the staff. This was also the first night we met Peter and Beatrice, who happened to walk in and were accosted by Ian. Ian was so drunk he thought Peter was a waiter and grabbed him by the arm and demanded more whisky. All very embarrassing, as I tried to point out to Ian that Peter was a guest. Not one bit bothered by his faux pas Ian invited Peter and Beatrice to join us. And so it went on, more shouts from Ian for whisky and grunts and mumbles from the Texan. Some of the other guests were clearly getting annoyed and the head waiter came and asked the three drunkards to leave, which just made Ian more aggressive.

Eventually the manager came and had words with all three and the Texan stood up and tried to leave but he just fell over, and some of the staff had to assist him up the stairs to his room. Ian, on the other hand, was still remonstrating and refusing to leave and his wife Heather just shrugged her shoulders and said, 'I can't make him.'! At this point my wife offered to help Ian and tried to persuade him to leave, and to the delight of all he agreed, as he said she reminded him of an old auntie. I don't know whether or not it was a compliment but he duly got up, assisted by Mags, and was helped up to his room. The Texan was eventually taken to hospital that evening after trying to get in his car but falling over and cutting his head in the process. And it came as no surprise the following morning when we heard he had been fired!

But Ian and Heather were still there and we got to know them a bit better over the next week. They had signed up to a timeshare deal, or so they said, but during our conversations it became clear that they had been travelling around Mexico for some time staying in hotels for free. They were clearly a couple of scam artists signing up for timeshares and getting freebies before pulling out at the last moment after they had had their free stay. But it was all starting to catch up to them and they almost got us involved in one of Ian's moments of madness.

The hotel's (which was all-inclusive) bar closed every night at midnight and we – Margaret and I, Peter and Beatrice, and Ian and Heather – had become friendly, dining and drinking each night until closing. Now there were no other bars or hotels nearby and so we usually just called it a night, but tonight Ian was drunk again and wanted more. As we were all sitting at the table Ian got up and wandered off. Then, to my horror, I saw him wander into the hotel's large glass walk-in wine store. He then proceeded to help himself to a couple of bottles of wine. Now none of the others at my table had seen this but I had and so did some other guests and also some of the hotel staff. But Ian was so drunk he obviously thought no one had seen him and tried to hide the wine as he walked out to the pool area. When he came back he invited all of us out to sit by the pool where he said he had a few bottles of wine. Peter and Beatrice were up for another drink and so would I have been, had it not been stolen. I made my excuses to Ian and declined his offer, before pulling Peter aside and telling him what had just gone on. Peter then also declined Ian's offer, and we all said goodnight, leaving Ian and Heather to drink their ill-gotten gains.

The following morning the shit had hit the fan, and we watched as Ian and Heather were escorted into a glass-walled office with the manager. A security guard stood outside the door and the police had also turned up. They had been caught very early in the morning trying to leave the hotel without checking out and with their suitcases all packed. A few hours later, without even so much as saying goodbye (probably because they couldn't), Ian and Heather were escorted off the premises by the police. We would find out a few days later from the hotel manager that they were in jail, not for stealing the wine but for allegedly scamming numerous hotels over a six-week period and not paying their bills. We would never find out what eventually became of them, whether they were innocent or guilty. In my opinion they were clearly up to no good, but they were good fun just the same.

End of the holiday and resumption of the biking trip

After two weeks holidaying with my wife it was time to say goodbye and get back on the road. But first I had to get her to the airport, no taxis this time (too expensive) so we were going to get there on the Tiger. I moved the bags and tent that were usually on my pillion seat and strapped them to the top of my panniers. Then I lashed Mag's pink suitcase to my top box and we were good to go. With just over 50km to the airport, it looked a bit unwieldy, but once moving the extra weight was not noticeable and the Tiger coped well. We had lunch at the airport, said our goodbyes, and then I was off once more, en route for Valladolid some 160km away.

I thought I'd stop at the first service station en route for fuel rather than go into town. Bad idea, there was none. After 20km I came across a sign saying; next fuel station 155km, but my onboard computer said I only had 75km of fuel remaining. So I had to turn around and ride back into town, a wasted hour! The skies had now darkened and day had turned into night although it was only three o'clock, and lightning bolts crashed into the ground in the surrounding forests. It didn't look good and riding back I got a bit wet as the rains started. Not wet enough for waterproofs yet, so I filled up at the gas station and set off again for Valladolid. I was now riding right into the storm and within a few minutes I was soaked through; well at least it was

*End of our holiday in Mexico: the Tiger is fully loaded with Mags
and her suitcase for the trip to the airport.*

warm rain. Visibility was reduced to almost nothing as the rain was so heavy and the skies were pitch black, illuminated every now and then by massive bolts of lightning arcing across.

Thankfully there was virtually no other traffic as visibility was terrible and I strained to see through my visor. I could feel the rain hammer into me through my riding suit, like being shot with ball bearings it was so heavy. Maybe I should have stopped but I pressed on regardless as it was only just over an hour's ride to my destination for the night. After about half an hour, I rode out through the other end of the storm and into brilliant sunshine and the dreaded heat under a baking sun. By the time I reached my hostel for the night I was completely dry. It had been an interesting couple of hours and not a bad start to the first day back in the seat after my holiday.

I had decided to ride some long legs over the next few days or weeks as the schedule that I didn't really have when I began this trip was now definitely behind schedule! Due to unforeseen delays; waiting for the Tiger arriving at the beginning, coming from Bogota to Panama, and having to go back to Scotland for my brother's funeral, I'd lost three weeks' riding time. And not forgetting my last two weeks holidaying with my wife, which was sort of planned but not for this late in the trip. It was now 1 August and I needed to reach Alaska before winter came. I reckoned as long as I got there in September I would be just about OK; the average temperatures for September are roughly between ten and zero degrees – about the same as when I was in Tierra del Fuego – uncomfortable but manageable.

Away from the touristy areas Mexico is now like Colombia was ten years ago, with a lot of areas that you daren't go to due to the high number of drug and crime-related murders. I'd heard lots of horror stories from other travellers and another guest I had met at the hotel last week, Tom. Tom was a US State Department official who worked here in Mexico and he had advised me to let the British Embassy know of my route because of the threat here. And sadly the body of American Adv rider Harry Devert had just been found along with his burnt-out bike; he had gone missing some weeks earlier riding through Mexico. So taking this into consideration and the fact I was short on time I decided to blast through the rest of Mexico and head straight to the USA.

Doug, the Texan I met at my hotel, was kind enough to mark my map with places and things that I should see on my way north. Most I had already planned to go and see, but Doug gave me local knowledge of where to go and which routes to take. They had also been very kind with their offers of hospitality, which if I took theirs and all their relatives up on, I would never getting out of Texas. But I planned to go and visit Doug and Raschelle at least for a few days in Dallas.

Valladolid to Tuxpan (The longest day)

Setting off from Valladolid I took *Ruta* 180, which runs east to west across the top of the Yucatan Peninsula before turning south-west. As roads go the ones here in this part of Mexico are the most boring I had been on since riding down the east coast of Argentina, similar in that there is nothing to look at and they are long, straight and flat. After a while I got bored and took the coast road for a short time from the town of Campeche before rejoining the main route at Champoton. Not forgetting I was trying to make time, I had to keep resetting the satnav, as it kept diverting me away from the tolls, most of which are on the bridges and are only a few pesos but the satnav was taking me miles off route to avoid them. After my two weeks' rest I was feeling good on the bike even in the blistering heat, so on reaching my planned stop (Villahermosa) I decide to push on as far as possible and headed for the town of Coatzacoalcos, a further 160km or so further on.

On reaching Coatzacoalcos, or I should say, the outskirts, the road was completely blocked off with detour signs. It all went a bit wrong as the signs were haphazard and I ended up in a massive refinery of some sort along with lots of trucks. I got given directions to get to town so set off looking for the right road. I ended up going round in circles with the detours, so headed for the small town of Nancital a few miles from the refinery to look for somewhere to stay, as it was now getting dark.

Arriving outside a small hotel in the town square I got off the bike and saw that there were lots men leaning over the balconies of some of the rooms. As I took off my helmet you would have thought I had two heads the way they were looking at me. Anyway, I walked into the reception, which had a bar in the same room and it was full of men drinking. It was early evening on a Saturday and they all stopped what they were doing and looked around at me; I felt like I was in a movie as it all went quiet! There was no one at reception and I felt really uneasy, so I turned around and left, I just didn't feel comfortable. After riding around a few more hotels, which were all full, it was now dark and I was getting nervous and anxious as a big pickup truck was following me around town and revving his engine all the time. Maybe he was just following the one-way system, but I was getting paranoid because of some of the horror stories I had heard. It was late, I was tired, I'd nowhere to stay and I was letting my imagination run away with me!

So I decided to break the unwritten rule of adventure riding; don't ride at night (last time I did in Argentina I could have killed myself when I crashed), and set off for the perceived safety of the dual carriageway and the toll roads. I had passed motels earlier in the day so hoped I might find one somewhere up the road. I programmed the satnav to look for the nearest accommodation, and it was telling me that there was a motel 23kms away. So off I went and after leaving the toll road in search of the motel I rode down a dark back road for some 16km, only to find that the road was again blocked, with no obvious detour. So I had to turn around and head back for the toll road. I rode for another 60km and eventually found a small motel just off the slip road – deep joy. It was now 10pm and I had been riding since 8am and covered a distance of 1,054km, epic! It had been a long hot day and I'd drunk 6ltr of water, a coffee and a Coke. I was starving and thankfully there was a small tortilla vendor parked up right outside the motel. As I was walking round the outside of the van to order something to eat I got the fright of my life! There was a loud squawk and shriek and a flurry of white feathers at my feet. Looking down I saw a chicken tethered to a piece of string that I had walked right into, yanking the chicken violently, hence the squawking. It seemed OK, if a little distressed, so I ordered some food and went back to my motel to eat. Normally I can eat anything, but the contents of the tortilla were inedible and I had to throw what looked like balls of fat away and just eat the tortillas.

After a great night's sleep I got up early and set off into a cool misty morning, which didn't last long before the sun showed its head and started baking me. However, I felt remarkably fresh and pushed out (only because there was nothing to look at or photograph) another 560km on the long, straight, boring roads. The only good bit was near the town of Cordoba, where I took *Ruta* 150 and *Ruta* 122, which goes around Veracruz and up through a pass (small by Andes standards) before dropping back down to the coast again, a nice little change for an hour or so.

I eventually arrived in Tuxpan on the east coast of Mexico and had a wander round town. There wasn't that much to look at or do so after getting something to eat I went back to my hotel. I prepared the bike for the next day; bit of adjustment (chain), minor repairs and fog-lamp mounting bolt again. Tuxpan didn't seem overly friendly as some guys shouted something at me when I was working on the bike. There didn't seem to be any other tourists around and I hadn't seen another gringo since leaving Valladolid.

Tuxpan, Mexico to Rio Bravo border, USA

I got out of Tuxpan around half past eight in the morning and took *Ruta* 180, which follows the Gulf of Mexico northwards. The 130km or so were quite enjoyable as it had plenty of twists and turns and the scenery wasn't too bad either. However, it soon changed back to the same long, wide, straight, boring roads of the previous days. Apart from cars and 34-wheeled trucks there was nothing much else to look at. The trucks do, however, move over to let you past, as do most of the cars, so average overall speed was good. On reaching the town of Tampico, which sits right on the coast, the road turns inland and heads north-west. After about 80km I took *Ruta* 81 followed by *Ruta* 85 all the way into Monterrey and these were similar to *Ruta* 180, all much of the same long, straight and boring, but fast. The temperature was also rising as I headed inland and I was having to consume vast amounts of water from my Camelbak, which I refilled at every fuel stop. I also just missed two massive thunderstorms, which I could see in the distance but thankfully they had moved away by the time I got there.

There was a massive police presence everywhere as I rode inland. There were police checkpoints all over the place, (some military as well) with big black 4x4 pickup trucks and very large fast-looking patrol vehicles. These were not ordinary policemen; they dressed in black, wore military-style helmets and body armour, most had their faces covered with ski masks, and they were all very heavily armed. As I passed through Tampico there was a massive police operation going on in the centre of town. Dozens of heavily armed policemen on both sides of the road were stopping cars; it looked like a full-blown drug bust operation or something. But, I think it was just a traffic violation or insurance check or something as there were tow/recovery trucks loading cars that had been pulled over.

When mobile, there were usually two men in the front of the pickups with three in the rear, one of which was stood up in the frame (turret) over-watch position. They travelled in convoys of up to six vehicles and never fewer than two (just like the military) from what I saw. Two convoys passed me at speed with blues and twos flashing, going in the direction I had just come from earlier in the day. In the afternoon I was riding along minding my own business when I saw blue and red flashing lights behind me and closing in fast and I thought I was getting pulled. But as I pulled over to the right an angry-looking policeman made some gestures at me as they sped past. I obviously hadn't got out of the way quick enough. There were six vehicles in this particular convoy and they were going somewhere in a hurry! Still, they didn't seem to be bothered by speeding bikers as they obviously had bigger, badder things to be getting on with.

I arrived in Monterrey with the intention of staying a night or two but it was big, busy, and modern with tall glass buildings and I didn't like the look of it as I rode through. So I decided to find a cheap motel on the edge of the city and head straight for the US border in the morning. It turned out to be a bad choice of motel, as unbeknown to me when I checked in there was a train line directly behind the motel. Every hour or so during the night I was woken by trains sounding their very loud horns as they trundled past. So when I was woken again at 5am I decided to get up and get an early start for the border, which was about two hours' ride away. After a fuel and bank stop I cleared the city just in time to see the sun rise over the hills that surround Monterrey, and it was stunning so I stopped to take some photos.

Arriving in Nuevo Laredo the border town I followed the signs to the crossing. I paid a few dollars to get through the barrier and asked the guard where the immigration and *aduana* office was. He just shrugged and waved me through and I realised I must have somehow ridden past them. I was now on the bridge across the Rio Bravo looking across towards the US border control. I briefly thought about just riding over to America as I was already through the Mexican barrier, but there was the small matter of my $400 deposit, and being Scottish I wanted it back. So I did a U-turn and rode down the other side of the road back into Mexico, and was immediately stopped by the border entry police. They told me to open and empty all my luggage. I tried to explain my error and that I hadn't just arrived but was leaving, but the border guard insisted that I open my luggage. At this point I lost my temper and said 'I'm not opening all my luggage, I'm trying to fucking leave.' He then asked, '*Hablar Espanol?*' And I said, '*No*, hablar Ingles.'

Thankfully someone came over who did *hablar Ingles*, before I got myself into trouble by not complying. I explained my mistake and the fact I'd missed the exit immigration offices and was given directions to get there. They were around the corner and under the bridge on a road (not very well signposted) that runs beside the Rio Bravo. Passport stamped I then stood for half an hour in a queue to get my deposit (which I had paid on entry to Mexico) for importing the bike back only to be told I was in the wrong place again! Now hot and extremely bothered, I made my way to another office where at last I got my $400 back. Back on the bike I once again joined the queue on the bridge over the Rio Bravo. There were five or six lanes all packed bumper to bumper with cars, buses and trucks, with no room between them to filter. I was now at meltdown, with the heat and the queuing; I had to turn off the Tiger's engine as it was overheating and so was I. We moved a few feet every few minutes and at one point I thought I was going to pass out it was so hot. Eventually after about an hour shuffling across the bridge, I got to the American side.

8.
USA ~and~ Canada

Rio Bravo to San Antonio

Passing through the US border at first seemed easy as I showed my passport at the barrier and got waved through. I was then directed to join a queue of people that snaked away for over a hundred metres from the border control building. There must have been a thousand people in it; my heart sank and I cursed under my breath. One and a half hours later I reached the front and the immigration desk. I handed over my passport and ESTA (Electronic System for Travel Authorisation). As the border official looked at them she asked me, 'What hotel are you staying in?' Doh! Now, I should have realised as it is standard practice when entering any country, that you need an address. But I'd forgotten and I didn't have one. Normally I'd just lie but I couldn't think of a hotel off the top of my head, so just said I was travelling by motorcycle and living in a tent. 'No, you need a hotel,' she replied. I explained again that I didn't have one. 'Use your phone and get on the internet and book a hotel,' she told me. 'I don't have a phone,' I replied, getting annoyed by the petty bureaucracy.

She eventually called a supervisor and I explained my situation to him. He checked my passport and ESTA and I was pleasantly surprised as he said, 'I don't have a problem with that. Let him in.' Hooray, someone with common sense. I then asked about bike insurance, but she didn't know anything about it. I still had another desk to visit to pay some immigration tax, which was only a few dollars, and I asked again about bike insurance; again the officer said he didn't know anything about insurance. So five hours after arriving at the border I was through and with no insurance, and I thought South America was bad. Before setting off I changed my bike's speedometer so that it was reading MPH as I was now back to riding in miles rather than kilometres.

My first destination here in America was San Antonio, where the infamous battle of the Alamo took place in 1836. It was the beginning of the end as far as Mexican control and ownership of what is now Texas was concerned. The ride to San Antonio was extremely hot, hotter than Mexico and I had to stop because I was feeling sleepy again, a combination of long days, early starts and the heat. I eventually arrived in San Antonio and headed for the downtown area and the infamous Alamo. Remember the Alamo! became a famous battle cry for Texans after the massacre. The first thing I noticed now that I was in the good ol' USA was; it was not as cheap as South America, the hotels and motels were really expensive. Anyway I was here now and glad to be out of Latin America and speaking English, no more sign language. I managed to get a reasonably priced motel in the town centre for a few days and only a short walk from the main tourist area. In the evening I had a quick look around San Antonio and it looked like a great place.

The Alamo, Texas hospitality and Fort Worth Rodeo

After breakfast I made my way to the Alamo, where remnants of the original building still stand in the town centre and which is now a museum and tourist attraction. The Alamo visitors' centre is made up of the original church and the long room, which was part of the defensive ramparts where those who chose to stay were slaughtered. America was expanding and immigrants, settlers and a

222

small military force had moved into Texas, which was part of and ruled by Mexico at the time. This at first had been encouraged by the Mexican government, but their views and policy had changed, so General Santa Anna and his Army set forth on a campaign to re-establish Mexican authority over the region and drive out the regular and volunteer Texan Army. Between 160 and 200 men gave their lives for freedom and independence during the siege amongst whom were the famous; Davy Crockett, Jim Bowie and Colonel Travers to name but a few. The interesting thing for me as a Scot and Brit was the fact that there were 22 Brits mentioned on the roll of honour, four of whom were Scottish. All of the defenders, who including the aforementioned, were killed in the final assault, which took place at 4am on 6 April 1836.

The other interesting thing from a military perspective were the detailed orders (which are on display) that General Santa Anna issued. Not only had he named who was in command of each assaulting column, who would take over in the event the commander was killed and what their respective tasks were, he went right down to individual tasks such as what time soldiers were to sleep and rise, what the ladder men were to carry (crowbars) and that they were to wear shoes or sandals. Assaulting troops were not to load their rifles but were to fix bayonets only. And he gave the now famous order that no quarter was to be given to the defenders!

A great day and a must-see for any visitors, very informative, and surprisingly the Hollywood movie starring John Wayne was quite accurate in its portrayal of the event. I then went around the other tourist spots and also visited some other military memorials (Vietnam and Korean wars) in the city.

After two great days in San Antonio I set off for Austin on interstate 35, the main route north. The roads here are boring but I enjoyed them just the same. They are as smooth as a baby's bum,

Arriving in Texas, USA.

ABOVE *Me and Doug at the College baseball finals.*

LEFT *Outside Doug's house in Austin.*

no potholes, no sleeping policemen, so I could relax and cruise along fairly quickly. I had been invited to Austin by Sam, the Texan anaesthetist I'd met in Colombia. When I arrived at Sam's I met his two kids, Skye and Angus (good Scottish names), who informed me that Sam had gone for a bike ride. When Sam arrived back we all went to a local outdoor swimming pool where we spent the rest of day swimming and sunbathing. Sam and I then went for supper in a fantastic hilltop restaurant with super views overlooking Austin. Back at Sam's place we spent the evening sitting on the porch drinking beer and brandy. We swapped stories of our time in the Army and his neighbour, Jim, told us tall tales of being a fisherman on the Bering Sea.

The next morning I was up fairly early with a bit of a headache and I had to wake Sam to say goodbye. I was off again on interstate 35 to Dallas to take up Doug and Raschelle's offer of hospitality. They were the couple I'd met whilst on holiday with my wife in Mexico. But first I took a visit to the Gas Monkey Garage of the TV show *Fast and Loud*. I didn't manage to see any of the stars of the show as they weren't around, but it was nice to see the garage and wander around their gift shop, which was a bit expensive, so all I bought was a Gas Monkey sticker.

Arriving at the palatial house owned by Doug and Raschelle I was made very welcome and shown to my room for the night. Doug and Raschelle told me that they were going to a wedding rehearsal that evening, so not long after I arrived they left me a virtual stranger all alone in their house. But before they left they gave me a beer, showed me where to get more from, ordered me pizza and showed me how the TV worked. They even put all my laundry in for a wash. 'The house is all yours, make yourself at home,' they said as they were leaving! I settled down to watch a movie and ate my pizza and washed it down with a few beers before retiring for the night.

The following morning Doug invited me to go with him to watch the World Series College Baseball where his nephew was playing with the St Louis Cardinals. Now I have never been to a baseball match before and it was quite difficult to understand what was going on, but it was a great way to spend a few hours, sitting on the bleachers (stands to us Brits), and Doug told me all I needed to know about baseball and what was going on. The Cardinals won very convincingly.

I was going to be camping a lot more now that I was in the States and I needed a new water container, as I'd had to use my original one for fuel after my fuel can got stolen at a border crossing earlier on the trip. Doug said I would be able to get one from Bass Pro, a gigantic hunting, fishing and outdoors retailer. You can get everything there, from guns to boats and anything that you could need or imagine for the great outdoors. As we entered the store Doug informed the staff that I was a British Army Commando veteran and I got a little bit of VIP treatment.

I was given a guided tour of the pipe range, which is an underground tunnel type shooting range. It is quite a safe range as the shooter is at one end and he fires at a target at the opposite end so the rounds can only go in one direction. This was a rather sophisticated one with lighting and automatic electric target return along the inside of the pipe. Similar to the types I had used in Northern Ireland during my tours there, only without the electric targets. Next up was the bow range, which was huge, and there were fake animals of every type; you could fire arrows from bows or crossbows at the array of plastic wildlife. What a fantastic facility and very impressive. There were all types of weapons here too that you could buy over the counter and I was asked if I would like to enter a competition to win a gun. They were giving two away every day for the next year; it made me laugh – only in America. Back at Doug's, I said my goodbyes (as they were going to a wedding later that evening) and thanked them for looking after me. I didn't want to abuse their hospitality and headed for Cowtown (Fort Worth) on Doug's recommendation.

He had told me to go and see the cattle drive through the main street, and the rodeo. Again finding somewhere cheap was difficult but I got a small motel nearby, but had to then get a taxi into Fort Worth, which cost a few dollars. Fort Worth town centre seems unchanged, very western-looking (like in the movies), more or less like it has done since it was built. During the Second World War it was the busiest stock yard in the world, as cattle and horses were bought and shipped to Europe for the war effort. The cattle drive involves a small herd of Texas longhorns that are driven up the main road by a few cowboys every day for the tourists.

The longhorn cattle are very impressive with their exceptionally long horns, which are about two metres wide, huge! It is not quite the Pamplona running of the bulls but interesting just the same. Next up was a visit to the Saturday night rodeo. I had a great time watching the bronco busting, barrel races and bull riding, very entertaining and all very American with lots of flag-waving. To finish off the evening I then went to Billy Bob's Country and Western bar, made famous by the movie *Urban Cowboy*. The bar is absolutely massive, more like a vast complex with lots of bars, and dance floors with line dancers and bands performing in the different areas. Another great day, and I had thoroughly enjoyed my cowboy and country-music experience.

The following morning it was again time to be moving on. I hadn't got time to hang around in any place for too long as I needed to get to Alaska before winter arrived. Another early start and I took interstate 287 north out of Fort Worth towards Amarillo and then the interstate 40 towards New Mexico and Albuquerque. The roads are, as I said earlier, super-smooth with not a lot to look at except for vast open expanses of grassland. It had been a great week in Texas and I left Fort Worth feeling fully immersed in the American culture.

Amarillo to Albuquerque, New Mexico to Arizona (Feeling the heat)

Riding through Texas towards Amarillo not only was I feeling the heat (104 degrees) but the Tiger was feeling it too, as my coolant temperature warning light came on. I immediately pulled over and let the bike cool down for about twenty minutes. Whilst waiting on it cooling, I checked the fuse, the relay switch and the coolant level in the expansion chamber. After checking them and wiggling them about, the warning light went off and I continued riding for another hour and all seemed OK. I found a small campsite near Vega just west of Amarillo, New Mexico, and at last I was camping again, but too hot for the tent so using my basher for the first time, living the dream!

The next morning I got up really early not realising I'd crossed a time zone and the time was now an hour behind Texas. It was a dull overcast day and quite cold, and as I set off I had barely ridden a few hundred metres when it started raining heavily and got even colder. So it was on with the waterproofs and it made a nice change from the unrelenting heat. However, after only an hour riding in the cold I was surprised when the temperature warning light came on again. I had just passed a sign for McDonald's (free Wi-Fi), so I kept riding so as to get internet access to enable me to use the free phone app on Google. I wanted to try and locate a Triumph dealer so I could get the Tiger looked at.

About a mile from McDonald's the engine warning light also came on; not good, I thought. After letting the bike cool down I checked the coolant again and it was low. I got some coolant from the garage next door, leant the Tiger at an angle so the radiator cap was at its highest point and refilled it with fresh coolant. Surprisingly the radiator took about a pint of coolant so it was obviously losing fluid from somewhere. After refilling the radiator the temperature warning light was now off but the engine warning light was still on. I then checked the internet to find the nearest Triumph dealer. As luck would have it, there was one only 200 miles up the road in Albuquerque, but it was closed on Mondays and this was a Monday. I was headed that way anyway so I set off for Albuquerque and the bike now seemed fine except for the fact that the engine warning light was still on. I found a lovely campsite for the night on the Turquoise Trail in the Sandia Mountains only 15 minutes from Albuquerque. I planned to go to the Triumph dealer in the morning, to get the bike checked out and have a diagnostic done.

At the campsite I met Jim and Richard, a couple of evangelists here on a working vacation trying to save people and preaching the word of God. I spent the evening drinking wine and chatting to them about God and religion. Jim, the elder of the two, was 71 and had travelled the world as a missionary and was very knowledgeable, interesting and a really nice guy. Now, over my years in the Army, I had spoken with a lot of ministers/padres and asked a lot of questions, most of which they hadn't answered to my satisfaction. Jim, on the other hand, had answers for everything and knew the bible inside out, and was very persuasive. I still remain unconvinced, but two great guys and an enjoyable evening's debate.

The next morning I had coffee with Jim and Richard and also met Kirsty and John, who were from the Midlands. They were here on a road trip driving a car across the States so we talked for a while before I set off for PJ's Triumph garage. Arriving at the garage I met Bobby the service guy and explained my problem to him. Bobby informed me that they (Triumph Tigers) have had problems with the radiator caps failing here in this part of the States; it was due to the extreme temperatures perishing the rubber, which allowed the coolant to evaporate, causing overheating issues. He said they would replace the cap as a matter of course and check out the cooling system as well as carrying out the diagnostic. He also thought that they might be able to do it under warranty. However, on checking, my bike is just outside the warranty period by two months, but he rang Triumph USA and they agreed to do the work under warranty anyway – winner!

Whilst waiting I also met PJ, the owner of the garage, and had a good chat with him about my trip and my current problem. He instructed the mechanics to flush the radiator completely and refill it with fresh coolant, and give the bike a full and proper check-over. So the good news was; diagnostic and coolant all sorted, warning lights reset and the Tiger was now running perfectly, and all done under warranty. The bad news was that I needed a rear shock absorber overhaul or maybe even a new one. I had noticed it was becoming a bit bouncy and the rear tyre was skipping over some road surfaces, which I now knew was due to the damping and rebound not working properly. PJ's said they could do it, but it would be three or four days at least waiting on parts. I couldn't wait around that long and as it was not terminal and I was riding on super-smooth highways it could wait. I was going to call ahead somewhere and book it in to have the work done further up the road, wherever the next Triumph dealer is on my route.

So, four hours after arriving at PJ's we had some photos taken and I was off back on the road again. I headed north-west towards Four Corners, the Navajo reservation where four states – Colorado, Arizona, New Mexico and Utah – meet (the only place it occurs in the USA. There is a tourist spot there where you can physically stand in four states at the same time. Apart from the novelty of being at the state lines there was not a lot to see or do here, so I took a few photos before setting off west and heading for the town of Flagstaff. I stopped at a

ABOVE LEFT *Posing with PJ, the owner of PJ's.*
ABOVE RIGHT *Four Corners. The only place in the USA where four states (Utah, Colorado, Arizona and New Mexico) meet.*
RIGHT *Camping on the Navajo Indian reservation, New Mexico.*

Lunch stop at the Hackberry General Store, Route 66 Arizona.

trading post to get some cash and got chatting to a local resident from the Navajo tribe, who told me where the next camping sites and towns were. Up ahead it looked very dark and ominous and it looked like rain, but he confidently told me it never rained here. So off I went, but it was getting late and I decided to wild camp. Taking a small sandy track off the main road I eventually find a suitable spot and pitched my tent behind some sand dunes on the Navajo Indian reservation.

I was awoken at 3am by high winds and pouring rain, again at 5am and it was still hammering it down at 8am. And apparently it doesn't rain here! There is sand everywhere and I had breakfast in the tent with extra sand for roughage. Everything had that horrible gritty sensation you used to get eating sandwiches at the beach as a kid, yummy. I also took the time as I was sitting in my tent to write up my blog whilst I waited on the rain subsiding. After an hour or so it was still raining and it was bloody freezing as well, due to the high altitude (around six or seven thousand feet). But I decided to go, so I packed up and put on four layers and waterproofs for the first time in months and rode off into the rain. It continued to rain all day.

Over the past few days I'd mainly been on highways, which helped with the fact I had no compression or rebound damping on the rear suspension. I had also dipped in and out of the famous Route 66 both in New Mexico and Arizona, and visited a few of the historic cafés on the route that are now mainly tourist attractions. My next stop was the Skyway Walk at the Grand Canyon, and then the Hoover Dam.

Grand Canyon, detour to California
(Strange encounters with the police)

After riding in the rain and freezing conditions all day, as I neared the Grand Canyon the rain stopped and it was now red-hot again. It was nearly seven o'clock in the evening so I decided to stop short, find somewhere to camp and then visit the canyon in the morning. There weren't a lot of good spots so I pulled into a small café called Castle Rock, which has a sign saying tourist information. Inside I met an elderly woman called Francis who sounded Australian but was actually English. I asked about campsites and she told me there were none but I was welcome to pitch my tent behind the café. No showers, but a toilet and Wi-Fi access, so ideal. I also meet Ken the chef and he offered to help try and find somewhere to fix my rear shock absorber.

Next morning I breakfasted in the café before setting off for the Grand Canyon; the road up had only just been built and it was a nice ride in the early morning sunshine; perfect tarmac and the first twisty road I had been on for some time. The only problem was that the Tiger was weaving badly in the bends due to the rear shock not working properly, so I had to take it easy. Arriving at the visitor centre I was surprised to see at least fifty coaches and hundreds, maybe thousands, of tourist, and it's only 8am. It was more commercial than I was expecting; I had to leave the bike and pay for a bus tour, which costs $35 and takes you round the three viewing points at the canyon. So it was on and off the bus time, not too bad as it was only a few minutes between each location.

The Grand Canyon is up there with any of the natural landscapes I had seen on my trip, maybe even the most spectacular. The views into the canyon and the sheer scale of it were amazing, and I spent a good couple of hours wandering around and taking photos. Looking over the edge of the cliffs sent butterflies through my stomach as there are no fences, so you can go as close to the edge as you dare. At one point there was a little Asian guy shouting at me to be careful (in broken English) and getting really panicky as I tried to get a closer look over the edge to the Colorado River 4,000 feet below. I was walking around in my riding suit and the temperature was unbearable and it's only just gone eleven in the morning. So I decided to hit the road and head for the Hoover Dam 40 miles away. First I needed to stop at the café and get back on the internet to try and find somewhere to sort my rear shock.

I rang two Triumph dealers; one in Las Vegas and one in Utah and the answer was the same, they can't repair it and I need a new one (£700), but they can't get one for two or three weeks, which will be September. Not what I wanted to hear, as I needed to be in Alaska in a couple of weeks before winter arrived! The guy in Utah, however, gave me the number for Race Tech, a specialist suspension garage in Corona (just south of Los Angeles), California, some 350 miles south-west of where I was. So I called them and spoke to Sydney (a female) and she told me they could repair, refurbish and rebuild it for $300 (about £200). I told her about my trip and the fact I needed it done as soon as possible and she said they could do it the next day – winner. I told her I would be there for the shop opening at 8am and then headed off for the Hoover Dam, which is en route.

The Hoover Dam, formerly called the Boulder Dam, was built in 1935 and is a spectacular feat of engineering. Once it was finished and started damming the Colorado River it changed the surrounding landscape completely, creating huge lakes where before there were none. It also produces hydroelectric power and surprisingly supplies water to areas as far away as Mexico. After an hour or so it was again time to head south and cross the Mojave Desert. I took the highway that runs right by Las Vegas, which I would have liked to have visited. But it wasn't really on my list of places to go so I rode right past. Crossing the Mojave, I could feel the temperature getting hotter, hotter even than Mexico and Texas. My eyeballs were literally drying out with the hot air coming up the front of my helmet, and once again I was drinking copious amounts of water. I passed a giant thermometer at least 100ft tall and it read 108 degrees! Thankfully the Tiger was not bothered by the heat because of the work I'd had done by PJ's in Albuquerque. Route 15 interstate was long, straight, wide and very, very busy with cars racing by at high speed.

I pushed on and arrived at Race Tech at 7pm and there were still people working, one of whom was Sydney, and I asked if I could camp on the small grassy area in their car park until the morning. She said yes no problem, and told me that the engineer would be in early to get my shock done, so I put my tent up and cooked some pasta for my evening meal. Everywhere was now closed and the small industrial estate was in darkness except for the odd street lamp. I sat there alone and washed my pasta down with some wine before retiring for the night, living the dream.

So there I was, tent up, bike parked alongside, outside a motorcycle specialist repair garage sleeping soundly. I dreamt that I could hear voices, only it wasn't a dream; I could definitely hear voices. I opened my eyes to find that the tent was completely illuminated in white light and the voices were repeating, 'Hey in the tent.' I was half asleep and confused, was I being abducted by aliens? As I started to regain my faculties and awaken properly the voice called out again, 'Hey in the tent.' I was still trying to make sense of it all. As I slowly got out of my sleeping bag I realised it wasn't aliens but still wondered who it could be. Again the voice called out, 'Hey in the tent,' and it then dawned on me that it must be the police. But what did they want?

Unzipping my tent and peering out into the brilliant white light, I was confronted by three of California's finest (two male and one female). They were standing in a semicircle around my tent, hands on guns and flashlights blinding me, and telling me in raised voices to get on the grass. Their squad cars were similarly positioned in the car park with lights on full beam. So I duly sat on the grass in my underpants and the cop nearest me asked, 'What are you doing?' I wanted to be sarcastic and say I was sleeping until I was rudely awoken, but I resisted the temptation as they didn't look too friendly. I didn't state the obvious. I told them I was waiting on the garage opening to get some work done and the garage had said I could camp here.

They asked if I had any guns or knives, to which I replied, only a Swiss army knife. They then asked me for ID and my vehicle documents. As I started to rise to move towards my bike to get my passport they all get really twitchy, grabbing at their side arms and shouting at me, 'Don't move, get on the ground!' I thought fuck me, I'm going to get shot! So I asked if it was OK to get up and get in the pannier to get my passport. They all seemed very on edge. I gave them my passport and I asked if there was a problem. They said they needed to check to make sure I was not a murderer or wanted for anything. Again I considered saying something sarcastic like; if I was a murderer I wouldn't be camped outside a motorcycle garage in an industrial estate with a motorcycle, but again I didn't as they didn't seem to have a sense of humour.

I tried to engage them in conversation but they were all really serious. They were still stood around me with their flashlights and squad cars and hands still on pistols. The female officer asks where my registration plates were from and if I'd been stopped before? Now I had resisted being sarcastic up until now, so I replied no, 'only in South America and I had to bribe them, hopefully I won't need to bribe you?' Well that went down like a lead balloon; if there had been any tumbleweed it would have blown by. They all just glared at me and the female officer said; 'We don't take bribes here!' As I said, no sense of humour! I handed my papers over and they radioed in my details and requested some checks. After a few minutes the checks were all done and word came back that I wasn't wanted for anything. I was then given my passport and documents back. They then all just turned around and walked off, not even a handshake or an 'enjoy your stay'. At least in South and Central America the police were friendly; even the ones that took money off me always did it with a smile and a 'have a good trip' or a kind word.

Now that my strange encounter with the police was over it was still only about 1am and I was tired, so I got into my sleeping bag and fell off back to sleep. I was next woken at 4am by a noise under my tent and what sounded like rain on top. What the fuck is going on now, I wondered? The water sprinklers had come on, which I hadn't seen when pitching my tent. One of them was right under my tent and the other just at the front – very annoying as they were loud. It sounded like the tent was being hosed down every few minutes and this lasted for an hour or so. Thankfully none of the water came in and I eventually dozed off to sleep again. After one of the weirdest nights of my trip I awoke at 6.30 and was having breakfast when the mechanic arrived. He introduced himself as Tony, originally from Australia; he was going to be fixing my shock absorber for me and said it would be a few hours.

I went for a wander around Corona whilst I waited, and three hours later it was all fixed. But it was good news bad news time again. Tony told me in plain-speaking Australian that the shock absorber was fucked, not what I wanted to hear. The shaft that runs through the centre had got a score/scratch on it, which was not good as this is what the seals slide over. So it either needed replacing or re-chroming, both of which are costly and time-consuming. The good news was that the scratch was at the top end of the shaft so would only affect the shock when it was at full extension. He had done his best to smooth the scratch out and had rebuilt the shock, and told me that it might last a week or it might last six months. Ever the optimist I hoped it would last at least until the end of my trip, which would only be another month or so. I was back on the road before lunchtime and the bike felt superb; what a difference the rebuilt shock had made. I hadn't realised how bad it had got what with it gradually getting worse and riding every day, but now I could feel the improvement.

My original plan had been to ride up through the Colorado Rockies, but now that I was over on the west coast I decided to go to San Francisco and visit my friend of over 25 years and former Army colleague Rik. Rik retired from the Army the year before me and we hadn't seen each other since, and he just happened to be on holiday there with his wife and two kids. The ride up from LA was the same as all the other highways I'd been on – long, straight, hot and boring. As I arrived in San Francisco it was 7.30pm and it had got a lot cooler so I had to zip up. Trying to find somewhere to stay proved very difficult as it was a holiday weekend, so everywhere was full and very expensive. I went to the posh hotel where Rik was staying but he wasn't in, so I left a message for him at reception. Whilst there I asked them how much it would be for a room. The cheapest room they had was one with a fold-down bed which they wanted for $200 for. They also wanted another $40 to park my bike; I politely declined and went looking elsewhere. I eventually found a motel just up the road; it still cost me $200, but at least the parking was free and it was a proper bed.

After checking in, I called Rik's room and told him where I was, and arranged to meet for a beer or two to catch up. Rik arrived at my motel on his own and told me his wife and kids were jet-lagged as they'd only just arrived and were already in bed. There was a bar directly opposite my motel so we headed straight there. We didn't venture far as we spent the whole night drinking, chatting about what we've been up to since retiring and reminiscing about our time in the Army. It was a late night as one beer followed another and another until we eventually had had enough. Needless to say, the next day I had a bit of a hangover.

I had arranged to meet Rik and his family for brunch down at the harbour area before heading off. Rik was also off on a bike trip to the

Golden Gate Bridge with his wife and kids. Only difference was, they were on bicycles and Rik was on a tandem with his wife. Rik joked about it being the start of divorce proceedings as they wobbled across the street on a trial run. I was also going to the bridge, but I knew I would get there a bit quicker and without any earache! Still feeling slightly the worse for wear after our quiet night out I said goodbye before resuming my trip north.

It had been an interesting, eventful and strange week and it was great to meet old friends. Now that I was on the west coast I decided to change my plan (that I didn't really have) again and I was going to ride straight up the Pacific Coast Highway and head directly for Alaska. Time was now definitely short and winter was fast approaching. With a bit of luck I would still get there before the first snowfall. Well, that was the plan; at least it was for the moment anyway, but things might change.

San Francisco to Chinook, Washington

Leaving the city of San Francisco I headed for the Golden Gate Bridge, which would take me north across San Francisco Bay. At the bridge I took a few photos and met a few people; it was very busy with lots of tourists. I was soon off on my way and it took me a while to clear the traffic. I followed the main highway (101) for about a hundred miles before turning off towards the town of Jenner and the old Highway 1, which follows the California coastline. What a brilliant road; after weeks of riding on highways with broken suspension it was a joy to be back on a seriously twisty road and the rear suspension was working perfectly (thanks to Race Tech).

Highway 1 runs for about one hundred miles and it follows every curve on the rugged coastline, as it snakes its way north. It winds its way up and down and in and out of every cove on perfect tarmac. The corners have some serious cambers so you can really throw the bike into them, however some do tighten up, which nearly caught me out on a couple of occasions. The temperature had dropped as well now that I was on the coast and sometimes it was freezing, as cold sea mist rolled in off the Pacific and the road rose and fell along the coastline. That night I found a nice little campsite and paid hiker/biker rates but was told that if any more biker/hikers turned up, I would have to share the small camp area, not a problem.

Another biker (the pedalling kind) did turn up and her name was Anna. She was cycling across America to start college and was a seriously hard-core cyclist. Today she had just cycled 85 miles (I had ridden 135) and was now sleeping on a small mat on the ground with no tent, just a small bit of tarp. She also survived by dumpster diving (or as we in the UK call it, bin raking) for food thrown out by shops. She offered me a bit of rotting vegetable and cottage cheese, which I politely declined. She said all cyclists do this. Well, I've met plenty and none had ever mentioned it to me, until now. I told her about Beth, the weird old lady cyclist I met in Colombia, and joked that that would be her in the future.

The next day I was off back on Highway 1 for a bit before it rejoins Highway 101, which is similar in that it hugs the coast but is a bit wider and faster. The weather was still the same with freezing mist rolling in from the Pacific. Occasionally the road moved a little inland and the temperature would rise dramatically. So one minute I was boiling and the next I was freezing. Still, the road was fantastic and the scenery utterly amazing. There are double yellows along most of the route but there is plenty opportunity to nip past the numerous RVs (Recreational Vehicles) of all shapes and sizes that are everywhere, most of them pulling cars behind them.

There are several scenic routes along the way where you can leave Highway 101. One worth a mention is the Avenue of the Giants, which runs through a giant redwood tree forest; it is thousands of years old and the trees are absolutely huge. Some of the other scenic routes are just that, but I did come across some wild elk (or reindeer as we call them) grazing in a field.

The following day I had trouble finding somewhere to camp but eventually found a State campsite that cost me $26. They insisted on giving me a pitch with electricity and water as it was all geared up for RVs. As it was late and I was tired I stumped up! The next day was more of the same and again I couldn't find a campsite as I rode through Oregon, so I rode all the way to Washington State, where I found one overlooking the great Columbia River. The campsite was full of fishermen in their RVs as this was the salmon run season and they were all here to try and catch them. I had averaged over 300 miles a day for the past 11 days and the roads had been fantastic. As I said before, that's why it's called Riding the Americas!

Whilst sitting by my tent cooking my evening meal a couple wandered past and stopped to ask me where I was from and what was I doing there. They were mother and son Gill and Troy, both here to fish for salmon. Troy told me he had a boat and asked if I would be interested in going salmon fishing with them in the morning? I gladly accepted his offer, and then he told me he would pick me up at 5.30am! So an early start – bummer – and another change to my loose plan. Four-thirty soon arrived and it was still dark and cold too. I forced myself to get up and get ready for my salmon fishing trip. I had a quick cup of coffee and sorted out my gear for the day then waited on Troy coming to pick me up. As promised, at 5.30am my host for the day arrived and off we went to the harbour to begin our day's fishing. Arriving at the quay side it was still dark and there were hundreds of 4x4s waiting in line to launch their boats into the river. Luckily Troy's was already in the water as he had a berth, so all we had to do was unload the vehicle and reload the boat and we were off.

Once on board the boat Troy gave us both a full safety brief before we set off, which I must say was very thorough. It was pretty misty and visibility was down to about 100 metres. There were small boats full of fishermen everywhere, I've never seen so many small boats in one place, and they're all headed out into the Columbia River to catch salmon. On the way out Troy educated me on the salmon; where they swam, what depth they swam at, what types there were, how many you were allowed to catch, what time of year they came up river to spawn, what lures he used, what bait is best, and lots of other very interesting information.

It wasn't long before we got our first bite and it was on Troy's mum's rod. Unfortunately as she reeled the salmon in near the boat it got off the hook and swam back into the murky depths. The law requires that barbless hooks are used, so salmon getting off the hook is quite common. As we bobbed about on the Columbia River estuary among the other boats we talked a lot about all sorts of things. As the mists lifted I could not believe the number of other boats on the river, hundreds, maybe thousands, and they were everywhere you looked as far as the eye could see. The river estuary is about four miles wide and the sea is 10 miles further down, where river and sea clash in a notoriously dangerous stretch of water. Thankfully we were not going down that far.

We were still sitting chatting when my line started whizzing out; I had a salmon on it. I was immediately up and reeling frantically and I couldn't believe how difficult and how physical it was; I reeled and pulled for maybe 15 minutes or more trying to land it and it was very tiring. But I did eventually land it and it was an impressive 24lb. Another thing I couldn't believe was how excited I was, like a kid at Christmas time – what a great experience. Another hour or so passed and Troy's mum caught another two and again they both got off the hook at the last moment, very disappointing. Then it was my

At the Grand Canyon with the Colorado River in the background.

ABOVE LEFT *Overlooking the Golden Gate Bridge, San Francisco.*
ABOVE RIGHT *Salmon Fishing on the Columbia River: me, Troy and my 30lb catch.*

LEFT *Avenue of Giants, Northern California.*

turn again as my line whizzed out once more and I had another one. The fight this time was harder and again very physical but eventually I reeled it up to the surface and it looked huge. Once it was finally on board it weighed in at an impressive 30lb.

By 11 o'clock we were done; you are only allowed to catch one fish each and as I didn't have a licence Troy decided not to risk breaking the law and we headed for home. I was still excited and had been grinning from ear to ear with my two catches. I can honestly say that it had been one of the best non-biking experiences on my trip. Unfortunately I couldn't take any of the salmon with me but I was satisfied with the fact that I'd caught them. Back at the campsite I said my goodbyes and thanked Troy for a fantastic experience and I was off once more on the road.

I had decided on Troy's recommendation to stay on route 101 north and follow it around the Olympic mountain range in the north-west corner of Washington State. And I'm glad I did – it was a brilliant fast sweeping road and virtually devoid of traffic, as most vehicles take the direct route north to Seattle. On the way round I found a nice little campsite and spent the night on the banks of Crescent Lake before heading for Hurricane Ridge; this is a viewing point in the Olympic National Park and it overlooks the whole mountain range. I left early to get there and paid $5 at the ranger barrier to gain access to the park. It was still misty but the ranger assured me the view at the top was clear. The road up was a motorcycle delight, only 17 miles long, very twisty, with no traffic and spectacular views. The speed limit was 35mph, which I stuck to, honest! On the way up I passed some small deer by the side of the road. Arriving at the top I was greeted with spectacular views across to Mount Olympus and the rest of the mountain peaks, some of which still had snow on them.

At the top I met David, an Asian guy travelling on a small Honda scooter, and I was amazed at the amount of kit he had on it! After a quick chat and a few photos I headed for the ferry at Port Angeles which would take me over to Victoria on Vancouver Island, Canada. I met several other bikers whilst waiting to get on the ferry. Brian, from Oregon, was riding round Canada and back down into Oregon and I spent some time chatting to him on the crossing. We had to ride across Vancouver Island to get another ferry back to the mainland so we rode together across for the other ferry. On the ferry we met another biker, Duncan, who by coincidence happened to be; English, educated in Scotland, Ex-21 SAS, a gynaecologist and amazingly knew Dan and Sara (small world). Dan and Sara are the Canadian bikers I met in Argentina and I was going to be staying with them, as they were on a break from their RTW trip.

I said goodbye to Brian as we left the ferry and I headed into Vancouver city to find the address that Dan had given me. I got there with no problems and was greeted by Dan and a nice cold beer. Sara was working in a local hospital during the day so Dan and I spent a few days touring around Vancouver, eating and drinking. We also had a night out with some of their friends, another interesting guy who had escaped from Vietnam in the last days of the war. Dan also took me to a local bike shop to get a new chain fitted on the Tiger, as the one I had put on in Mexico had been stretched when my rear shock wasn't working properly. I only stayed for a couple of days as I had arranged to meet another former Army buddy, Dave. Dave lived on Vancouver Island where I had come from a few days earlier. However he worked here in Vancouver as an environmental wildlife officer. I had arranged to pick him up and he would be riding pillion, so I moved my luggage around and cleared the pillion seat. After picking up Dave we made our way to the ferry terminal. And whilst waiting at the ferry port it was small world time again as who did we bump into but Dan and Sara who were going to the island for a wedding.

Back at Dave's I met his wife and young son before changing and heading off to meet some other expat Brits for a barbecue. Another great night followed; eating pulled pork, drinking copious amounts of beer and listening to Dave and his mates singing. I got up later than usual on what was a Saturday morning. Dave offered me the option of staying for a day or two more, which was tempting; however, conscious that the weather window for getting to Alaska was ever shortening I reluctantly had to refuse his offer. All packed and I was ready to go, I bade farewell and hit the road again, North to Alaska!

As I had already crossed to Vancouver once I decided to catch another ferry from the north of the island at Nanaimo, which went across to Horseshoe Bay –a good bit further north than Vancouver city so I would miss the hassle of riding through the city traffic and all the stress that that brings. The ride to the ferry took just over an hour and as I arrived I'd just missed one. I had to wait another three hours for the next one, but no problem, I just relaxed and had lunch whilst I waited.

Horseshoe Bay to Yukon (Feeling more like an adventure again)

Arriving in Horseshoe Bay the weather was sunny and I was looking forward to riding north. I'd be riding on route 99, which follows the Squarnish river estuary for a bit as it winds and twists its way north. The road was perfect motorcycling territory again and the mountain scenery was fantastic. On the left in the distance there were mountain peaks, some still with snow on them, and there were ice glaciers in the gorges and saddles. I was headed for Whistler, where the 2010 winter Olympics were held. It was only a couple of hours' ride away, and is now a big tourist attraction offering all sorts of outdoor pursuits. Arriving in Whistler I saw two bikes with UK number plates turning into a car park, so I followed them in to say hello.

They were two young riders from England, both called Sam, and they were just three weeks into a six-month trip, riding north to south. We talked for a while and they told me that they were booked into a hotel for the night. I, on the other hand, was not and as it was getting late I needed to get going to look for a campsite. I went to three different campsites around Whistler and they were all full due to it being the height of the holiday, so yet again I decided to ride on in the hope of finding a campsite further up the road. It was now starting to get dark so I had to make a decision about where I was going to stay. A memory of a brief I was given some years earlier whilst in the Army came into my mind.

Back in the early nineties when I was a sergeant on exercise here in Canada I got charged with disobeying a direct order whilst on adventure training. Basically we had not come in at the stated time. What has that got to do with this? you ask yourself; well, the brief we got that night was: 'The transport will pick you up at midnight. If you miss it, you need to get a taxi or you can take your chances with the bears!' So I had a choice: keep riding in the hope of finding a campsite or take my chances with the bears. Well, I was going to take my chances with the bears again and wild camp. The bears are North America's equivalent of South America's gangsters and criminals; everyone tells you they are everywhere, are dangerous and to be careful, etc. But they're not!

I turned off the main road about 20 miles past Whistler onto a forest track and found a nice little spot to pitch my tent. I then made a nice pasta with chorizo that I fried first before adding some chilli sauce. All the time I was thinking, I hope bears don't like chorizo, as the aroma filled the forest around me. As I said, I've been here before a few times with the Army and tried to remember the brief for camping in bear country and put it to good use. After eating I washed everything thoroughly, packed all my rations in the top box and ditched all the dirty water far away from my tent; I also hung my garbage a good way away as well. I then went to bed and slept soundly all night, and woke to a lovely bright morning having not heard or seen any bears. By the way, the charge against me was dropped on a technicality.

I was on the road by 7.30am and continued north-east on Highway 99 which had now started to open out a bit with fast, flowing corners and nice straights. The terrain had also started to change from mountainous to rolling hills. I soon reached the junction with Highway 97, which runs north towards the city of Prince George. This road was a little busier with traffic as it is the main route north, but thankfully not too busy. The road is much the same as the latter part of Highway 99, with long fast sweepers rising and falling over the rolling countryside as it works its way ever northwards. What surprised me about the countryside was the amount of farmland that borders each side of the road. There were green fields with crops, fields full of bales of hay and cattle ranches all the way to Prince George, as well as pine-covered hills and mountains in the distance. Not what I had expected.

It was going to be another long day as campsites again proved to be few and far between. I arrived at Burns Lake after covering about 500 miles, and rode around up and down different roads looking for the campsite that was supposed to be here, to no avail. So yet again I decided to ride on, and thankfully after another 70-odd miles, I found one just outside the small town of Houston. It was a really nice one as well; cheap, good Wi-Fi and hot showers. On arriving I meet Lyn and Ed, two boys from the blackstuff (Tarmac layers) who were working just up the road. However, they were not working now but were sitting drinking Budweisers next to their RV. They offered me a beer and we sat talking for a while. After a few beers, I made my excuses (otherwise I would end up like them, drunk!) and went for a shower. I cooked a good meal and ate before calling it a night, as I was dog tired after a long day's riding.

It rained all night but when I woke in the morning the sun was out, although as I was now further north it had got noticeably colder whilst riding. So I layered up and for the first time in months I was wearing three layers. I set off and headed for New Hazelton, still on Highway 97, and there was less traffic now that I was leaving civilisation again. Not long after New Hazelton, I was greeted with my first sign saying Alaskan Highway, informing me that I am nearing my destination. After filling up and having lunch at the services next to the turning, I turned right onto the Alaskan Highway. A few miles up the road I met a Canadian who was on a 50cc scooter and I stopped for a chat. A few miles further up the road I met another two Canadian bikers at a junction and stopped for a chat with them as well.

After saying goodbye to my fellow adventure riders I headed off in search of the elusive campsites again. Riding along I got my first sight of a black bear, sitting by the side of the road eating daisies. As I pulled in to try and get a photo it scarpered over the bank. Now, bears are like London buses – you wait ages for one and then three come along at once. Over the next few miles I saw another two bears and both ran off before I could get a photo. One of them, however, sat in the gutter and I pulled up right alongside him; he was no more than 10 feet from me down the bank and looked at me nonchalantly. I tried to get my camera out but he just sauntered off into the undergrowth, and it was amazing how quickly he disappeared, so no photos yet.

I rode on for a bit and found a nice provincial campsite on the shores of Kinaskan Lake. Whilst I was setting up the warden came around to collect the fee for camping. I got chatting to her; she was a nice old lady, originally from Germany. She said I needed a campfire and that she would give me wood for it, but I told her I was fine, as

I had a stove. I asked her how much it was to camp and she said she would give me a British Columbia disabled ticket (I must be looking bad), which meant I could camp for free. There were no showers, no Wi-Fi, and few other campers, so I sat by the lake eating cheese and pasta. And schoolboy error, I only had half a bottle of wine left from yesterday to wash it down with.

After a great night's sleep by the lake, I got up early and washed in its cold clear waters before setting off ever northwards. The temperature was dropping so again I layered up. This time I was up to four layers; base, fleece, waterproof liner and riding jacket, and I was still cold when I was riding. The road was now getting a bit rougher; not as rough as some roads I'd been on but there were lots of areas that had been repaired with gravel, and there were also no road markings. Still, it was dry (for now), quiet, and I was alone and feeling isolated for the first time since leaving South America, but I was feeling more adventurous again too.

Passing over the Cassiar Mountains the skies darkened and I rode into a massive storm, with lashing rain, low visibility and high winds, and the temperature plummeted drastically. This was my first cold rain since Tierra Del Fuego. It was also a foretaste of how quickly things could change and of how severe the weather could be up here. It was not good as I was blown around and buffeted by the strong winds, making riding difficult and for the first time in ages I questioned, why was I doing this? Within minutes I was soaked right through and my feet and hands were freezing, even with the heated grips on. Thankfully the storm only lasted about an hour and as I rode into the next valley it was drier and brighter, but still cold. I rode through a forested area that had suffered fire damage and all the trees were like charcoal skeletons for mile after mile, very strange-looking.

I soon passed a sign saying welcome to the Yukon and shortly afterwards arrived at a junction informing me that I was about to join the Alaskan Highway (AlCan), which was not strictly correct as I'd been on it for some time. The Alaskan Highway actually runs from BC, where it's named Highway 97 North, before becoming Yukon Highway 1 and then finally Alaskan Route 2, which would take me to the city of Fairbanks. It was built after the Second World War by US and Canadian military engineers to link mainland USA with Alaska, as the USA perceived this to be a threat and likely route for Russian troops in the event of war.

Yukon to Fairbanks Alaska

So in reality I was on the Yukon route 1 part of the AlCan. Further up the road I pulled into the small (one pump and a wooden shack) service station to refuel and as I was about to leave I had a small world moment. I was just pulling away when another adventure biker rode on to the gravel forecourt, so I stopped to say hello. He was all wrapped up like me with six or seven layers on and wearing a ski mask under his helmet, but I could clearly see that he was Asian. He was riding a BMW GS 800, and I immediately knew who he was before he had even introduced himself; my friends Dan and Sara had told me about him. Still on our bikes I leant over and said to him, 'Are you Faizal?' And he replied, 'Yes, are you Steve?' He had also been told about me by Dan and Sara – bizarre, small world! Faizal is on a round the world trip from Malaysia; he started in a group of five all sponsored by Tourism Malaysia, Bank Rakyat and BMW Motorrad Malaysia. The sponsorship had ended and the rest of his group had gone home, so he was now funding his own trip and was accompanied by a young American called Jesus, who arrived a few minutes later riding a Triumph Bonneville. Faizal had met him earlier on his trip whilst in Mexico and they had arranged to meet up for this leg of his ride.

After a quick chat we decided to ride together as we were all heading north to Prudhoe Bay. Sometime later, we were riding along at a fair pace and Jesus's bike seemed to run out of fuel. We stopped and Faizal gave him a couple of litres and we set off again. However, we had only ridden a couple of hundred metres when Jesus stopped again. He seemed to be having a problem with his bike. I pulled alongside and he said he thought there was air in the fuel line. I asked him if he was on reserve and what the capacity was. He wasn't sure what the reserve capacity was but when he switched over the tap (to reserve) the bike started and ran OK. So off we went again, but not long afterwards he pulled over, only this time he had run out of fuel. I gave him my spare four litres and that got us to the next petrol station. Faizal and Jesus wanted to push on to the town of Whitehorse, another hundred miles further up the road, but I was tired as I had already been riding all day and had ridden over 400 cold miles, so I decided to leave them and find a campsite for the night.

I found another nice little provincial campsite by Teslin Lake and pitched my tent; it was another quiet site with only a few campers. I met a young German (yes, they're everywhere) couple here on a work visa. We chatted for a while by a campfire, drank some wine and they smoked a joint. And believe it or not, considering I'd ridden all the way through the Americas and met dozens if not hundreds of backpackers, they were the first that I had met who were doing drugs. In the middle of the night I woke up as I was cold and the temperature had dropped to around zero, so for the first time on the trip I had to double bag. My Vango tent is not made for these cold conditions as it has mesh vents which let in the air, and up here the air's cold. The next day I was up early and it was still very cold as I rode off, so I was now wearing five layers. I rode to a small hamlet called Beaver Creek just a couple of miles from the Canadian border crossing with Alaska. I pitched my tent for the night in a little trailer park next to a grocery store, which wasn't bad as they let me use their showers and Wi-Fi.

That evening I sat on the porch of the grocery store checking my emails and it was surprisingly hot, but that didn't last as the temperature dropped quickly when darkness descended. I got a message from Faizal saying that he was in Dawson, which is on the Top of the World Road in Northern Yukon. It is an alternative route to Alaska and the one I was thinking of coming back down on. Another cold night followed and I had to put my sealskin hat on to sleep in, and again I was double bagging. In the morning I had another message from Faizal saying he was setting off but I was unable to reply as the internet wasn't working properly. So I set off, and this time I had six layers on. The road was quiet with just the odd pickup and RV. The scenery was amazing; snow-capped mountains in the distance and the forests already in their autumn colours, with winter fast approaching.

After another long day's riding I eventually arrived in Fairbanks and found a little guest-house. It was almost full except for a conservatory glass-type building that was separate from the main house and in the garden. I booked us all in and sent a message to Faizal and Jesus. They turned up a few hours later and we settled into our digs for the next two nights. We then went out for food and some beers and got to know each other a little bit. The next morning I had arranged to get new tyres from a BMW Harley dealer (Harley Davidson Farthest North Outpost) in Fairbanks so rode over to their garage to collect them.

They said on the phone that they couldn't fit them, which I thought was a bit odd, so asked again when I arrived why they couldn't do it. The girl on the counter sent for the manager and I had a discussion with him about their bad business practice of selling tyres to Adv riders, and not fitting them just because I'm not on a BMW or Harley

Davidson. He started going on about not knowing the correct torque settings, and health and safety (H&S) etc. I told him I would take the wheels off in the car park and refit them myself, and that all I wanted them to do was fit the new tyres which they were selling me. He then said I couldn't work in the parking lot (car park); not very helpful. They were also not happy with fitting the existing tubes and wanted to sell me new ones; I asked what was wrong with them and the tyre fitter said it was difficult to fit tyres with old tubes – bullshit! I was getting very frustrated but eventually after I spoke to the General Manager they agreed to fit them, but I had to sign a disclaimer first. They allowed me to take my wheels off but only on a gravel area at the edge of their parking lot.

Both wheels off, the Tiger was on the centre stand and propped up on one of my panniers and a milk crate as none of the mechanics would lend me any motorcycle jacks. Then I was walking towards the shop with the wheels when I heard a crash! I looked around and the Tiger was on its side, with no wheels – nightmare! Unbeknown to me the centre stand had been slowly sinking into the gravel, resulting in the fall. A few mechanics helped me pick it up and I again propped it up (still no offer of a jack). Eventually the tyres were fitted and then came the real sting; it cost another $105 (£60) on top of what I'd paid for the tyres after I had done all the work – rip-off! Of all the garages I had visited on my trip, this had been the most unhelpful and awkward, quoting bullshit to me about torque settings and H&S, unbelievable!

Anyway, I now had new rubber for the final push north. The ride up here had been long and cold but the scenery was amazing. It had also been the most desolate, lonely riding I had done since way back in South America and it felt like an adventure again. No phone signals or Wi-Fi (even Bolivia had Wi-Fi) for most of the trip up through the Yukon and Alaska, and nearly 2200 miles covered in the six days since leaving Vancouver, averaging 366 miles a day in very cold riding conditions. It was now the end of August and after getting my tyres fitted and a day's rest and relaxing in Fairbanks with Faizal and Jesus we were ready to ride the Dalton Highway. And I would have it all to do again when I returned from Deadhorse. What I didn't know was that it would get much colder!

Fairbanks to Prudhoe Bay (The Dalton Highway), Alaska

Deadhorse and Prudhoe Bay were about 500 miles further north on a gravel and dirt road called the Dalton Highway; it would take two days to ride up there and two days to ride back. The weather forecast said it should be dry for a few days then they were expecting the first snows on Tuesday, by which time we should be back in Fairbanks. The Dalton Highway and the Trans-Alaska Pipeline System run through the Atigun Pass (1,415m) in the Brooks Mountains on their way to the oilfields at Prudhoe Bay, on Alaska's North Slope. We were told that winter had already arrived at the notorious Atigun Pass as featured on the Discovery Channel's *Ice Road Truckers*. It has a reputation as one of the most dangerous roads in the world. Locals told us that we would be lucky to get through as conditions on the pass were bad and it was snowing, but we set off anyway. For me it was a personal goal and it was the same for Faizal. I also knew we were cutting it a bit fine with the weather, but we were going to find out the hard way just how brutal and unforgiving Alaskan weather could be even this early in the winter…

We set off after having breakfast in Sam's Sourdough Café and it was a cold but bright sunny day. The first 65 miles were all paved except for the odd few miles of gravel and we then reached the sign informing us that we were about to go on the Dalton Highway. It would now be all gravel and hard-packed dirt for the remainder of the ride. About another 60 miles on we reached the petrol station at the Yukon River Camp, where we refuelled. Not long after leaving the petrol station and crossing another small bridge, I looked in my rear view mirror and saw Faizal pull over. I pulled in and looked back down the road and I could see Jesus stood in the road and his bike lying on its side. I turned around and rode back to find Jesus had crashed his Bonneville; he was OK but was obviously a little shook up.

He had come off at around 50mph after hitting one of the many potholes on the Dalton. Unlike mine and Faizal's off-road adventure bikes, which have 21in front wheels and long travel suspension, Jesus's bike is a road bike with a 17in front, short travel suspension and not designed for the punishing Dalton gravel track. Thankfully he was not injured and the bike had stayed on the road and was not too badly damaged. A few rips on his clothing at the knee and elbow were all that was sustained. The bike had a broken front brake lever and the engine foot brake and engine casing were severely ground away but not holed through. Luckily for him he was on a Triumph and I had a spare brake lever that fitted his bike, so we were off again quite quickly.

We soon arrived at the sign informing us that we were now in the Arctic Circle and stopped to have a few photos taken. The weather was still holding, cold but sunny, and we arrived at our destination for the night, Coldfoot, a small collection of buildings left over from when the road was built, which now had a restaurant/bar, a petrol station and a hotel (sort of). The hotel was the largest building here, single-storey, made from wood, with two-person rooms, like an old barrack block, and very expensive for what was effectively an old workers' camp. There were no mod cons, just a bed and a hot shower (not en-suite), and there was a laundry room that you had to pay to use. The cost to have a room for the night was $199 (about £130), so we decided to camp at the back of the building, which was free.

Both Faizal and I had small tents that were just about adequate, but Jesus only had a bivi bag so I lent him my basher and helped him erect a top cover over his sleeping area, which was good thing, as during the night the temperature dropped below zero and we had our first light covering of snow. It was also double bag time again and I slept warmly and snugly. I awoke around eight the following morning and on crawling out of my tent saw that the tents and Jesus's basher were all covered in snow. My two fellow travellers were still asleep; Faizal, who had been snoring all night, was still snoring and there was no noise or signs of life whatsoever coming from inside Jesus's basher. I thought maybe he was dead, so gave him a prod and he groaned. I went for a wash and then had breakfast in the restaurant before returning over an hour later to our campsite.

Faizal was still snoring and Jesus was also still dead to the world, so I packed my tent, refuelled the Tiger and got ready for the road. I sat in the café watching for signs of life from my new riding buddies but there were none. Faizal eventually got up and pottered around and started boiling rice for breakfast. I continued to sit in the café overdosing on coffee. Eventually Jesus made an effort and got out his sleeping bag and took forever to get packed; I went over and tried to hurry them up as it was now 11am and I'd been up for three hours. I was having to remind myself I wasn't in the Army any longer, as I wanted to start shouting at them to get a move on! But instead I told them I'd wait over at the café again, where I had another coffee and tried to stay calm.

Faizal at last joined me in the café, which was getting busy now with truckers and hunters who had just come down from Prudhoe Bay. They informed us that there was a lot of snow and ice on the Atigun Pass and that we wouldn't get through! Not good. One guy with a flatbed trailer on the back of a huge 4x4 truck offered to put our bikes on it and take us over the pass. We considered his offer but politely declined as that would have been cheating! After an age Jesus eventually made it to breakfast, then he went back, packed, got into his riding gear, refuelled his bike and at last, just after midday we got on the road. Jesus is what is known in the Army as an admin case (bad personal administration); about 20 miles up the road he pulled over and we all stopped to see what was wrong. He had forgotten to put his ski mask and neck warmer on and his neck and face were freezing in the cold Alaskan air. At last properly dressed we set off and thankfully rode for a good bit, stopping only occasionally to take photos.

As we got closer to the Atigun Pass it started snowing, only lightly though, and the gravel was still visible and good to ride on. However, arriving at the foot of the pass we could see it looked worse as the road climbed up into the mountains. We also saw that all the trucks were stopping and putting on their snow chains; this was not a good sign, and we were slightly worried, but we pressed on. I was leading and kept a steady throttle as I started to ascend the icy road, which also now had a couple of inches of snow on top. There were still some areas with gravel showing, offering some grip. I checked my mirrors every now and then to make sure the others were still behind me as we slowly started to climb. A few hundred metres from the top I hit hard-packed ice and it was a struggle to stay upright as the rear stepped out. I squirmed and slid but managed to keep going and eventually made it to the top of the pass. Going over the top, which was almost flat for a good hundred metres or so, I had to put both feet out as stabilisers because the front and the rear were both sliding around. I made it over the top and started descending the other side, which was also icy.

I glanced in my mirrors for the first time in a while as I started going down the other side and I couldn't see the other two, so I pulled over to the side and waited a while before deciding to ride back up to see where they were. I thought the worst. I now had a problem; I couldn't get turned around. Every time I tried to turn the bike on the

Jesus, Faizal and me about to set off for the Dalton Highway.

Jesus's Bonneville after his off.

Heading north on the Dalton Highway.

Riding away from the Atigun Pass.

Riding the Dalton Highway.

steep slope I started sliding sideways and I was in danger of dropping it. I had no option but to leave it there, so I parked up and decided to walk back. As I was walking back up a truck pulled over and gave me a lift as I was some way down from the top. He also informed me that he had heard on the CB radio that one of the bikes was in a wreck (that's American for crashed). Cresting the top I saw a safety truck with orange flashing lights and further down I saw Jesus's bike on its side and Faizal and the truck driver trying to lift it. After we got it back on its wheels Jesus told us that this was his second crash; he had crashed on the way up, decided he was not going to make it, turned around and then crashed trying to make his way down. And this time he had broken the gear shifter so was definitely not going any further even if he wanted to. He would be lucky to make it back to Coldfoot.

The safety patrol guy told him there was a mining camp nearby and they might be able to fix his shifter to enable him to return to Coldfoot. Jesus had had enough and so had the Triumph Bonneville, and he decided he was turning back. The safety guy advised me and Faizal go back too, as it was only going to get worse. Well, I was already over the top and getting to Prudhoe Bay was why I had come on this trip, so I wasn't going to turn around, and I said I was going continue regardless. Faizal had come all the way from Malaysia and he also said he wanted to go on. Jesus looked like he was going to burst into tears – I think he thought Faizal, who he had been with for some time, would have gone back with him. So we bid farewell and good luck to Jesus and the safety car escorted him back down the mountain to the mining camp. I got another lift in a 4x4 back up and over the pass to where I'd left the Tiger. After remounting, Faizal also got over the top without any further problems and we continued on towards Prudhoe Bay. Once on the north side of the mountains and clear of the pass the snow subsided and the sun even came out. The gravel track was wet in places and in some places bone-dry, so the last 170-mile ride to Prudhoe Bay was cold but enjoyable.

Prudhoe Bay was not a pretty sight, just a massive oil town; with oil rigs, construction buildings, industrial complexes, office complexes, huge stores, huge garages with hundreds of huge vehicles parked in them, and some accommodation buildings. And there was a fuel station somewhere, which took us quite a bit of time to find and turned out to be one of those self-service ones. We had trouble getting fuel as we couldn't even get into the metal container where the machine was that took your credit card. We eventually managed with the help of a worker who had come by to refuel his truck. We then headed off looking for the Prudhoe Bay Hotel. There are a couple of hotels; well, that's what they call them, but they are really just massive barrack-type buildings, housing oil industry workers. Thankfully we found the hotel quite quickly and checked in. It cost $115 each and for that we got a bed in a two-person room, free Wi-Fi and three meals in the big self-service, eat all you can canteen. Like the Coldfoot accommodation the toilets and showers were communal and unlike the Coldfoot camp there was a no alcohol policy here! However, the food was superb; Faizal and I ate like kings and then got a good night's sleep in preparation for the return down through the Atigun pass in the morning. The weather forecast for the following day was not good and we were both a little bit apprehensive to be honest, which would prove to be justified!

Prudhoe Bay to Atigun Pass (Coldfoot Ice Road Bikers)

Waking up the following morning in the Prudhoe Bay Hotel, it didn't sound good. We could hear the wind howling and the rain lashing down like a demented drummer on the wooden building. It was also freezing, and this was only 1 September, not what we had wanted.

But worse was to come at breakfast when we read the weather board next to the reception, advising that all vehicles going down the Dalton were to fit snow chains before going over the Atigun pass as it was blowing a blizzard and completely iced over. We waited a few hours to see if the rain would subside but it did not and we didn't want to pay a small fortune again to stay another night. So once again we decided to press on; how hard could it be?

At ten o'clock, all layered up (six layers) with full riding suit and an extra set of waterproofs over the top, we set off into the rain for the ride south through the Atigun Pass. The Dalton gravel was now wet but surprisingly grippy, except for the odd bit that was sludgy and slippy. Just for good measure there were the obligatory roadworks and the tractor had just raked a few miles of road. This made it difficult to ride in as the bikes weaved around in the soft freshly turned road surface, a bit like sand riding. As we were nearing the pass we could see up ahead that the weather looked worse, as the whole mountain range was shrouded in white. As we got closer, trucks coming towards us were flashing their lights at us and gesturing for us to stop. What did they want we thought, as we rode on past. A few miles from the pass we were again being flashed at and flagged down by an approaching truck. So we pulled in to see what was wrong, and the concerned driver told us to turn back as conditions were very, very bad!

The next truck also stopped us and told us to go back to Prudhoe as we would not get through the pass, but we rode on as we had no option but to try, because we probably didn't have enough fuel to get back to Prudhoe Bay. And the weather forecast said it was going to get worse over the coming days, so onwards we rode towards the forbidding bleak whiteness of the blizzard ahead. At the foot of the North Slope, which would take us up the pass, trucks were again fitting snow chains. We stopped in the layby with all the trucks and had quick chat about our options, and decided we would go for it!

What we also found out was that the North Slope was steeper than the South slope, which we had obviously come up over without too much difficulty, but we were about to find out how much harder it was riding up the north side.

It was snowing heavily as we started our ascent and all was going well. As we climbed, however, it started to get slippier and windier, and the snow was getting heavier. We were making good steady progress and about a third of the way up I decided we needed a photo, otherwise no one would believe us. I saw what looked like a layby and pulled over to take a few photos as we would not get an opportunity further up as it got even steeper. Photos (evidence) taken, we set off again and had only ridden about 50 metres when the back end slid out on me and I was down. Faizal, who was still parked in the layby, came to assist me with lifting the Tiger. With Faizal pushing I tried to get going again but only managed to spin the rear, which then slipped out on the slope and down I went again. We struggled again to lift the Tiger, not easy on a very steep snow- and ice-covered slope. Trying to get going the same thing happened again and I was on the ground. After four attempts to get going, four falls and four times lifting the fully laden Tiger, we were both already feeling the strain. We were sweating with the effort, not good when it's around minus 10 degrees.

I realised that I was not getting going from where I was, so I need to reassess the situation and my options. Looking back down the road, about fifty metres away there was a sliver of gravel showing through the ice and snow, so I decided to try and get down to it – not easy. I couldn't turn the bike around so I put the Tiger in first gear, switched off the ignition, stood beside it and then gently eased it off the side stand. I pulled in the clutch and the Tiger started rolling backwards. As it started to gain momentum I released the clutch and let it slide back with me slipping beside it. Every few feet I had to lean it down on the side stand, which acted like an anchor brake to stop it gaining too much momentum. I repeated this process over and over until I reached the bit of gravel, then I remounted and got ready to try and ride up again. Faizal was back on his bike in the layby and we were both ready to try again.

I selected second gear slowly, released the clutch and I was off. Knees squeezing the Tiger and an ever so gentle hold on the bars and with a steady throttle, I started to climb the slippery ice-covered pass. It was like riding on a tightrope wire – one slip and you're off – so I didn't even look back as I concentrated on the road ahead. I was making good steady progress but it was hard to see as the snow was swirling around and my visor was all iced over. I had to open it, but now I was getting blasted by snow in the face and eyes, nightmare! As I neared the summit the wind was getting stronger and it was blowing me towards the verge and into soft drifting snow. I tried hard to stay on course as I could now see the summit, but I got blown into the verge and had to stop or risk falling over. I tried in vain to get going again but it was impossible, as the Tiger squirmed and slid around on the icy slope. I had also noticed that Faizal was nowhere to be seen.

So rather than risk a fall, I dismounted as lifting the bike on my own would be impossible on the steep slope and ice. I would wait on a passing truck and see if I could get assistance. Now what I didn't know was that all the big trucks on the Dalton had been stopped for safety at either end of the pass as it had been reported by passing 4x4s that both me and Faizal were stuck on different points. I flagged down a passing 4x4 and the driver gave me a push. Thankfully that was enough to get me out of the snow and ice verge and I rode the last 50 metres to the summit where I parked up, relieved. I know going down will be tricky, but theoretically a lot easier.

Now I needed to find out what had happened to Faizal. The next 4x4 that came up pulled over and I thought he was going to offer me assistance. But no, he just started berating me shouting; 'Fucking idiots, what are you doing up here? You're holding up the fucking oil industry,' amongst other things. So I shouted back; 'We're on a fucking adventure so fuck off and thanks for your help!' He drove off still shouting but it was carried away in the wind. The next trucker was more helpful, informing me that he had tried to help Faizal but he had also fallen four or five times and was now on his way back to Prudhoe Bay. I thought, he can't be, he hasn't got enough fuel. Unbeknown to me he had made his way to the bottom of the pass and was attempting another run at it.

The surprising thing was, apart from the two guys who assisted us, quite a few other 4x4s passed both of us but didn't even stop to see if we needed help, which we clearly did. I flagged down the next 4x4 driver who thankfully stopped, and I asked for a lift down to the bottom to see if I could find Faizal. We had only driven a few hundred metres down when out of the blizzard I saw Faizal riding slowly towards us. He was slipping and sliding but he was upright and moving forwards and upwards. As I jumped out of the 4x4 Faizal and the BMW crashed and they were both on the ground at probably the steepest area on the whole pass! He was now only a few hundred metres from the summit. Over the next two hours we pushed, pulled, lifted, and tried to ride the big Beemer up the slope. The outcome was always the same, as we fell again, again and again. I forget how many times but it was exhausting trying to get his bike to the top. At one point Faizal told me to ride his bike as he was exhausted and literally out on his feet. I tried, but his bike seemed alien to me and the inevitable happened; I rode a few feet with him pushing before I too was on the ground and again we struggled to lift the big Beemer.

A passing 4x4 stopped and Faizal offered the driver any amount of money, whatever it took to take his bike over the pass for him. Even if the truck driver had said yes, which he didn't as he had no room, what chance would we have had of lifting a 300kg plus BMW on to a

4x4 on a steep icy slope – no chance! It was hard enough just getting it back on its wheels. Faizal needed a pep talk, so I told him we were going to get to the top regardless of how long or how hard it was but we would get there. Whatever it took we would get there, even though I was not convinced myself, and I'm no stranger to working in the Arctic, having done nine winter tours in Norway whilst in 29 Commando. That's over two years of experience, so I knew how hard this environment was to work in and this was proving to be as hard as anything I'd ever done in the past.

It's a challenge, a proper adventure and nobody said it would be easy. I was already at the top, so I knew Faizal would get there eventually. But we were both now exhausted, so I offered more encouragement and told him we needed to keep trying. He didn't seem convinced but we tried again and again with the same outcome every time. The slope was now just too steep and icy and we are both too tired and physically drained with the efforts of continually lifting, pushing and trying to ride his bike.

We were about fifty metres from the top when another 4x4 came by and it stopped. Two of the biggest, burliest hunters I have ever seen, dressed in camo gear, got out and asked if we needed help. Boy, did we need help and we gladly accepted. Faizal got on his bike and we started to push but almost immediately he was down as the rear spun out on the slope. Then the two giants suggested that we just manhandled it, and pushed it. So with the engine off, we used brute force; well, they used brute force, Faizal and I just hung on as we started pushing and headed towards the summit. Nearing the top Faizal had had enough and dropped off, leaving me and the two hunters to get it the last few metres to the top. We thanked them and then they left us to our own ends.

I was now thinking that the worst-case scenario was that we might need to camp up here for the night and grizz it out until the morning.

Problem was, we didn't have food and it was horrendously cold and windy so we had to push on. I told Faizal the hard work was done and that going down would be easy; first gear, no revs, no braking, and just let gravity do its job. He didn't seem convinced, but I knew we could ride down the pass. So I gave him another pep talk and offered more encouragement telling him we would rest for a few minutes and then get going. Not before we had another photo though. And schoolboy error, all this time I'd had my helmet over my forearm and it was now full of wind-driven snow, nightmare!

We couldn't stop too long as we were both drenched in sweat with our efforts and it was well below zero up here and still blowing hard. As I set off I had only ridden a few feet when I hit a big deep bit of soft snow and fell immediately. As Faizal came to help me lift the Tiger I could see in his eyes that he was worried, and so was I. Thankfully this would be mine and Faizal's last fall, well at least for today anyway. A transport escort vehicle arrived and as we set off it escorted us down the south side of the mountain. As I started rolling downhill I let gravity do its thing. I tried to relax, no braking at all only engine braking and no sudden movements on the bars and slowly we made our way to the bottom of the pass. I kept checking my rear-view mirrors to make sure Faizal was behind me and OK. I was doing a steady 9mph and was tempted to engage second gear but thought it best not to. I got to the bottom and had time to get out my camera and take a photo of Faizal as he arrived with the escort vehicle. We had made it, we had got over the Atigun pass in the most terrible, challenging conditions (with a little help from two big men) and everyone had said we would not make it!

As we rode away from the pass the snow turned to rain and the track was now a sludgy, slushy mixture and quite tricky to ride on. It rained heavily all the way back to Coldfoot and we arrived at 7pm; it had taken us nine cold hard hours to cover the 240 miles from

ABOVE *Me and Faizal preparing to leave Prudhoe Bay for our ride back across the Atigun Pass.*

LEFT – TOP TO BOTTOM *Thumbs up before the ascent of the Atigun Pass; one of my many falls; almost at the top and visibility is getting worse; Faizal makes it to the top.*

BELOW *Faizal and the BMW after crashing off the Dalton Highway.*

Deadhorse. Over two of those hours were spent on the pass, which is only a couple of miles long, epic! On entering the café at Coldfoot we were surprised to find that we had become minor celebrities, as everyone had heard of our endeavours from passing truckers. Everyone had heard of the two mad bikers in the Atigun Pass and were keen to listen to our tales of conquering the ice road. We met two other bikers, Steve, an American, and Matthias, a German, who were keen to hear our tales as they wanted to ride the pass too. We told them how bad and hard it was but they were going to go in the morning anyway.

I saw this quote on the wall in Coldfoot: 'Those who cross the Arctic Circle have entered the Northern domain of the polar bear and are entitled to all the privileges of this frozen realm of blizzards; including freezing, shivering, exhaustion, and any other privilege and miseries that can possibly be bestowed.'

Well we had entered the domain and experienced all of the above, and I think we had earned the right to call ourselves Ice Road Bikers! We had also earned and needed a good night's sleep in a bed for the night as we were both cold, wet and exhausted, so we stumped up the $199 for a room in the Coldfoot accommodation block.

Coldfoot to Fairbanks (More crashes)

After a good night's sleep, before we set off in the morning I had some serious business to take care of. My friend and former Army colleague Davy Grey had nominated me (after doing his somewhere hot with a little wine bucket) to do the ice bucket challenge. I thought there couldn't be a better place to do it than here in Coldfoot, Alaska. So I did the challenge sitting beside the Coldfoot sign with the temperature just below zero. Faizal filmed it and Steve and Matthias, the two bikers we had met here, poured the large bucket of ice and water over me and boy, was it cold. The worst part was the large brick-sized bit of ice that hit me on the head; now that hurt! Ice bucket challenge completed I dressed and we said our goodbyes to Steve and Matthias, who were going to attempt to ride over the pass. I met Matthias a few days later in Fairbanks and he told me they made it to the top of the south slope but turned back as they didn't think they could make it down the other side.

It was a lovely bright day but still freezing and I wondered what could go wrong now as we set off for the ride back to Fairbanks. And nothing did until after refuelling at the Yukon River Camp fuel station. We set off for the last bit of gravel track before rejoining the tarmac; I had only ridden a few miles when I noticed that Faizal was not behind me. Road conditions had been good all the way down, wet and dry gravel in the middle with sludgy mud at the edges after yesterday's rain but still fairly good. So I pulled in and waited for a few minutes and the next vehicle that came past told me that Faizal had crashed and was in the ditch. They also said he was OK, but it still was not good as the verges are steep and the ditches deep on the Dalton highway. I rode back to where he had crashed and there were two 4x4s parked up and one was our old friend the highway safety guy; that's three times we've seen him in as many days. Faizal and his bike were 15 to 20 feet down the bank with the two guys trying to help him push it back up.

After taking a photo of his predicament first, which amused the two helpers, I assessed the situation and thought there was no way that we were going to push or ride the BMW back up the muddy grassy verge. Faizal was thankfully OK, but a little bruised as he and the BMW had tumbled down the bank with the bike landing on top of him. He told me it was a slow speed crash after losing concentration (whilst fumbling in a pocket for a knife) and drifting into the mud at the side, which then sucked him over the edge. Yes, I was bemused too – why do you need a knife whilst riding along? Anyway the bank was clearly too steep to push or ride a bike back up. So I wandered along the bottom of the heavily overgrown ditch, which was bordered by small trees and dense undergrowth, to find an alternative way out. The bank was less steep about thirty metres back up the road, but getting there was going to be difficult as it meant manhandling the GS 800 around in the ditch and more manhandling, riding through the undergrowth and whatever else!

With Faizal riding and our two helpers and me doing the manual work; pushing, pulling, lifting and basically bulldozing our way through the thick vegetation, we made it back up through the undergrowth and up the bank onto the road. Thankfully it didn't take too long and not too much effort. Since I'd teamed up with Faizal, I had spent more time pushing, lifting, pulling and generally recovering his BMW GS 800 than I had the Tiger in over six months! But it had been great riding with him and I couldn't have done the Atigun Pass without him. The remainder of the day passed without incident and we got back to Fairbanks safely but still cold and wet through.

Arriving in Fairbanks we decided to wash the Dalton grime off the bikes before finding somewhere to stay the night and headed for a wash-down in town. Now Fairbanks is a fairly large town in a large state but it was about to be small world time again. As we were washing our bikes another rider rode in and it was Jesus, the young American rider. He had had his gear shifter welded at the oil camp and had then ridden back to Fairbanks. When he arrived back piss-wet through, an old couple had taken pity on him, and he had been staying with them for the past few days. Whilst washing the bike I noticed that my front left fork had blown and it was leaking fork oil; far too expensive to get done here, so I decided to nurse it back to Seattle where I planned to end my trip. After washing the bikes Jesus left us and went back to spend the night with his kind old hosts, and Faizal and I went in search of lodging.

The only accommodation we could get was a hostel that consisted of old western-style mining tents. These were half wood – floors and the lower half of the walls – with canvas upper halves and roofs. Thankfully they had small heaters in them and we slept soundly, except for when some noisy German hikers arrived in the middle of the night. The following morning we set off for what I thought we'd agreed was Sam's Sourdough Café for breakfast before riding south. But as we rode past some traffic lights Faizal took a right turn. I rode on thinking he had just made a mistake and waited at the café. We had no means of communicating and that was the last I saw of him. At the café I met Matthias, the German rider who had attempted to ride over the Atigun Pass, and failed. We had breakfast together and after finishing there was still no sign of Faizal. We didn't have phones so I set off on my own; there's only one road south, so we might bump into each other, I thought.

After riding for a few hours I passed a convenience store so decided to go in and get some food as I was going to be camping. Pulling into the car park I came to a halt; there was no snow, no ice, it was dry and I fell over; what was going on? I must be tired, how had that happened? I just fell right over, dropping the Tiger in the process. I was helped by a guy who appeared from nowhere and we picked the Tiger up. I noticed that the right-hand indicator was broken; not only that but it had a hole punched right through the plastic tank protector. So I spent the next hour gluing and taping it all back together, all the while with my new friend, who seemed to be the village idiot, talking to me, offering advice and trying to help. Eventually I'd stuck it all together and said a quick goodbye to my annoying and very strange helper. I stopped several more times on the way back in the hope of finding Faizal, but he was nowhere to be seen. How could we not find each other, I wondered, as there is only one road south? You would have thought our paths would cross somewhere, but no. Small world, big road!

I spent the night at Beaver Creek where I had camped on the way up and decided to camp out again. It was a very, very cold night and in the morning everything was covered in ice. I had slept in my clothes and was double bagged in my tent and it was still bloody freezing. But I had to get up and get going. Whilst packing my tent I constantly had to stop and put my hands in my armpits for a few minutes to reheat them. The alloy tent poles were sticking to my hands it was so cold. I used the Wi-Fi in the café and managed to get a message to Faizal, arranging to meet him at a hotel in Whitehorse.

I eventually met up with Faizal later in the day in Whitehorse and we went for a few drinks to celebrate our ride north and say goodbye to each other properly. After a meal we spent the evening in the bar next to our hotel, which had a Karaoke night, and we had a great time reminiscing about the Ice Road. After breakfast the following morning we parted ways as Faizal was getting a ferry from Alaska back to Seattle and I was riding, so more cold days ahead! It had been good to have a travelling companion for a while as I had ridden the whole trip solo except for a couple of days back in Chile and Costa Rica. And as I said before, I couldn't have done the Atigun Pass on my own.

Riding the infamous Dalton Highway had been everything an adventure ride should be and it was great after riding for so long on tarmac. It had been more demanding than I thought and expected it would be and it had had everything I had wanted and more. It had literally been the icing on a fantastic motorcycling adventure cake. The Dalton had thrown everything at us in the last few days; danger, challenging conditions, crashes, wind, rain, snow, ice, and sub-zero temperatures. I had been as cold as I have ever been on any of my winter deployments to Norway and had had to work just as hard, if not harder. I also experienced all sorts of emotions; anxiety, awe, excitement, fear, frustration, exhilaration, hope, happiness, pleasure, pride, relief, satisfaction and suffering, but it was worth it and I'd do it all again. I'd had to call on all the skills that I had learnt in the Army (mainly recovery) and apply all of the Commando qualities; Courage, Unselfishness, Cheerfulness (in adversity) and Determination! Living the dream! It had been a great six and a half months with a lot going on, full of ups, downs, highs and lows. But it wasn't over yet; I still had over 2,400 cold miles to ride back down to Seattle.

As I said Faizal was getting the ferry back to Seattle, which takes five days, before continuing his journey. I was also headed for Seattle where I intended to ship the Tiger back to the UK. I had looked at finishing my trip here in Alaska but the shipping costs (£4,000 plus) were extortionate. New York was also an option but with winter having already arrived I didn't fancy the 4,000-mile ride across North America. I'd also promised to visit another old Army friend in Banff, BC. So Seattle it was, and it was going to be cold all the way and test my sanity and resolve yet again.

I was now on my own again with my trip nearing the end. It didn't look like it was going to get any warmer on the ride back south, and so it proved, as the next few days were very testing; freezing cold, misty, raining all day long with the temperature hovering just above zero. There was not a lot to look at due to poor visibility except for the bison grazing by the roadside. I arrived in the little town of Fort Nelson somewhere in Northern British Columbia freezing and piss-wet through for the second day in a row. My hands and feet were falling off and I was shivering uncontrollably, so I booked into a motel and had the first bath I had had in years (I normally shower) to heat myself up.

Fort Nelson to Dawson Creek (The coldest day)

When I woke up in Fort Nelson the following morning it was freezing and it was snowing again. Not what I wanted to be riding in but I couldn't stay here, it's a one-horse shitty little town, so I wrapped up and set off. The snow was light at first but it got heavier as the day went on, though thankfully it wasn't lying on the road. Visibility was bad and my visor was freezing on the inside and covered with snow and dirt on the outside that was thrown up from the road by passing trucks. The front of the bike was all iced over with dirty grey ice covering the windshield and the wing mirrors with big dirty grey icicles hanging off them. I don't know what the temperature was but it was most definitely the coldest day's riding on the trip so far and probably the coldest I had ever ridden in. I was having to stop every 50 miles or so and run up and down the side of the road to heat myself up.

Again there wasn't a lot to look at as I rode along, but I at last got a close-up photo of a black bear; unfortunately for him he was dead and lying beside the road covered in snow. I wanted to stop but needed to keep heading south where I would eventually get to warmer weather. After five hours riding in freezing snow and bad visibility I reached the town of Fort St John and the snow had now changed to freezing rain. I passed a neon temperature sign reading 2 degrees, so it was getting warmer. But I pressed on for the town of Dawson Creek, only another 40 or so miles. I checked into a motel to warm up and dry out. Watching the news I was surprised to see that some parts of Canada were experiencing a heatwave, but up here in Northern BC winter had definitely arrived.

Dawson Creek to Jasper (Still freezing)

Looking out of my motel window in the morning I was dismayed to see that the Tiger was covered in a light layer of snow. Packing my gear I found that I couldn't get into my panniers as the locks were frozen and so was the petrol cap lock; I eventually managed to get into them with a little help from WD40. Very cold again but surprisingly it wasn't snowing as I set off. I now had just over a thousand miles to go and I was going to take the slightly longer more scenic route down through Jasper National park. And I was hoping that the weather would heat up a bit.

It did get a bit warmer but that would change later; as I rode down route 40 and entered Alberta, the temperatures plummeted and it started snowing again. All the hills and trees had a light covering of snow and were shrouded in mist so once again I had nothing to look at. But the road was a pleasure to ride, fast sweeping bends and, despite Mother Nature's attempts to ruin my trip, I was still enjoying it, sort of. Arriving at the Jasper National Park entrance the park ranger informed me that it was snowing up ahead; oh well no change then, I thought.

Riding had become a mind game, not very physical as the roads were well paved and there was no snow on them, but just keeping going and covering ground was a mental challenge. I arrived in Jasper town after six and a half hours riding in the freezing conditions for the sixth day in a row and booked into the Athabasca hotel. All my ex-comrades and anyone who has exercised in Canada will know this hotel from doing adventure training here. I caught the weather forecast on TV – they were explaining how unusual the snowfall was at this time of year, and that it was to continue for the next few days. The following week the forecast was for the high 20s, no use to me as I was here now and riding up to Banff tomorrow to see another ex-29 Commando veteran and friend, who lived there. I only had a few days left so I took the opportunity to get on the internet and look for a flight home to the UK. I found a reasonably priced one and booked it for three days' time. Then the realisation hit me that my trip was nearly all over.

Jasper, Banff, Merritt (More snow and more police encounters)

As I was preparing to leave the hotel in Jasper one of the locals informed me that the road to Banff was all snowed in and that I wouldn't get through. Well, I couldn't stay here as I had booked a flight back to the UK on Saturday; I was also going to meet my old friend and former Army colleague in Banff. Stopping in a service area for lunch I met Dave, from Liverpool, on a two-week bike holiday, and we had lunch together. After that we rode together for a few miles down towards Banff before we parted ways. The mountain tops were obscured by low cloud so not a lot to look at again. The Icefield Parkway road that I was riding along was pretty uninteresting to ride on, not as twisty as I'd hoped for. The temperature had now risen and it was now eight degrees, positively red-hot! The last forty miles into Banff is dual carriageway and I counted five unmarked police cars on the way down, all having pulled someone over, thankfully not me, but my time would come!

I arrived quite late in Banff and went straight to the Banff Centre where I was meeting my mate Colin. He had been here in Canada for about five years now and was working at the centre as a security guard. Unfortunately he was also working tonight, but we had supper together, which he kindly paid for. We reminisced about our time in the regiment together, and caught up on each other's lives and what we had both been up to since we last met. But it was soon time for Colin to go to work so we said our goodbyes and I got a few photos before heading off for my digs for the night. I was staying in the local YMCA, which was nice and also cheap.

I woke in the morning and was horrified to find the whole of Banff under about eight inches of snow. I had a small panic attack as I'd booked a flight for two days' time and it looked like I was going to be stuck there. I couldn't cancel the flight so I was going to have to get on the road in the snow yet again! I went outside to load the Tiger and it too was covered in deep snow. I was filled with dread, as the thought of riding in deep snow was not very appealing to me, but I had a flight to catch so I steeled myself and prepared to hit the road. I couldn't hang around here waiting on the weather getting better.

Packed and dressed I set off and refuelled at the local petrol station, where the woman at the till told me to be very careful out there. All the other people at the station were looking at me like I'd got two heads or maybe they just thought I was mad!

Snow was everywhere and the road was covered in deep slush but ride-able. As I got onto the main route north the road was very wet but no slush or snow. Thirty miles further on as I turned west towards the town of Golden it was now completely dry. Again there was not a lot to see as the mountains were still shrouded in cloud but the roads were clear and it was quite warm again, seven or eight degrees. All was going well until I passed the town of Revelstoke, when I saw red and blue flashing lights behind me. I duly pulled over, not knowing what I had done, as I wasn't going particularly fast. The unmarked patrol car stopped behind me and out got the stern-looking police officer. He told me I was lucky to be alive after what I had just done, but I was confused. He told me the overtaking manoeuvre I had done about five miles up the road was dangerous. I thought for a moment and asked what overtaking he was he talking about.

He reminded me about the truck I overtook on double yellows further back up the road. Apparently, as I overtook a truck there was another truck coming in the opposite direction, and again he said I was lucky I wasn't dead as that is what kills people. I told him that there were definitely broken yellow lines on my side of the road and it didn't seem dangerous to me. To which he replied, 'They were double yellow when you pulled back in, and you must also have been speeding.' It had taken him five miles to catch me, he said, before asking, 'What speed were you doing?' I replied, 'I don't know, as I was looking at the truck coming towards me.'

He then gave me the obligatory lecture about how many accidents happen here and what can happen if you're involved in an accident.

He also said that he didn't like attending accidents, and I thought, maybe you should change jobs then. He then asked me to produce my driver's licence, vehicle documents and insurance. And I thought, that's me fucked now as I don't have insurance, haven't had any since leaving Mexico!

I produced my licence and my passport and before I got anything else out he asked to see the passport. He then looked at my V5 and asked how I had got the bike here and where I'd been. Then he wandered back to his car. Now, I hadn't given him my insurance as I didn't have any, so I waited nervously whilst he was on his radio checking me out. When he came back I was still thinking the worst and had been trying to think of an excuse as to why I didn't have insurance. He said if I was a local he would be impounding my bike but as I was Scottish he was going to be lenient with me. He handed me my documents back and informed me he was giving me the smallest charge that he could. Thankfully he never asked to see my insurance and I got a ticket for an unsafe pass on the left. Total: $84 Canadian (£52) if I paid within 30 days at any government office.

Well I was on a flight out of there in a few days' time so it crossed my mind not to pay it, but I might want to come back here someday. I don't know what computer databases they use but I wouldn't like to get turned around at the airport for an unpaid fine, so I would pay anyway just in case. The remainder of the day went without incident, the temperature continued to rise and the sun also made an appearance. As I said, the roads hadn't been that great on the way down from Alaska and neither had the weather or the scenery due to low cloud and snow obscuring my view, but it had been a different type of challenge and all part of adventure riding; who wants it easy? And in a perverse sort of way it had been enjoyable too, living the dream even though it was a very cold dream.

Merritt to Seattle (The final frontier and final day)

After nearly two weeks of riding in snow, rain and sub-zero temperatures I awoke to a dry bright sunny day but it was still bitterly cold. The road was quiet and had nice long fast sweeping, flowing bends as I made my way back down towards the American border. Due to the cold in the mountains I still had all six layers of riding gear on. But as I came down into the lower valleys towards the coast it was getting warmer.

Riding along I thought I was hearing things but I could also feel something through the rear brake pedal. There was a grinding noise coming from my rear brake when I was braking, and on checking I found that I had no pads left at all. This was due in some part to the fact that my left front fork seal blew out on the Dalton highway. I had been using the rear more to stop the front end diving and pumping out suspension fluid, thus accelerating the rear pad wear. I had already tied a piece of towel around the fork leg but that was saturated now. With no rear brake, I was having to use the front more, and suspension fluid was spraying all over the front brakes and up the side of the bike My plan was just to nurse the Tiger back to Seattle and the cargo company with a view to getting everything fixed when I get back to the UK, but however hard I tried not to use the rear to stop damaging the disc, sometimes I instinctively used it. And with still such a long way to go I would have to get some new pads from somewhere.

I still had the small matter of my speeding fine to take care off. Normally you would ride right past Canadian border control and on through to the US side and passport/immigration control. But as I needed to pay my fine I stopped between the two border control buildings in no man's land. The Royal Canadian Mounted Policeman (RCMP) had told me I could pay the traffic violation fine at any government building or border crossing point. So I quickly nipped in to the Canadian building and informed the border guard why I was there. He looked bemused and said he had never dealt with a traffic violation before and wasn't sure whether I could pay there. After some internal enquiries and a few phone calls he confirmed that I couldn't pay it there.

Ever helpful, he started looking on the internet to find out where I could pay and thankfully found somewhere just up the road. There was a government insurance office half a mile away back up the road I had just come down that would accept my payment. Whilst we were chatting he received a phone call, and looked at me and asked, 'Where is your bike?' 'Outside,' I replied. 'Where outside?' 'In no man's land, between the two buildings,' I said. He then asked if I knew what day it was and what significance it had. I looked at him blankly and shrugged my shoulders. Then he told me it was the anniversary of the 9/11 attack on the Twin Towers in New York. And that the USA was on heightened security alert for terrorist attacks and that I had caused a small security incident.

Just as he informed me of my gaffe, I heard the door behind me opening and in rushed three of the USA's finest border guards, who asked me in strict tones; 'Is that your bike?' With stern unsmiling faces they then told me that I needed to move it immediately, as I had caused a bomb scare! I apologised for my mistake but they were not amused and didn't seem too friendly. I explained why I had stopped in no man's land as they escorted me out of the building and back to where the Tiger was parked. I explained again that I had to go back up the road to pay a fine. They then told me that I couldn't go back and I had to enter the USA. I asked why I couldn't just turn around as I needed to go back up the road to pay a fine. 'You have crossed the imaginary line between Canada and the US, so you need to enter,' they said. No flexibility or common sense.

I pleaded my case and again explained my circumstances, and again asked why I couldn't just turn around as I hadn't actually entered the

USA. They started to give me the same answer as before, but then saw my registration plate and asked where I was from and why I was here. I gave them a quick dit about my trip, explained again about the ticket and miraculously they were struck by some common sense. They then told me to turn around quickly on the one-way road and cut through a car park opposite and that would take me back onto the road into Canada, which I hadn't actually left anyway. Less than ten minutes later my fine was paid and I returned to the border and crossed without further incident into the USA.

Now the shipping company (James Cargo) that were shipping my bike back had said they needed a temporary import certificate to ship the bike out of the USA. After clearing passport and immigration I again parked my bike, making sure it was in a correct parking area, and I made my way to the import office and asked for one. I had now crossed into the USA at three separate crossings (Texas, Alaska and now Washington) and had never been given one. I was now told that they wouldn't issue one as there was no need. I told them that the shippers said I needed one to ship the bike back to the UK. After wasting an hour and lots of phone calls the border agent confidently informed me that I didn't need an import certificate as a tourist because I hadn't actually imported the bike. She gave me her name and contact details to pass to the shippers in case they had any questions. So, confident that I didn't need an import document, I thanked her and was on my merry way. I would find out later that I did in fact need an import certificate to get the Tiger back to the UK and, as I didn't have one, it would be delayed and cost me extra!

My rear brake pads still needed replacing so now that I was in a more populated area I kept a lookout as I was riding along for a bike shop to try and get new ones. I eventually passed one, so dropped in to see if they had a set of pads for my bike. They didn't, but gave me directions to Triumph Seattle. My satnav hadn't been working since way back in Alaska but I found the Triumph shop fairly easily. I had a quick chat with the manager and some of the staff who were all interested in my trip. They offered to fit the pads for me but it's a quick five-minute job so I just borrowed their tools to save me unpacking. The rear disc was damaged and would probably need replacing but the new pads were fitted and I was gone.

I had pre-booked into a motel near the airport and also only 14 miles from the shipping company warehouse for ease of dropping the bike off the next day. That evening I washed the Tiger in preparation for her trip home. I had a nice ride the following morning to the warehouse, which I found fairly easily with a little help from a Harley Davidson rider. I dropped off the Tiger, helped load her on to a truck and that was it, trip over, I was now a pedestrian!

End of the Adventure: the Tiger is loaded ready for the journey back to the UK.

In the taxi back to my motel I couldn't believe it was all over, but it was and I'd achieved what I set out to do. I had ridden solo (except for the Dalton Highway) from Buenos Aires to Ushuaia, the tip of South America, and then all the way up through South, Central and North America to Prudhoe Bay, Alaska, right at the top of the continent. I had covered 29,000 miles and in the process tested mine and the Tiger's abilities and sometimes questioned my sanity as well.

I made countless new friends and met some amazing, fantastic people along the way, all of whom contributed in some way to the experience. Their generosity and kindness has been humbling; I had help from complete strangers and am grateful for it, so thanks to all who helped me in any way. It has been a life-affirming once-in-a-lifetime experience; full of ups and downs, highs and lows, joy and pain, including personal bereavement, but nobody said it would be easy. That is why it's called adventure riding, and this has been a truly amazing motorcycle adventure.

I'd like to thank my friends and family for their support and encouragement throughout my trip from beginning to end. And I would especially like to thank my wife Margaret, firstly for allowing me to embark on my dream trip and secondly for her continued support and strength during the harder times on my journey.

For me it was all about the riding and achieving my aim, and life on the road was great. I loved it and could have ridden forever, but I also love my wife and family. And after a lifetime of going overseas on operations, I was looking forward to going home… until the next time?

Steve and the Tiger Riding the Americas.

The End!

In memory of my brother

WILLIAM ROY STEWART

1963 – 2014

Final Statistics

BIKE	Tiger 800 XC 2012
DURATION OF TRIP	Six and a half months (193 days)
ACTUAL RIDING DAYS	109
START MILEAGE	6,217
END MILEAGE	35,217
TOTAL TRIP DISTANCE	29,000 miles
MOST MILES IN ONE DAY	659
FEWEST MILES IN ONE DAY	50
AVERAGE DISTANCE PER DAY	263 miles
COUNTRIES RIDDEN THROUGH	15 (Argentina, Chile, Bolivia, Perú, Ecuador, Colombia, Panamá, Costa Rica, Honduras, Guatemala, Nicaragua, Belize, Mexico, USA, Canada)

Fuel and consumption

FUEL USED	2,601 litres
AVERAGE MILES PER LITRE	11
COST	£2,020
AVERAGE COST PER LITRE	77p

Servicing

SERVICES	5
AIR FILTERS	6
OIL CHANGES	5

SPARK PLUGS		3 sets
TYRES	Metzeler Karoo 3s	5,907 miles
	Full Bore	8,353 miles
	Heidenaus	11,000 miles
	Heidenaus (present)	3,740 miles so far
BRAKE PADS		
	Rear replaced	17,815 and 35,179 miles
	Front replaced	20,000 miles (approx.)
CHAIN AND SPROCKET		
	Both replaced	23,340 miles
	Chain replaced	29,097 miles due to being damaged by having no rear shock damping

All servicing except for one done myself.

Mechanical issues

- Bike cutting out at low revs, not idling properly, coughing and spluttering after lots of desert and gravel/dirt track riding, fuel injectors cleaned, problem solved.
- Side stand cut-out switch seized, WD40 easy fix.
- Rear shock blew; refurbished and rebuilt in Corona, California.
- Overheating problem in New Mexico, radiator cap perished due to extreme heat and allowed coolant to evaporate. Fixed by Triumph USA under warranty.
- Front left fork seal blew in Alaska.

Breakages/repairs

- Chain guard broke and fell off in Patagonia due to excessive side wind.
- Main frame down tubes fractured below where they meet the rear sub frame. Spot welded in Colombia. Frame replaced by Triumph UK on return.
- Punctures: 1 front.

- Left wing mirror replaced.
- Left front indicator replaced.
- Left pannier hammered back into shape.
- Front wheel rim dented on left side after hitting massive pothole, rim hammered back into shape.
- Crash bars pulled back out from engine casing.
- Left fog-lamp mounting point on main light cluster repaired with steel epoxy.
- Two top yoke bolts replaced after they went missing (fell out somewhere).
- Chain guide broke; repaired with cable ties.
- Right-hand plastic tank guard/cowling shattered after fall due to extreme cold weather.
- Front mudguard mounting points broken due to stand falling when getting new tyres fitted.
- Both fog lamps' lenses cracked due to falls.

Crashes and falls

ON ROAD	1
ON GRAVEL	1
SLOW SPEED FALLS IN THE SAND	3
BIKE BLOWN OVER BY WIND	
IN PATAGONIA	4
DROPPED BIKE	4
FALLS IN SNOW AND ICE	too many to remember!